A Revitalization of Images

A Revitalization of Images

Theology and Human Creativity

Gregory C. Higgins

CASCADE *Books* • Eugene, Oregon

A REVITALIZATION OF IMAGES
Theology and Human Creativity

Copyright © 2019 Gregory C. Higgins. All rights reserved. Except for brief quotations in critical publications or reviews, no part of this book may be reproduced in any manner without prior written permission from the publisher. Write: Permissions, Wipf and Stock Publishers, 199 W. 8th Ave., Suite 3, Eugene, OR 97401.

Cascade Books
An Imprint of Wipf and Stock Publishers
199 W. 8th Ave., Suite 3
Eugene, OR 97401

www.wipfandstock.com

PAPERBACK ISBN: 978-1-4982-2450-5
HARDCOVER ISBN: 978-1-4982-2452-9
EBOOK ISBN: 978-1-4982-2451-2

Cataloguing-in-Publication data:

Names: Higgins, Gregory C., 1960–, author.

Title: A revitalization of images : theology and human creativity / Gregory C. Higgins.

Description: Eugene, OR : Cascade Books, 2019 | Includes bibliographical references and index(es).

Identifiers: ISBN 978-1-4982-2450-5 (paperback) | ISBN 978-1-4982-2452-9 (hardcover) | ISBN 978-1-4982-2451-2 (ebook)

Subjects: LCSH: Imagination—Religious aspects—Christianity. | Creation (Literary, artistic, etc.)—Religious aspects—Christianity.

Classification: BR115.A8 H54 2019 (print) | BR115.A8 H54 (ebook)

Manufactured in the U.S.A.   03/04/19

For Eileen, Emily, and James

Contents

Preface | ix
Introduction | xi

Chapter One: The First Creation Story | 1
Chapter Two: The Second Creation Story | 20
Chapter Three: Biblical Journeys | 39
Chapter Four: Biblical Vision of Jacob's Ladder | 58
Chapter Five: Biblical Longings for the Future | 78
Chapter Six: Biblical Numbers | 97
Chapter Seven: Music and Art in the Bible | 114
Chapter Eight: Elements of Nature in the Bible (Fire, Wind, Water) | 132
Chapter Nine: Persons in the Bible | 151
Chapter Ten: Parables in the Bible | 172

Bibliography | 191
Subject Index | 203
Author Index | 205
Scripture Index | 207

Preface

I would like to thank a number of people who have assisted me in various ways with the writing of this text. First, I need to thank the faculty and students of Christian Brothers Academy in Lincroft, New Jersey, where I have taught for over thirty years. Second, thanks to my fellow St. Rose of Lima parishioners in Freehold, New Jersey. Third, special thanks to Benjamin and William Pickett, Bexley and Callie King, as well as Ryan, Colin, and Brandon Schneider. Finally, my deepest thanks to Eileen, Emily, and James to whom this work is lovingly dedicated.

Introduction

THE TITLE, *A Revitalization of Images* plays off the title of the 1949 work by the British theologian and philosopher Austin Farrer (1904–68), *A Rebirth of Images*. Farrer argued in a number of works that the key to understanding both the nature of theological reflection and the dynamics of the Christian spiritual life lies in recognizing the critical role that images play in shaping how we think and act. The "birth of Christianity," states Farrer, "is a visible rebirth of images."[1] Israel preserved the images of Joseph and his brothers, the kingship of David, and the Suffering Servant, to name but a few. "Christ in his earthly life had made the decisive transformation of the images, and he had given his Spirit to continue the work in the minds of the disciples, to lead them into the knowledge of all the truth."[2] Not only did Christ transform the images handed down in Israel through his life, death, and resurrection, but the New Testament writers witnessed to that transformation in their own imaginative ways. As Farrer writes in *The Glass of Vision*,

> In the apostolic mind . . . the God-given images lived, not statically, but with an inexpressible creative force. The several distinct images grew together into fresh unities, opened out in new detail, attracted to themselves and assimilated further image-material: all this within the life of a generation. This is the way inspiration worked. The stuff of inspiration is living images.[3]

This process, in turn, provides us with a model for doing theology. "Theology is the analysis and criticism of the revealed images . . . Theology tests and determines the sense of the images . . ."[4] Theology tests the images, and is tested by them. Without this activity, the images can become lifeless. The task, then, of theology is the continual revitalization of biblical imagery in the ongoing life of the Christian community.

1. Farrer, *Rebirth of Images*, 14.
2. Ibid., 16.
3. Farrer, *Glass of Vision*, 43–44.
4. Ibid., 44.

In order to accomplish this task of revitalization, those doing theology need to be conversant with past thinkers as well as engaged in the present life of the church. To that end, in each chapter we begin with a biblical image that has figured prominently in the writings of Christians down through the centuries. "Image" is broadly defined to include things ranging from "Jacob's Ladder" to the creation stories. We examine two important thinkers from the past who have drawn upon the image when discussing the Christian life. Next, we turn our attention to a contemporary thinker who has employed the image in his or her own theological work. The theologian may support or challenge the traditional interpretation of the image. In the final section of each chapter we examine how theologians representing the wide spectrum of current theological positions use the image to propose their own understanding of the Christian life. In each section we will include the theological perspective of an orthodox, liberal, postliberal, and postmodern thinker.

Revitalization and Contemporary Theology

The approach in *Revitalization* mirrors three noteworthy features of Christian theology. First, a person surveying the field of contemporary theology cannot help but be struck by the wide array of approaches, positions, and concerns. This pluralism exists not only in terms of the theologies presently being developed in the academy, but, I suspect, within the minds of most Christians gathered for worship at their local church. On some issues, we fiercely uphold the orthodox position; on other issues we land squarely in the liberal camp, and on still more we see the different sides of an argument and don't know where we stand. We treasure the orthodox commitment to faithfulness, we applaud the liberal questioning of the *status quo*, we recognize with the postliberals that Christianity calls us to live in a way that the world may not understand, and we acknowledge the deeply fragmented nature of the world that is emphasized in postmodernism. The challenge, of course, is to draw upon this diversity in such a way that it becomes an asset rather than a liability to our theological reflection. The selection of works under consideration in the present text reflects in some small way the deeply pluralistic state of both our own thinking and the theological landscape.

Second, in each chapter *Revitalization* presents numerous examples of the ways in which theologians, both past and present, read Scripture.[5] Along the way, a host of questions arise that appear with great frequency

---

5. See Davis and Hays, *Art of Reading Scripture*.

in contemporary theological debates. Is meaning a property of the text or a creation of the individual reader or the interpretive community? The pre-modern readings of the biblical text that produced such intriguing and spiritually powerful typological and allegorical interpretations can also frequently strike the modern reader as strained. Is it possible to develop a way of reading the Bible that taps into what Farrer calls "the life-giving power" of Scripture that complements the historical-critical method of interpretation?[6] The diversity of positions raises the question of truth. Is it possible to have multiple legitimate readings of the Bible, and if so, is it possible to identify illegitimate readings? The text will, I hope, provide ample opportunity to engage these questions.

Third, a focus on images reminds us that while theology requires systematic thought and critical inquiry, it also involves a creativity of mind and spirit. Again, Farrer provides us with a way of thinking about this dimension of theology. He writes, "Man expresses himself by language, and language, being repetitive noise, is capable of musical arrangement."[7] Creative theological writing enlightens the mind and touches the soul. We can only hope that more than a handful of thinkers under consideration in *Revitalization* will inspire us to make a little music of our own.

---

6. Farrer, *Glass of Vision*, 51.

7. Ibid., 114.

Chapter One: The First Creation Story

WE BEGIN OUR STUDY of how both past and present Christian thinkers incorporate some of the most enduring biblical images into their descriptions of the Christian life, fittingly, "In the beginning . . ." The opening chapter of Genesis presents the progressive unfolding of God's creation of the world and all the living creatures that inhabit it. This first of two creation stories in the Bible captures the theological and pastoral imaginations of two of the most influential figures in the fourth-century Christian church: Basil of Caesarea and Ambrose of Milan. Both bishops devoted a series of homilies to the Hexaemeron, the six days of creation. Their works demonstrate how they approach the biblical narrative and discern a spiritual meaning in the most minute detail in the text. The six-day creation story also illustrates the challenges that contemporary Christian thinkers, such as the theologian Sallie McFague, face when seeking to employ that classic image in their own theology. Can the image of the six-day creation still inform the theology, spirituality, and morality of a Christian community that no longer shares Basil and Ambrose's understanding of the universe, their theory of the origins of species, or their acceptance of the Mosaic authorship of the text? Can the six-day creation story still speak to Christians who are deeply troubled about the state of the environment and the role that humans have played in disturbing it? Is it possible to ground a theological position in Scripture, to critically engage the work of esteemed thinkers within the Christian tradition, and to respond in a way that is credible and meaningful to contemporary Christians? Before we turn our attention to Basil and Ambrose, we need to survey our options for how best to answer these difficult questions.

Spectrum of Theological Approaches

As we survey the contemporary theological landscape, we discover a wide range of possible strategies for the dealing with the gap between the world of Basil and Ambrose and our own. The spectrum runs from traditional orthodoxy to liberalism, postliberalism, and postmodernism. Each of the four brings its own set of theological and philosophical convictions to bear on the problem. As a result, each has its own particular concerns and points of emphasis. At times many of the approaches share a common point of view, while at other times their differences are irreconcilable. We will draw upon all four perspectives as we approach the question of the ongoing vitality of the image of the six-day creation story for the life of the church.

In the approach that emerged in the early orthodox theology of the church, all Scripture is ultimately interpreted in light of the life, death, and resurrection of Christ. As divinely inspired texts, the Old Testament contained "types" or foreshadowings of Christ. Jonah's three days in the belly of the whale, for example, prefigured Christ's three days in the tomb (Matt 12:40). Augustine expressed the logic of this approach to the Bible succinctly when he stated that, "in the Old Testament is concealed the New, and in the New Testament is revealed the Old."[1] Theologies centered on the concept of Logos were especially marked by this sense of continuity. The Logos (the Word) that became incarnate in Christ Jesus was also the same Logos by which the world was created. All of creation, especially human reason, therefore, participated in the rationality of the Creator. The second-century Christian theologian Justin Martyr spoke of the seeds of the Word scattered throughout the teachings of Greek philosophers. At its deepest level, the Logos theology of the early church rested on a deep continuity between creation and redemption, and therefore rejected any system of thought, such as that found in the various forms of Gnosticism, that saw the material world as a creation of an evil principle and the salvation wrought by Christ as a freedom from the confines of darkness and materiality.

The drawback of the orthodox position was later codified in the principle, "Error has no rights." Armed with the objective truth that all rational human beings should embrace, orthodox Christians at various times in history have subjected those in error to scorn, "correction," or worse. The Christian truth-claims stood in judgment of other tradition's claims, but orthodoxy provided little insight on how to judge the Christian tradition itself. Abolitionists, for example, challenged orthodox Christians citing biblical verses on slavery. Similar episodes can be found throughout the Christian tradition involving the treatment of indigenous peoples by Christian missionaries to condemnations of various scientific theories that today we accept without question. For this reason, many thinkers in the Christian tradition have been drawn to our second approach.

The liberal tradition accepted the orthodox belief that truth is universal, but did not regard the Christian tradition as its sole repository. This approach identified an "essence" of Christianity within the vast plurality

---

1. Augustine, *Instructing Beginners in Faith*, 70.

of the biblical writings. This essence formed the kernel—to use one of the most common images in the liberal tradition—that could be separated from the husk of culturally bound and theologically dispensable framework in which it was presented. For example, the twentieth-century biblical theologian Rudolf Bultmann pursued a project of "demythologizing" the New Testament so that the original *kerygma* or proclamation (God's offer of authentic human existence to the individual in the present moment) could be recovered without asking modern Christians to accept the outdated three-tiered view of the universe (heaven above, earth in the middle, and hell below) assumed by the biblical writers. Christians could then incorporate truths uncovered by physicists, geologists, and biologists within their religious beliefs. Christian belief could be revised in ways that are responsive to the developments in all areas of human inquiry without sacrificing what is essential to the gospel message.

The critics of liberalism saw in its attempt to reshape Christian belief a dangerous inclination to accommodate the church to the prevailing beliefs and attitudes of the wider culture. The line between Christian commitment and national pride, for example, could be blurred and one mistaken for the other. When the young Swiss pastor, Karl Barth, read a letter in 1914 supporting Kaiser Wilhelm II's war policies signed by many of the liberal professors he revered, he feared that liberal theology had led Christian thinkers down a dangerous road from which it must urgently retreat. Among his many concerns, Barth believed that Christians should not feel compelled to revise their theological claims according to the canons of modern rationality. Such a policy endangered Christian identity and weakened the ability of the church to witness to the truth. Barth's theology was a repudiation of the working assumption underlying much of Christian thought since the Enlightenment that human knowledge could be secured on an indubitable foundational principle, thus guaranteeing that certain canons of reasonableness would prevail across all communities of rational human beings.

Whereas the liberals stress the universality of reason, postliberals emphasize the particularity of the Christian narrative. Human understanding is inextricably bound with the narratives by which humans view the world and their place in it. The task of Christian theology is not a matter of correlating its truths with those discovered in other disciplines. Rather, it involves Christian self-description. The Christian narrative, stretching from the beginning of creation to the final consummation of the kingdom, in the expression of the postliberal theologian, George Lindbeck, "absorbs the world" that Christians inhabit.[2] The Christian way of life involves becoming proficient in the

---

2. Lindbeck, *Nature of Doctrine*, 118.

language of Christian narrative and acquiring the virtues that characterize the Christian way of being in the world. Unlike orthodox theologies that see the truth of Christian claims as consisting in a correspondence between statement and objective reality, the postliberal approach sees no way of definitively proving or disproving Christian claims in this way. While certainly not ruling out the possibility that doctrines do in fact correspond to the nature of God or Christ, the postliberals insist that we cannot step outside the language we used to know if, or in what way, the propositions we make are true. We can only apply a regulative test as to whether a proposition coheres with the way of life described in the Christian narrative.

Postliberalism has its critics on both the orthodox and liberal sides. First, the orthodox have reservations about the postliberals' account of truth. The Evangelical theologian, Alister McGrath, has taken issue with Lindbeck on this very point. "The possibility (which Lindbeck seems unwilling and unable to consider) is that the discourse that he identifies Christian doctrine as regulating . . . may represent a serious misrepresentation, or even a deliberate falsification, of historical events; and that it may represent a completely spurious interpretation of the significance of Jesus Christ."[3] Identifying claims that are compatible with the Christian narrative is an element of Christian thought, but it does not address the critical question of whether these claims are in fact correct. On the liberal side, the ethicist James Gustafson writes, "George Lindbeck's commendation of 'the ancient practice of absorbing the universe into the biblical world' does not come naturally to anyone I know. It is hard to determine what *the* biblical world is; there clearly are many. Even if one could, it is not easy to *absorb* neuroscience and genetics, black holes and quarks, viruses and broken limbs, Alzheimer's disease and bipolar disorder, Palestinian-Israeli and Northern Ireland tensions into biblical, theological, or other religious discourse."[4] If all of this suggests that the contemporary theological scene is fragmented, it is the next position that emphasizes this fact.

Postmodernism is a broad term covering a variety of positions, and as such, defies precise definition. In general terms, postmodernism is marked by a deep and abiding suspicion of any system of thought that claims to have been given some privileged access into the true nature of reality or that attempts to provide a grand narrative in which all of reality can be properly understood. As the postmodern thinker John Caputo puts it, "The secret is that there is no Secret, no capitalized Know-it-all Breakthrough Principle or

---

3. McGrath, "Evangelical Evaluation," 38.

4. Gustafson, *Examined Faith*, 9. Gustafson's own theology is grounded in the Reformed tradition. See *Ethics from a Theocentric Perspective*, chapter 4.

Revelation that lays things out the way they Really Are and thereby lays to rest the conflict of interpretations. When we open our mouths, it is only we who are speaking, poor existing individuals, as Kierkegaard likes to put it, and we would be ill advised to think that we are the Mouthpiece of Being or the Good or of the Almighty."[5] As the claims of a group (operating within its own interpretive framework) grow more and more absolute, the suspicion of the postmodern thinker rises. Typically, however, this is coupled with a realization that none of this removes us from the reality of having to navigate our way in this world. We may be awash in a world of interpretations, with no certain way of adjudicating conflicting interpretations, but at the same time, we are compelled to act, to name injustice, and to treasure some ideals while rejecting others.

The critics of postmodernism fear that such a position endorses relativism, a state in which one interpretation is no better or worse than any other interpretation. Caputo counters, "I do not recommend ignorance and I am not saying that there is no truth, but I am arguing that the best way to think about truth is to call it the best interpretation that anybody has come up with yet while conceding that no one knows what is coming next."[6] For the postmoderns, our inability to know definitively which position is right ("undecidability") speaks to the traditional concept of faith. "If we really do not know who we are, then faith is really faith. Undecidability protects faith and prayer from closure and in keeping them thus at risk also keeps them safe."[7] Keeping beliefs at risk paradoxically keeps them safe from the danger of dispassionate engagement. Postmodernism is "the willingness to get along as best we can *without* capital letters and *without* final authoritative pronouncements, without a Knowledge of the Secret, and to splash about in the waters of undecidability."[8] The spirit of postmodernism, then, is one of disruption of all final answers. Critics fear that this leaves us with chaos; supporters insist that it is the crucial realization we need to make in order to find our way among the fragmented world in which we live.

---

5. Caputo, *On Religion*, 21.
6. Ibid.
7. Ibid., 130.
8. Ibid., 126–27. Emphasis original.

Basil and Ambrose

Similarities in the *Hexameron*

If a reader were to compare the *Hexameron* by both Basil and Ambrose, he or she would be struck by the deep similarity between the structure and purpose of the two works. Both are comprised of nine sermons delivered extemporaneously during Holy Week. Basil delivered his sermons around 378 in Caesarea and Ambrose presented his in the following decade in Milan. Both are a combination of philosophical debate, moral exhortation, and catechetical instruction. Each author prefaces his scriptural commentary with a spirited defense of the Christian doctrine of creation *ex nihilo* ("from nothing") and then engages in a detailed examination of each of the six days of the creation story narrated in the opening chapter of Genesis.

Basil and Ambrose both had a working knowledge of ancient scientific works on natural history, zoology, and botany. In his study of Basil, the theologian Stephen Hildebrand notes Basil's familiarity with Plato's creation story found in the *Timaeus*, Aristotle's theory of the interaction of elements, and the Stoic concept of a divine law inscribed in the nature of plants and animals.[9] Both Ambrose and Basil, however, display a keen interest in refuting any cosmological theory that suggested that God shaped preexisting material. Ambrose repeats Basil's principle, "It is absolutely necessary that things begun in time be also brought to an end in time."[10] Not only is this a point of doctrine that both church leaders would feel compelled to defend, it also supports a particular reading of nature and human history. If we could go back to the start of time, says Basil, we would discover that "the world was not devised at random or to no purpose, but to contribute to some useful end and to the great advantage of all beings, if it is truly a training place for rational souls and a school for attaining the knowledge of God, because through visible and perceptible objects it provides guidance to the mind for the contemplation of the invisible" (I.6). Unlike ancient atomistic thinking that suggested that "the universe was without guide and without rule, as if borne around by chance" (I.2), Basil insists that the universe bears witness to the power, providence, and beauty of God. It is a school, a training place, for gaining knowledge of God. Through the creation we can glimpse into the mind of the Creator (I.11). Additionally, a universe that has a beginning in time and an end in

---

9. Hildebrand, *Trinitarian Theology*, 115–16.

10. Basil of Caesarea, *Hexameron*, I.7. Ambrose repeats this idea in *Hexameron*, I.10. All citations of the *Hexameron* from both Basil and Ambrose are taken from the translations in the bibliography unless otherwise noted.

time naturally turns the mind of those who contemplate it to the end of time, to a "future age with a spiritual and never ending light" (II.8).

Basil and Ambrose both regard the first creation story as a divinely inspired text and proceed accordingly in their close reading of it throughout the *Hexameron*. Where modern scholars focus on issues such as the relationship between the priestly account of creation (the modern designation given to the first creation story that was edited into its present form by the priests during the Babylonian exile) and the ancient Babylonian creation story *Enuma Elish*, Basil and Ambrose approach the text with an eye toward spiritual truth and moral exhortation. This becomes immediately apparent as we read their commentary on the events described during the first day of creation: the spirit of God sweeps over the waters on the formless earth covered in darkness; God separates the light from the darkness, and day and night are created. Relying on a Syrian interpreter whom he trusts, Basil argues that the spirit or wind of God sweeping over the waters might be better understood as "warmed with fostering care" as in the case of "a bird brooding upon eggs and imparting some vital power to them as they are being warmed" (II.6). This powerful maternal image of God suggests a vision of the world imbued with the life-giving power of God. Ambrose emphasizes the moral lesson found in the opening verses of Genesis: humans, not God, created evil. "If evil has no beginning, as if uncreated or not made by God, from what source did nature derive it?" It stems from our deviation from the path of virtue. "Our adversary is within us, within us is the author of error, locked, I say, within our very selves. Look closely on your intentions; explore the disposition of your mind; set up guards to watch over the thoughts of your mind and the stupidities of your heart" (I.8.31).

Basil and Ambrose continue to draw spiritual and moral lessons from each of the subsequent days in the creation story. No element of the created order is too insignificant for our contemplative consideration. The assessment of the Greek Orthodox theologian Doru Costache regarding Basil applies equally well to Ambrose: "the exploration of creation and the effort to picture a worldview ultimately became for St. Basil a quest for the marks of the Creator's wisdom and the meaning of human life."[11] The variety of trees, for example, reflects the differences between virtuous and deceitful persons. While we may marvel at the symmetry of the pine cone, says Ambrose, the tamarisk tree reminds us that duplicitous individuals often intermingle with people of good will. "For, just as there are men everywhere who are double-dealers at heart, who, while they show themselves to be gracious and unaffected in the presence of good men, cleave to those who are most

11. Costache, "Christian Worldview," 28.

vicious—so in a similar way these plants have a contrary tendency to spring up in both well-watered regions and in desert lands. That is why [Jeremiah] compared dubious and insincere characters to tamarisks" (III.16.69). Likewise, crabs stealthily place a pebble within the shell of the oyster to prevent it from closing, and then insert their claw and devour the oysters. "There are men who, like the crab, exercise surreptitiously their guile on others and fortify their own weaknesses by the use of certain inherent characteristics. Thus they weave a web of deceit around their brethren and find their sustenance in another's anxieties" (V.8.23). The natures of various birds, too, provide models of human virtue and vice. We should emulate the love and care of the bird known as the waterfowl who "adopts the nestling of the eagle when disowned or not recognized and allows him to mingle with her own brood. She exercises over him the same maternal care as she does her own, providing food and nourishment impartially" (V.18.61).

Basil and Ambrose: Differences in Biblical Interpretation

There are literally dozens of similar moral reflections offered by Basil and Ambrose based on the nature of various plants, sea creatures, and land animals, but they do have one key difference in their respective approaches to biblical interpretation.[12] Basil preferred staying close to the "literal meaning" of the text, though we might today describe it as "the plain meaning." Ambrose on occasion employs an allegorical interpretation that allows for pairing different elements in the biblical story to persons or events outside the passage under consideration. These two methods of biblical interpretation have traditionally been associated with two different centers of thought in the ancient world: the literal with the city of Antioch and the allegorical favored by readers in Alexandria. Scholars today, however, insist that this distinction does not always hold up in practice, so it needs to be understood as a generalization.

Basil expresses his reservation regarding the use of allegory in Homily IX.[13] "I know the laws of allegory, although I did not invent them of myself, but have met them in the works of others. Those who do not admit the

---

12. For a discussion of the differences between Basil and Ambrose, see Swift, "Basil and Ambrose on the Six Days of Creation," 317–28.

13. Richard Lim argues that Basil does not categorically rule out the use of allegory, "but that, instead, he is warning his specific, and largely unsophisticated, audience not to abandon the literal meaning of scriptures in favor of more arcane spiritual meanings" in his "The Politics of Interpretation," 362. Hildebrand points out that Basil does in fact employ the allegorical method in his commentary on the Psalms; see his *Trinitarian Theology*, 122–39.

common meaning of the Scriptures say that water is not water, but some other nature, and they explain a plant and a fish according to their opinion. They describe also the production of reptiles and wild animals, changing it according to their own notions, just like the dream interpreters, who interpret for their own ends the appearances seen in their dreams" (IX.1). According to Basil, sticking to the plain meaning of the text guards against the introduction of wild speculation into the act of interpretation. The historian Philip Rousseau describes Basil's starting point: "one had to take the text at face value . . . simply, without burrowing away to find difficulties and complexities that were not there. The truth, Basil felt, was by its nature 'naked' and therefore easily discovered."[14] The waters above the firmament and waters below the firmament are simply that: water. Those who regard the waters above the dome as powers praising God, while regarding the waters that have fallen to earth as powers of malice, are introducing false and dangerous ideas. Rather, "let us consider water as water" (III.9).

In the course of his commentary on the creation of the heavenly bodies, Ambrose offers an allegorical interpretation in which the moon represents the church and the sun represents Christ. "Deservedly is the moon compared to the Church, who has shone over the entire world and says as she illuminates the darkness of this world: 'the night is far advanced, the day is at hand.' . . . Looking down, then, the Church has, like the moon, her frequent risings and settings. She has grown, however, by her settings and has by their means merited expansion at a time when she is undergoing diminution through persecution and while she is being crowned by the martyrdom of her faithful" (IV.8.32). The moon, of course, does not produce its own light, but merely reflects the light of the sun. In the same way, "Not from her own light does the Church gleam, but from the light of Christ. From the Sun of Justice has her brilliance been obtained, so that it is said: 'It is now no longer I that live, but Christ lives in me'" (IV.8.32). As the patristics scholar Michael Heintz observes, "[A]llegory, rather than being for Ambrose simply a means around the awkwardness of the literal sense, functioned catechetically as a vehicle through which his hearers saw the events recorded in the Scriptures as enacted in the present-day life of the community, particularly in its sacramental or ritual life; that is, allegory served to engage his listeners more deeply in the liturgical life of the local church."[15] For example, the Spirit sweeping across the waters at creation is a foreshadowing of the Spirit moving over the waters of baptism. Allegory, therefore, provided the link by which Ambrose joined the narrative world of

---

14. Rousseau, *Basil of Caesarea*, 323.
15. Heintz, "Ambrose of Milan," 120.

the Bible with the world inhabited by those who crowded into the cathedral in Milan to hear him preach.

Basil and Ambrose's Aesthetic Vision of Creation

Despite their differences regarding the appropriateness of offering an allegorical interpretation, Basil and Ambrose share a deep conviction that "the world is a work of art, set before all for contemplation, so that through it the wisdom of Him who created it should be known" (Basil, I.7). Both thinkers employed a variety of artistic metaphors when speaking about the relationship between God and the created order. God is the divine Artist (Ambrose, I.6.22); the artistry and order of the natural world guide us in forming an idea about God who is the source of all beauty and wisdom (Basil I, 11), and every element of the created order, depending on the preferred metaphor in that homily, lends its voice to a hymn praising God, adds its step to a dance celebrating God (Ambrose, III.4.18), or offers another chapter unfolding God's story of salvation (Basil, 9.2). Basil's opening comments to his congregation at the start of his sixth homily captures his sense of wonderment at the beauty and splendor of the creation wrought by the hands of God. "If, at any time in the clear cool air of the night, while gazing at the indescribable beauty of the stars, you conceived an idea of the Creator of the universe—who He is who had dotted the heavens with such flowers . . . or again, if at times you observed with sober reflection the wonders of the day and through visible things you inferred the invisible Creator, you come as a prepared listener and one worthy to fill up this august and blessed assembly" (VI.1).

Among the wide variety of artistic metaphors that both Basil and Ambrose employ, musical ones figure most prominently. Both the heavens and the earth sing a song of praise to the Creator (Ps 19:1–4). Following an ancient belief, Basil believed that the universe itself emitted a pleasant song as the seven planets held in place in crystalline spheres revolved around the earth. "Certainly, this is not more incredible than the seven circles through which nearly all philosophers with one consent agree that the seven planets are borne, and which they say are fitted one into the other like jars inserted into each other. And these, carried around in the opposite direction to everything else, when they cleave through the ether, give out such a melodious and harmonious sound that it supposes the sweetest singing" (Basil III.3; see Ambrose, II.2.6). On the terrestrial level, the four elements of earth, air, fire, and water interact in a similarly harmonious fashion. "The earth is dry and cold, the water is cold and moist, the air is moist and warm, and the fire is warm and dry. Thus, though their combining qualities each receives the faculty of mixing with the other; and, in fact, each through a common quality mixes with its neighboring element, and throughout the union with that which is near, it combines with its opposite ... Thus, it becomes a circle and a harmonious choir, since all are in unison and have mutually corresponding elements" (Basil, IV.5).

The birds sing a chorus of praise to God from sunrise to sunset and throughout the night. "It is customary for the birds at nesting time 'to charm the sky with song,' in joy that their allotted task is done. This usually happens, following, as it were, a ritual pattern, at dawn and at sunset, when the birds sing the praises of their Creator, at the moment of transition from day to night or night to day" (Ambrose, V.12.36). A chorus of song heralds the start of a new day. "Would that the nightingale were to give forth a song to arouse a sleeper from his slumber! That is the bird accustomed to signal the rising of the sun at dawn and to spread abroad joy more penetrating than morning light. Still, if sweetness is lacking in their song, we have with us the moaning turtle-dove, the cooing pigeon, and 'the raven who with deep tones calls down the rain.'" During the day, the "natural chant" of swan's song fills the air with "strains of most tuneful and delightful music" (Ambrose, V.12.39). In the evening, birds "conceal themselves in their hiding places, saluting the close of day with a song, lest they depart without offering such thanks as a creature owes to glorify his Creator" (Ambrose, V.24.84). The descent of darkness does not end the birds' performance. "Night also has its songs wherewith to soothe the hearts of men who lie awake. The night owl, too, makes a contribution of song" (Ambrose, V.24.85).

As Ambrose approaches the end of the *Hexameron,* he turns his attention to the creation of man and woman in the divine image. After extolling the musicality of the birds of the sky, Ambrose switches his artistic metaphor to portraits when describing the unique place humanity enjoys in creation. Based on the passage from Isaiah, "Behold, Jerusalem, I have painted the walls" (49:16), Jerusalem is interpreted allegorically to refer to the soul. "That soul of yours is painted by God, who holds in Himself the flashing beauty of virtue and the splendor of piety. That soul is well painted in which shines the imprint of divine operation ... Precious is that picture which in its brilliance is in accord with that divine reflection" (Ambrose, VI.6.42).

Just like pollution and the effects of time can obscure the brilliance of a famous portrait, sin has a corrosive effect on the soul. The Christian life, then, becomes a continual process of preservation and restoration. "Man has been depicted by the Lord God, his artist. He is fortunate in having a craftsman and a painter of distinction. He should not erase that painting, one that is a product of truth, not a semblance, a picture, expressed not in mere wax, but in the grace of God" (VI.8.47).

When the human soul displays its beauty in all its brilliance to God and neighbor, it is the most splendid portrait on exhibition in God's gallery that is filled with countless exquisite works.

Sallie McFague's *Life Abundant*

While the theologian Sallie McFague shares Basil's and Ambrose's sense of wonderment at the beauty and harmony of the natural world, her theological vision is tempered by an anguished concern about the present state of our environment. In her 2001 work, *Life Abundant*, McFague calls for a revision of our current cultural and theological worldview so that we can envision a way of life that is focused on the well-being of the planet rather than on satisfying the insatiable demands of a consumer society. "My reflections coalesce around this point: what I have learned about who God is, who we are, and where we fit into the scheme of things tells me that the one thing needful in a theology for twenty-first century North American middle-class Christians is an alternative view of the abundant life from that of our consumer society. *Life Abundant* is about this reconstruction."[16] Her book falls into three parts: a discussion of the theological positions underpinning her proposal; a comparison of a worldview presented in neo-classical economics and that promoted in her ecological economic worldview; and an account of how we can better understand the meaning of God, Christ, and the world in our twenty-first-century context.

McFague begins by identifying "the relative absolute" that animates her theology. She defines a "relative absolute" as "a central conviction that is neither a foundation nor the 'essence' of Christianity, but a deeply held, abiding insight into God's relation with us . . . my relative absolute is that we give God glory by loving the world and everything in it."[17] This core conviction steers a middle course between "ideological absolutism" and "radical relativism."[18] While "theological statements . . . are risky, partial uncertain assertions made by relative historically bound creatures about universal matters—God, world, and human beings," they also represent a thinker's deepest conviction about what is most universally true.[19] It is from the vantage point of this "relative absolute" that McFague evaluates two

16. McFague, *Life Abundant*, 11.
17. Ibid., 29.
18. Ibid., 61.
19. Ibid., 29.

competing worldviews: the neo-classical economic model and McFague's own "ecological economic model." "The first model sees the planet as a corporation or syndicate, as a collection of individual human beings drawn together to benefit its members by optimal use of natural resources. The second model sees the planet more like an organism or a community that survives and prospers through the interrelationship and interdependence of its many parts, both human and nonhuman."[20] Emphasizing the "relative" pole of "the relative absolute" McFague notes that as worldviews, both are *interpretations* of reality and *descriptions* of reality.[21] They are both models of socially constructed reality, and as such, are capable of being altered. Emphasizing the "absolute" pole, however, McFague insists that the choice between models is not a theologically neutral one. "A working definition of Christian theology," writes McFague, "as I understand it, goes like this: Theology is reflection on experiences of God's liberating love from various contexts and within the Christian community."[22] This returns us to McFague's "relative absolute"—our worldview is limited, partial, and historically conditioned, but the Christian tradition boldly stakes a claim that God's love is a liberating love offered to all creation, and so that by loving the earth, we give glory to God.

In the final part of *Life Abundant* McFague analyzes how God, Christ, and the life of Christian discipleship appear differently when viewed through the interpretive lens of the neoclassical economic model and the ecological economic model. We begin, then, with the contrasting understandings of the God-world relationship in the two models. The dominant image of nature in the neoclassical economic model is that of a machine. The physical world operates according to certain immutable laws that modern physics has been able to express mathematically. God in turn ensures the constant operation of these laws. McFague sees in this model a distant God who does not "interfere" with the normal functioning of the world. In the ecological economic model, organic imagery dominates. The world is metaphorically God's body. Distancing herself from a pantheistic interpretation of this image, McFague insists that while the world is *in* God, it is not identical to God. "With the metaphor of the world as God's body, God as the agent or spirit in and through all that is (as our spirits are the energizers of our bodies) we can imagine a united view of God and the world, which does not, however, identify them."[23]

20. Ibid., 72.
21. Ibid., 71.
22. Ibid., 40.
23. Ibid., 141.

The God-world relationship suggested in each of the economic models shapes how we view Christ and the nature of the salvation. The distant relationship between God and the world in the neoclassical model results in an understanding of Christ as the unique and unsurpassable union of human and divine nature in history. McFague criticizes the traditional understanding of the Incarnation as the singular moment in human history in which God dwelt among us in the flesh. "In the traditional picture, the incarnation of God occurs at one point and one point only in the world—in the man Jesus. God is not everywhere all the time, for apart from creating the world, God enters it just once."[24] The organic imagery of the ecological economic model suggests Christ is the chief exemplar of a divine-human interrelation that permeates all of creation. "By bringing God into the realm of the body, of matter, nature is included within the divine reach. This inclusion, however, is possible only if incarnation is understood in a broad, not a narrow fashion; that is, if Jesus as the incarnate Logos, Wisdom, or Spirit of God is paradigmatic of what is evident everywhere else as well."[25]

The life of Christian discipleship arising from the understanding of the God-world relationship and the nature of Christ takes different forms when viewed from the lens of each economic model. Individual rights and freedom from governmental intrusion are hallmarks of the neoclassical economic model, and solidarity and the common good are central themes in the ecological economic model. The views of the life of discipleship follow suit. "In the neoclassical model, the individual, freed from his or her sins by Christ, is expected to live a moral life, being generous to the poor and a good steward of the natural resources that we need . . . In the ecological model, human life is basically communal—sin is therefore a relational matter, being out of appropriate relations with God and neighbor (which includes non-human neighbors)."[26]

In short, each view offers a different vision of what constitutes "the abundant life." While it is commonly associated with an individual's luxurious lifestyle, the abundant life for McFague is the state in which all planetary life flourishes—"it is a vision of abundance that will include each and every creature, especially the most vulnerable and oppressed."[27]

24. Ibid., 159.
25. Ibid., 169.
26. Ibid., 132.
27. Ibid., 197.

The Revitalization of the Image of the Six-Day Creation

At the outset of our study of Basil, Ambrose, and McFague, we posed a series of questions regarding the image of the six-day creation story. Can the image of the six-day creation still inform the theology, spirituality, and morality of a Christian community that no longer shares Basil and Ambrose's understanding of the universe, their theory of the origins of species or their acceptance of the Mosaic authorship of the text? Can the six-day creation story still speak to Christians who are deeply troubled about the state of the environment and the role that humans have played in causing it? Is it possible to ground a theological position in Scripture, to critically engage the work of esteemed thinkers within the Christian tradition, and to respond in a way that is credible and meaningful to contemporary Christians? At first glance, given the many theological differences between Basil and Ambrose on the one hand and McFague on other, the prospects for revitalizing the image of the six-day creation seem dim. However, upon closer examination we discover a consensus in their thinking that makes it possible for us to forge several strategies that incorporate the theological insights of all three theologians.

This common ground centers on a cluster of artistic images concerning God, the world, and humanity. Ambrose praises the excellence of the "divine Artist and Craftsman" (I.6.22). Basil describes the world as "a work of art, set before all for contemplation, so that through it the wisdom of Him who created it should be known" (I.7). McFague observes, "Just as artists feel that they are embodied in their work, that who they are is expressed in their creations, so also God's glory is reflected in each and every creature, from the mite to the whale, from the acorn to the mountain, and in each one of us human beings."[28] As McFague observes, the interpretive lens through which we view these three realities produces a different understanding of the interrelationship among them. Viewed aesthetically, the God who creates is the source of all beauty; the world becomes an artistic expression, and we humans are seen as its caretakers, or perhaps even apprentices who complete the work begun by the master.

Ambrose, Basil, and McFague all seek to engender in their audience an overwhelming sense of awe and gratitude when considering the beauty of the natural world. For example, Ambrose's prose grows flowery when he considers the beauty of the sun. "It is true that it is the eye of the world, the joy of the day, the beauty of the heavens, the charm of nature and the most conspicuous object in creation. When you behold it, reflect on its Author.

---

28. Ibid., 145.

When you admire it, give praise to its Creator (IV.1.2). Basil likewise exhorts his listeners, "I want the marvel of creation to gain such complete acceptance from you that, wherever you may be found and whatever kind of plants you may chance upon, you may receive a clear reminder of the Creator" (V.2). McFague encourages a similar response when we consider that "love (and not indifference or malevolence) is at the heart of reality ... The *sanctus* is our response: the deepest religious emotions are awe and thanksgiving. If God is not a being or even just being-itself, but reality as good, then our astonishment and gratitude knows no bounds."[29]

As we have seen, Basil and Ambrose both speak of the natural world in terms of musical analogies. Basil describes a "general chorus of creation" that "harmoniously sings a hymn of praise to the Creator" (III.9). Given Ambrose's reputation as "the father of hymnody," it is not surprising that musical images abound in the *Hexameron*.[30] In the worshipping community "we hear the voice of people singing in harmony the praises of God" (Ambrose, III.1.5). Nature itself lends its voice to the song of praise, from the sweet song of the nightingale to the summer serenade of the cicada. "How sweet is the chant from the tiny throat of a cicada! In the heart of midsummer 'they rend the thickets' with their songs. The greater the heat at midday, the more musical become their songs ... " (Ambrose, V.22.76).

The many dimensions of music provide a number of possible uses for the image in contemporary theology. Different facets of musical composition, performance, and enjoyment resonate with each of the four theological approaches surveyed earlier. Those favoring the path of orthodoxy would appreciate the theologian Hans Urs von Balthasar's image of God's revelation as a symphony. "In his revelation, God performs a symphony, and it is impossible to say which is richer: the seamless genius of his composition or the polyphonous orchestra of Creation that has prepared to play it."[31] This insight dovetails nicely with Basil's vision of the Word of God moving throughout all of human history. "Consider the word of God moving through all creation, having begun at that time, active up to the present, and efficacious until the end, even to the consummation of the world" (IX. 2). The six-day creation is the opening movement in this divine symphony, and the natural world provides the instruments whose melodic sounds echo throughout time.

---

29. Ibid., 137.

30. For a discussion of Ambrose's thought on music, see chapter 7 of Stapert, *New Song*.

31. Balthasar, *Truth is Symphonic*, 8.

CHAPTER ONE: THE FIRST CREATION STORY

The liberal tradition, which regards religious statements as expressions of depth-experiences, sees in music the potent articulation of the yearnings of the human spirit. The civil rights leader Andrew Young relates the story of the time police had blocked protesters from marching to the Birmingham jail.

> When we go about two blocks from the jail, the police had blocked the street with the dogs and the fire trucks. When we got there, they said, "You can't go to the jail." And so everybody got down on their knees and started praying. And when people are in that kind of situation, it's not a verbal prayer, it's more a moan. And when the emotional, scared, religious people start moaning, something happens. And something happened not only to us but to the police.
>
> And somebody jumped up. A lady said, "God is with this movement. We're going on to the jail." And we started walking directly at the police and the dogs. And all of a sudden, the dogs weren't barking, and we started singing, "I want Jesus to walk with me." And when you get through and you looked back, you saw all of these fire trucks blocking the street. And some good little sister hollered, "Great God Almighty done parted the Red Sea one more time!"[32]

The spiritual, "I Want Jesus to Walk With Me" not only expressed the protesters' faith, but also impacted the police who had barred their way. The theological challenge for those in the liberal tradition is to capture Basil, Ambrose, and McFague's sense of awe and wonderment at the beauty of the natural world and express it in a way that inspires people to break through barriers.

Postliberal theologians emphasize the power of language to shape experience and reinforce communal identity in a fragmented world. The postliberal ethicist Stanley Hauerwas speaks of the power of art to shape our vision of the world. "Art, whether representational or not, reveals to us aspects of our world that we are usually too dependent on conventionality and fantasy to be able to see. Art shows us how difficult it is to be objective by showing us how different the world can look."[33] Just as Basil refers to the world as "a training place for rational souls" (I.6), Hauerwas regards the church as the training ground for acquiring the skills necessary to see the world as described in the Christian narrative. The church's songs,

---

32. Andrew Young as quoted in the episode, "The Soul of a Nation" in the PBS documentary, "God in America."
33. Hauerwas, *Vision and Virtue*, 39–40.

prayers and liturgical practices play an indispensable role in shaping the members' vision of the world. As Ambrose recognized, the Christian practice of baptizing and breaking bread only makes sense within the narrative world of the Bible in which creation, redemption, and sanctification are inextricably linked. The postliberal strategy for revitalizing the image of the six-day creation would be to highlight the connections between the practices of the Christian community (e.g., blessings) and the biblical narrative's depiction of the natural world as a contingent reality that owes its very existence to the love and will of God.

Postmodern thinkers, who are deeply suspicious of all definitive claims about truth, find in the improvisation of jazz musicians a fitting image of contemporary theology. In his recent work, *Theology as Improvisation*, the theologian Nathan Crawford writes, "My thesis is that theology is improvisation. I claim this because improvisation offers a way of thinking that is inherently open."[34] Crawford contends that improvisation requires being "rooted in a tradition" while at the same time remaining open to "reorienting and transforming the tradition."[35] The task of the theologian is to assemble the fragments of our highly pluralistic world into a coherent pattern without succumbing to the temptation of thinking that this coherence amounts to an all-encompassing account of truth. "The theologian needs a way of bringing the fragments together that does not seek to systematize or totalize them, but give them a certain coherence (although, this is, at times, quite loose) by thinking their similarities-in-difference."[36] Postmodern theologians bring the voices of criticism to bear on the attitudes and behaviors of Christians that have contributed to the environmental crisis, while at the same time, constructing what the postmodern Scripture scholar Walter Brueggemann calls a "counterworld of evangelical imagination." According to Brueggemann, "Creation faith is a doxological response to the wonder that I/we/the world exist. It pushes the reason for one's existence out beyond one's self to find that reason in an inexplicable, inscrutable, loving generosity that redefines all our modes of reasonableness."[37] The springboard into this "counterworld of evangelical imagination" is the six-day creation story. Whether it be a symphony, a spiritual, a hymn, or a jazz performance, musical expression in all its forms has the potential to revitalize the image of the six-day creation in the lives of Christians who see the beauty of God's creation, but fear for its long-term survival.

34. Crawford, *Theology as Improvisation*, 4.
35. Ibid., 5.
36. Ibid., 148.
37. Brueggemann, *Texts Under Negotiation*, 29.

Discussion Questions

1. What features of the six-day creation story do you find most striking? What questions do contemporary Christians have in terms of the story?
2. Which theological approach do you find most compelling: orthodoxy, liberalism, postliberalism, or postmodernism? Why?
3. How would you describe Basil and Ambrose's vision of the natural world?
4. Do you find the allegorical approach to biblical interpretation appealing or unappealing? Why?
5. How would you describe your own "relative absolute" in theology?
6. Do you agree or disagree with McFague's understanding of the relationship between God and the world?
7. How might music provide a helpful way for thinking about theology, creation, or the Christian life?

Suggested Readings

For an introduction to postliberalism, see Ronald T. Michener, *Postliberal Theology: A Guide for the Perplexed* (New York: Bloomsbury, 2013). For an introduction to postmodernism, see Kevin Hart, *Postmodernism* (Oxford: Oneworld, 2004). For background on Basil, see Andrew Radde-Gallwitz, *Basil of Caesarea: A Guide to His Life and Doctrine* (Eugene, OR: Cascade, 2012) and Stephen M. Hildebrand, *The Trinitarian Theology of Basil of Caesarea* (Washington, DC: Catholic University of America Press, 2007). For a discussion of Basil's exegesis, see John A. McGuckin, "Patterns of Biblical Exegesis in the Cappadocian Fathers: Basil the Great, Gregory the Theologian, and Gregory of Nyssa" in S. T. Kimbrough Jr., ed., *Orthodox and Wesleyan Scriptural Understanding and Practice* (Crestwood, NY: St. Vladimir's Seminary Press, 2005). For background on Ambrose, see the Introduction to Boniface Ramsey, *Ambrose* (New York: Routledge, 1997). For a discussion of Ambrose's *Hexameron*, see Stanley P. Rosenberg, "Nature and the Natural World in Ambrose's *Hexameron*," *Studia Patristica* LXIX (2013) 15–24. For a discussion of early Christian thought on creation, see Paul M. Blowers, *Drama of the Divine Economy* (Oxford: Oxford University Press, 2012).

Chapter Two: The Second Creation Story

As we move into the second creation and the story of the fall, we delve into a treasure trove of images that have fueled the Christian imagination for two millennia: Adam and Eve, the tree of knowledge, the cunning snake, and the banishment from Eden, to name but a few. Through these powerful and enduring images Christians have understood, among other things, the power of temptation, the relationship between men and women, and the painful riddle of disease and death. Our first thinker, Gregory of Nyssa (ca. 335–ca. 395), links our present discussion with the preceding chapter's discussion of creation. His older brother Basil ended his *Hexameron* before discussing the creation of humanity (Gen 1:26). Shortly after his brother's death, Gregory took up the mantle and devoted his energies to a treatise traditionally entitled, *On the Making of Man*[1] dealing with the creation of humanity in the first creation story as well as the creation of Adam and Eve and their fall. The complex dynamic in Christian thought between humans' exalted status as beings created in the image and likeness of God and their lowly status as fallen sinners informed the autobiographical reflections of our second thinker, the great Puritan sage John Bunyan (1628–88) in his *Grace Abounding to the Chief of Sinners*. We conclude with a groundbreaking reading of the second creation story in the seminal 1973 piece, "Eve and Adam: Genesis 2–3 Reread" by the feminist biblical scholar Phyllis Trible. Trible's reading of the Eve and Adam story challenged the centuries-old use of the story as a legitimation of gender discrimination.

Gregory of Nyssa's Interpretation of the Creation Stories

On the Making of Man falls neatly into two parts: in the first (chapters 1–15), Gregory beautifully describes the spiritual resemblance that exists between the nature of humans and the nature of God as a result of humans' unique status as beings created in the image of God; in the second part (chapters 16–27), the tone turns more somber as Gregory contrasts humanity's present state of instability and conflict with its original prelapsarian state of

---

1. The work is also commonly cited by its Latin title, *De Hominis opificio*.

blessedness.² One of the most distinctive features of Gregory's theology of the human person appears in the first half of *Making*. His theory of a "double creation" relies upon the presence of two creation stories in Genesis. In the first story, "God created humankind in his image, in the image of God he created them; male and female he created them" (Gen 1:27) while in the second story God first creates Adam and then Eve. "Thus the creation of our nature is in a sense twofold: one made like to God, one divided according to this distinction: for something like this the passage darkly conveys by its arrangement, where it first says, 'God created man, in the image of God created He him,' and then, adding to what has been said, 'male and female created He them,'—a thing which is alien to our conceptions of God" (XVI, 8). Gregory further clarifies what this "double creation" means later in *Making*. "I take up then once more in my argument our first text:—God says, 'Let us make man in our image, after our likeness, and God created man, in the image of God created He him.' Accordingly, the Image of God, which we behold in universal humanity, had its consummation, but Adam as yet was not . . . " (XXII, 3). The image of God in which humans ("universal humanity") were created is not gendered. It is incorporeal and the capacities that it imparts to humans apply equally to men and women (XVI, 17).

Royal imagery pervades Gregory's description of human nature in the opening chapters of *Making*. Human nature "by its likeness to the King of all" has "a royal and exalted character." Rather than donning purple robes, humans are "clothed in virtue, which is in truth the most royal of all raiment, and in place of the sceptre, leaning on the bliss of immortality, and instead of the royal diadem, [they are] decked with the crown of righteousness" (*Making*, IV, 1). This "dignity of royalty" (IV, 1) accords humans a privileged status in God's created order. To be sure, humans, like all other living things, take in nutrients and grow and, like other animals, have senses that allow them to be keenly aware of their environment, but according to Gregory humans alone have the gift of reason. Along with reason, humans possess the gift of free will, "for the soul immediately shows its royal and exalted character . . . [in that it is] self-governed, swayed autocratically by its own will" (IV, 1). Rationality and freedom, two hallmarks of the soul's status as bearing the image of God, play a critical role in Gregory's theology, but so too does love. "Again, God is love, and the fount of love: for this the great John declares, that 'love is of God,' and 'God is love': the Fashioner of our nature has made this to be our feature too" (V, 2).

The human capacity to reason soundly, to act freely, and to love purely are for Gregory reflective of the royal status that humans enjoy by virtue of

2. On the structure of *Making*, see Behr, "Rational Animal," 66.

their creation in the image of God, but this alone does not give us the full picture of the human condition. The key is found in the sequence in which the first creation story unfolds. About the same time that Gregory was composing *Making*, he also composed a short work dedicated to a discussion of the soul and the future resurrected state. In this dialogue between himself and his dying sister Macrina, Gregory plays the part of the disciple seeking the wisdom of the elder spiritual guide. In the midst of their discussion of the emotions (or impulses), Macrina explains, "The holy word tells how the Divine proceeded by a certain route and orderly sequence to the creation of mankind. For when the universe had taken shape, as the narrative says, man did not immediately come onto the earth, but the nature of irrational animal preceded him, and plants preceded the animals."[3] Coming last in the order, humans carry within themselves the appetites for sustenance and the perception of what would contribute to or threaten their overall well-being. When we read that we are to subdue the earth and have dominion over its creatures, Macrina states, we should take that to mean that our rationality should direct our passions and intentions to their proper end. "Therefore if reason, which is the distinctive property of our nature, should gain dominance over those traits which are added to us from outside (the word of the Scripture has also revealed this as if in a riddle, bidding mankind to rule over all the irrational creatures) [Gen 1:28] none of these impulses would work in us for servitude to evil, but fear would produce obedience in us, anger courage, cowardice caution, and the desiring impulse would mediate to us the divine and immortal pleasure."[4] The emotions or impulses, in other words, are not necessarily vices, but they have the potential to become them if they are not directed to the true, the good, and the beautiful.[5]

Gregory believes that the two creation stories convey "to us a great and lofty doctrine" (XVI, 9), namely, that humans are the mean, the midpoint, or the juncture between the height of divinity and the depth of brutality. "While two natures—the Divine and incorporeal nature, and the irrational life of brutes—are separated from each other as extremes, human nature is the mean between them: for in the compound nature of man we may behold a part of each of the natures I have mentioned,—of the Divine, the rational and intelligent element, which does not admit the distinction of

---

3. Gregory of Nyssa, *On the Soul and the Resurrection*, 55. Roth mentions that the character Macrina seems to argue two different positions in the dialogue regarding the passions. At times she speaks of the passions as attached to the original "passionless blessedness" of the soul (114) and at other times as them being part of the soul from the start (n. 20, 56–57).

4. Ibid., 57.

5. Behr, "Rational Animal," 238.

male and female; of the irrational, our bodily form and structure, divided into male and female: for each of these elements is certainly to be found in all that partakes of human life" (XVI, 9). The dynamism inherent in the soul calls to mind the graceful motion of trapeze artists soaring high above the crowd. Their energy and exertion propel them in a graceful movement high above the net. Their exchanges require intense focus, but when successfully completed, their act appears effortless. In a similar way, Gregory speaks of the heights the soul can reach when reason holds sway over the emotions and the power of love desires what is truly beautiful: "we find that every such motion, when elevated by the loftiness of mind, is conformed to the beauty of the Divine image" (XVIII, 5). In terms of his analysis of the human condition, Pascal echoes Gregory's insight when he observes, "Man is neither angel nor beast; and the unfortunate thing is that he who would act the angel acts the brute."[6]

What happens, then, if our attention is diverted from what is most beautiful? Like the trapeze artists who mistime their movements, the soul falls to what is below. The tendency of sin "is heavy and downward" and "our soul is more inclined to be dragged downwards by the weight of the irrational nature than is the heavy and earthly element to be exalted by the loftiness of the intellect; hence the misery that encompasses us often causes the Divine gift to be forgotten, and spreads the passions of the flesh, like some ugly mask, over the beauty of the image" (XVIII, 6). We exchange the highest good for a lesser good.[7] To ask why we would make such a turn is to enter directly into the mystery that stands at the center of the creation stories. As Gregory writes in his *Great Catechism*, "No growth of evil had its beginning in the Divine will. Vice would have been blameless were it inscribed with the name of God as its maker and father. But the evil is, in some way or other, engendered from within, springing up in the will at that moment when there is a retrocession of the soul from the beautiful" (V).[8] Theologically, God can not be the cause of evil, but why there is a "retrocession" of the soul at all is one of the mysteries of the human condition that the creation stories acknowledge, but do not explain.

For Gregory, what was lost in the fall is regained at the final resurrection. For while Gregory does not mention the "garments of skins" (Gen 3:21) with which God clothed Adam and Eve after the fall in *Making*, in *On the Soul and the Resurrection* he lists the features of human life that these garments of skins symbolize. "These are the things which we have received

---

6. Pascal, *Pensees*, n. 358, 99.
7. Scuiry, "Anthropology of St. Gregory of Nyssa," 37.
8. Gregory of Nyssa, *Great Catechism*, 479.

from the irrational skin: sexual intercourse, conception, childbearing, dirt, lactation, nourishment, evacuation, gradual growth to maturity, the prime of life, old age, disease, and death."[9] In the resurrection, the human life will "be set free as it were from the reins, and revert once more, released and free, to the life of blessedness and impassibility" (XXII, 2) In *On the Soul and the Resurrection* Gregory writes, "Incorruptibility, glory, honor, and power, which are agreed to be characteristic of the divine nature, formerly belonged to the one made in God's image, and are expected to be ours again. The first ear [1 Cor 15:35–38] was the first man, Adam. Since at the entrance of evil our nature was split up into a multitude like the kernels in the ear, each of us, denuded of the form of that first ear and mixed with the earth, at the resurrection will spring up again in the archetypal beauty."[10] Just as humans are the midpoint between divinity and brutality, we also stand in a symbolic midpoint in history between creation and redemption.

John Bunyan's *Grace Abounding to the Chief of Sinners*

Where Gregory emphasized the inherent instability of the human soul and the way in which our thoughts and desires can fluctuate from the heights of divine contemplation to the basest emotions of jealousy and greed, John Bunyan (1628–88) provides a first-hand account of the anguish and uncertainty that can plague the human person. Though ostensibly Bunyan's autobiography, *Grace Abounding to the Chief of Sinners* defies precise classification.[11] It is not the classic model of a conversion story—there is no parallel to the blinding light on the road to Damascus. Neither is it an academic work intended to advance a position on the relationship between nature and grace. It might best be seen as a mixture of Puritan theology and spiritual testimony—a stylized account of his life story as he understood it through his own reading of the biblical narrative. With his evocation of 1 Tim 1:15 in the title and his lacing of biblical allusions throughout his work, Bunyan's *Grace Abounding* offers a profound reflection on human existence lived east of Eden.

The tumultuous British political and religious history of the seventeenth century provides the background for approaching *Grace Abounding*. The political battles between the king and the Parliament as well as the

---

9. Gregory of Nyssa, *On the Soul and the Resurrection*, 114.

10. Ibid., 119.

11. See Greaves, *John Bunyan and English Nonconformity* where he warns that "extreme caution must be used when employing [*Grace Abounding*] to construct Bunyan's life and religious experience" (38).

theological tensions between the Church of England and the Independent churches both impact the course of Bunyan's life. During the Civil War (1642–51) Bunyan served in the Parliamentary army, but when his regiment was disbanded in 1649 he returned to his trade as a tinker.[12] In 1653 Bunyan became a member of the Independent church in Bedford and a few years later began preaching in public. Following Oliver Cromwell's death, the monarchy was restored under Charles II (1660) and public preaching by those not licensed to do so became a matter of importance to local magistrates. In November of 1660 Bunyan was arrested for preaching and sentenced to three months in prison. His release was contingent upon his assurance that he would not preach in public again. At the end of his initial sentence, Bunyan refused to offer this assurance and so he remained in prison for the next twelve years. In 1666 Bunyan published *Grace Abounding*. Granted a royal pardon in 1672, Bunyan was released from prison. That same year the congregation at Bedford called him to be their pastor. He was imprisoned again for six months in 1677, probably for refusing to attend the parish church, and in the following year *The Pilgrim's Progress* first appeared in print. During a trip to London he fell ill and died in 1688.

The last work that Bunyan completed before serving his twelve-year prison sentence was *The Doctrine of the Law and Grace Unfolded* in which he expounded his "covenant theology," an area of great interest among Puritan thinkers. A number of Puritan concerns clustered around the idea of covenant (e.g., election, assurance of salvation, justification by faith), but at the heart of the debate was the issue of the individual's relationship to God. Bunyan himself speaks of a "covenant of works" and a "covenant of grace" (Heb 8:8–13). The covenant of works existed between God and Adam before the fall. The Lord commanded Adam not to eat from the tree of knowledge under punishment of death (Gen 2:16–17). The Ten Commandments, in Bunyan's view, are identical in substance to the command given to Adam.[13] With the fall, all of humanity falls under the punishment for Adam's disobedience. In his work on Bunyan, Pieter de Vries describes the new condition created by the fall. "Bunyan regarded the fall as a radical breach between God and man. From a human perspective it may be said to constitute a severance forever, without any likelihood whatsoever to bridge the chasm between man and God. The gloomiest hues are hardly adequate to paint man's predicament. He is dead in trespasses and sin."[14] The only escape for this bleak situation is a sharing in the covenant of grace established between

---

12. Owens, "Introduction," ix.
13. Bunyan, *Doctrine of the Law*, 25.
14. de Vries, *John Bunyan on the Order of Salvation*, 99.

the Father and the Son. This is established through faith, understood not as a human achievement but as a divine gift. In terms of the experience of the individual, a life lived under the covenant of works would produce a personality that is "sensitive of conscience to a diseased degree, beset by fears and insistent ideas" as well as one marked by a "fearful melancholy self-contempt and despair" as William James described Bunyan.[15]

The Bunyan scholar Michael Davies argues that the distinction between the covenant of works and the covenant of grace provides the key to understanding *Grace Abounding*. "Far from being a random sequence of unconnected experiences, impossible to fathom or to follow by convert and reader alike, *Grace Abounding* can be read according to a lucid process of salvation, charting the sinning believer's journey from a guilt-ridden state of enslavement under the covenant of law and works (according to the terms of Bunyan's covenant theology) to the liberty offered by a covenant of grace, faith in which brings blessed release for Bunyan from incarcerating fears and doubts."[16] As we discover, the blessed release is not a permanent state of being for Bunyan. In fact, the reader of *Grace Abounding* is struck by Bunyan's on-going vacillation between the terror of a life under the covenant of works and the serenity of a life under the covenant of grace. "Thus, by the strange and unusual assaults of the tempter, was my soul, like a broken vessel, driven, as with the winds, and tossed sometimes headlong into despair; sometimes upon the covenant of works, and sometimes to wish that the new covenant, and the conditions thereof, might so far as I thought myself concerned, be turned another way, and changed."[17]

Viewed from the perspective of the person living under the covenant of grace, *Grace Abounding* recalls Paul's dichotomy between the old Adam and the new Adam. "Therefore just as one man's trespass led to condemnation for all, so one man's act of righteousness leads to justification and life for all. For just as by the one man's disobedience the many were made sinners, so by the one man's obedience the many will be made righteous" (Rom 5:18–19). Experiencing the covenant of works, Bunyan writes, "I was more loathsome in mine own eyes than was a toad, and I thought I was so in God's eyes too: sin and corruption, I said, would as naturally bubble out of my heart, as water would bubble out of a fountain."[18] In a later reprise from his afflictions, he experiences the covenant of grace when he considers the righteousness of Christ. "Now did my chains fall off my legs indeed, I was

---

15. James, *Varieties of Religious Experience*, 154.
16. Davies, "John Bunyan and Spiritual Autobiography," 73–74.
17. Bunyan, *Grace Abounding*, 48.
18. Ibid., 14.

loosed from my affliction and irons, my temptations also fled away: so that from that time those dreadful scriptures of God left off to trouble me; now I went also home rejoicing, for the grace and love of God . . ."[19]

Many readers of Bunyan's autobiography would most likely agree with Vincent Newey's assessment: "Reading *Grace Abounding* is like travelling in a mighty maze whose plan is far from clear, and where at every turn we meet some new and puzzling psychodrama suggesting not so much providential design as solitary struggle in a spectacular universe of the mind's making."[20] Bunyan begins by recounting the nightmares that he suffered as a young boy of nine or ten when fearful visions of the fires of hell plagued his sleep. After marrying his first wife around 1648, Bunyan became convinced of his sinfulness, but tried unsuccessfully to reform his life. Once after hearing a sermon on the evil of breaking the Sabbath, he soon began playing a game of "cat" in which the player strikes a wooden dart that has been placed on the ground with a cudgel and then hits the airborne dart. "But the same day, as I was in the midst of a game of cat, and having struck it one blow from the hole; just as I was about to strike it the second time, a voice did suddenly dart from the heaven into my soul, which said, *Wilt thou leave thy sins, and go to heaven? Or have thy sins, and go to hell?* At this I was put to an exceeding maze; wherefore leaving my cat upon the ground, I looked up to heaven, and was as if I had with the eyes of my understanding, seen the Lord Jesus looking down upon me, as being very hotly displeased with me, and as if he did severely threaten me with some grievous punishment for these, and other my ungodly practices."[21]

He first had his eyes opened when "the good providence of God" brought him to the town of Bedford. While he was there he "came where there was three or four poor women sitting at a door in the sun, and talking about the things of God; and being now willing to hear them discourse, I drew near to hear what they said; for I was now a brisk talker also myself in matters of religion: but now I may say, *I heard, but I understood not*; for they were far above out of my reach, for their talk was about a new birth, the work of God on their hearts, and also how they were convinced of their miserable state by nature: they talked how God had visited their souls with his love in the Lord Jesus, and with what words and promises they had been refreshed, comforted, and supported against the temptations of Satan in particular . . ."[22] The women at Bedford seemed to Bunyan to have found

---

19. Ibid., 59.
20. Newey, "'With the Eyes of My Understanding,'" 192.
21. Bunyan, *Grace Abounding*, 11.
22. Ibid., 14.

"a new world" about which Bunyan knew nothing. On his various business trips, he would make a point to stop by Bedford and listen to the women. Slowly, Bunyan writes, "I began to look into the Bible with new eyes."[23] As Newey observes, "A measure of spiritual progress, and also its means, this 'new' capacity for perceiving truth, comfort, and direction stands over against the 'blind, ignorant' state of his unregenerate self before his acquaintance with the Bedford Church."[24] Bedford becomes for him the sunny city on the hill. "About this time, the state and happiness of these poor people at Bedford was thus in a kind of vision represented to me: I saw as if there were set on the sunny side of the mountain, there refreshing themselves with the pleasant beams of the sun, while I was shivering and shrinking in the cold, afflicted with frost, snow, and dark clouds."[25] A wall surrounded the city and Bunyan sought passage through the narrow gate. Bedford represented the warmth of Christian fellowship, the light of scriptural understanding, and the security of spiritual assurance.

Bunyan's glowing account of his time spent with the church at Bedford and its pastor John Gifford should not be taken to mean that he had found uninterrupted peace once he became a member. To the contrary, he experienced temptations so real that he reports that "sometimes I have thought I should see the devil, nay, thought I have I felt him behind me pull my clothes."[26] There are to be sure breaks in the storms of inner turmoil. "Now had I an evidence, as I thought, of my salvation from Heaven, with many golden seals, thereon, all hanging in my sight; now could I remember this manifestation, and the other discovery of grace with comfort; and should often long and desire that the last day were come, that I might for ever be inflamed with the sight, and joy, and communion of him, whose head was crowned with thorns, whose face was spit on, and body broken, and soul made an offering for my sins."[27] However, he also mentions in an offhanded manner his long periods of intense struggle. "So soon as this fresh assault had fastened on my soul, that scripture came into my heart, *This is for many days* (Dan 10:14), and indeed I found it was so: for I could not be delivered nor brought to peace again until well-nigh two years and an half were completely finished."[28] Certain biblical passages, such as Esau selling his birthright, haunted him. "But chiefly by the aforementioned scripture,

---

23. Ibid., 16.
24. Newey, "'With the eyes of my understanding,'" 196.
25. Bunyan, *Grace Abounding*, 18.
26. Ibid., 29.
27. Ibid., 34.
28. Ibid., 51.

concerning Esau's selling of his birthright; for that scripture would lie all day long, all the week long; yea, all the year long in my mind, and hold me down, so that I could by no means lift up myself; for when I would strive to turn me to this scripture, or that for relief, still that sentence would be sounding in me, *For ye know, how that afterward, when he would have inherited the blessing he found no place of repentance, though he sought it carefully with tears.*"[29] The weight of the passage regarding Esau selling his birthright was counterbalanced by Paul's assurance of the sufficiency of grace, and the scales in his mind tipped from one side to the other.[30]

Such oscillation may run counter to the typical conversion account in which doubt and confusion are cast aside, but it aligns nicely with Gregory's understanding of the Christian life. Gordon Wakefield keenly observes, "If, following Gregory of Nyssa and the Greek fathers, perfection is understood not as a state so much as a continual advance towards a transcendent glory which we attain only as we see that it beckons us to heights we have yet to scale, it may be more compatible with Bunyan's analogy of pilgrimage."[31] Davies makes a similar point when he observes, "What *Grace Abounding* shows the reader is that conversion into faith offers an escape neither from sin nor temptation. Rather it presents their accommodation within a doctrine of grace and forgiveness . . . For this reason, the visible saint that Bunyan progresses towards is not one perfected or freed from sin and temptation but, through grace, is pre-eminently both saint *and* chief of sinners."[32] In this way, perseverance rather than freedom from temptation marks the discipleship of those who have become new creations in Christ (2 Cor 5:17).

Phyllis Trible, "Eve and Adam: Genesis 2–3 Reread"

In 1973 the Scripture scholar Phyllis Trible published a seminal article, "Eve and Adam: Genesis 2–3 Reread," in which she challenged the long-standing interpretation of the Adam and Eve story as an endorsement of "male supremacy and female subordination."[33] We will focus on four key elements of Trible's argument.

First, Trible challenges the traditional reading of the second creation story that sees the man being created before the woman. She does so based on the two possible senses of the Hebrew word *'adham*.

29. Ibid., 37–38.
30. Ibid., 53.
31. Wakefield, "Bunyan and the Christian Life," 131–32.
32. Davies, *Graceful Reading*, 152–53.
33. Trible, "Eve and Adam," 251.

Ambiguity characterizes the meaning of ʾadham in Genesis 2–3. On the one hand, man is the first creature formed (2:7). The Lord God puts him in the garden "to till it and keep it," a job identified with the male (cf. 3:17–19). On the other hand, ʾadham is a generic term for humankind. In commanding ʾadham not to eat of the tree of knowledge of good and evil, the Deity is speaking to both the man and the woman (2:16–17). Until the differentiation of female and male (2:21–23), ʾadham is basically androgynous: one creature incorporating two sexes.[34]

This androgynous being, therefore, is the one formed by God in 2:7: "then the Lord God formed man from the dust of the ground, and breathed into his nostrils the breath of life; and the man became a living being." Trible contends that the creation of "the woman" and "the man" happens only later in 2:21–23 and that the creation of the woman, following behind the garden, the animals, and the man represents the "climax, not the decline" of the creation.[35] Trible's contention that "the woman" and "the man" are created concurrently in Genesis 2:23 has not gone unchallenged. For example, Robert Kawashima counters, "Far from indicating the woman's emergence prior to or simultaneous with the man's, however, this sentence *logically presupposes* the prior existence of man. Specifically, this directly quoted speech [2:23], presenting Adam's point of view, demonstrates that he *already* identified himself as 'man' before the creation of the woman out of his male body."[36]

Second, Trible argues that the formation of the man's ʿezer, which is often translated as "helpmate" or "suitable partner" should not be taken to mean "servant" or "subordinate." "Thus ʿezer is a relational term; it designates a beneficial relationship; and it pertains to God, people, and animals. By itself the word does not specify positions within relationships; more particularly, it does not imply inferiority."[37] Rather, the creation of the woman from the rib "means solidarity and equality."[38] Related to this is the common misunderstanding that the man (ʾish) "names" the woman (ʾihshah) (Gen 2:23), implying a domination over her in the same way that the man exercises dominion over the animals by naming them (Gen 2:19). Trible insists that the text does not support such an interpretation. The typical literary form in the Bible for "naming" someone or something is to combine a form of "to call" and the name itself. For example, "Cain built a city and *called*

---

34. Ibid., 251.
35. Ibid.
36. Kawashima, "A Revisionist Reading Revisited," 50. Emphasis original.
37. Trible, "Eve and Adam," 252.
38. Ibid., 253.

the *name* of the city after the *name* of his son Enoch" (Gen 4:17).³⁹ The text does use the word for naming, but rather simply says the man "calls" his partner "woman." Trible concludes, "My translation is this: God is the helper superior to man; the animals are helpers inferior to man; woman is the helper equal to man."⁴⁰

Third, Trible rejects the frequent characterization of Eve as either flawed or devious in ways that the man is not. She cites various scholars who explain that the serpent tempted the woman and not the man because she was intellectually weaker, more prone to participate in astrological cults, or morally suspect. "But the narrative does not say any of these things," Trible counters. "It does not sustain the judgment that woman is weaker or more cunning or more sexual than man."⁴¹ Neither does the text say that the woman is a temptress or seducer. A close reading of the text also interestingly reveals that "the man does not blame the woman; he does not say that the woman seduced him; he blames the Deity." The only suggestion of a seduction or beguilement comes when the woman says, "the serpent beguiled me and I ate" (3:13). Only here occurs the strong verb *nsh'*, meaning to deceive, to seduce."⁴²

Fourth, Genesis 3 concludes with the fall from paradise into the world that we experience, a world in which all relations are distorted. Serpents strike at the heels of humans and humans try to stomp the lunging creature; women experience pain in childbirth; farmers till the soil under the scorching sun, and all creatures suffer the inevitable reality of death and their bodies return to the earth from which they were made. Trible insists, however, that "we misread if we assume that these judgments are mandates. They describe; they do not prescribe. They protest; they do not condone." Like an earthquake that overturns everything in its wake, the effects of the fall ripple throughout every aspect of creation, including the relationship between men and women.

> This sin vitiates all relationships: between animals and human beings (3:15); mothers and children (3:16); husbands and wives (3:16); man and the soil (3:17, 18); man and his work (3:19). Whereas in creation man and woman know harmony and equality, in sin they know alienation and discord.⁴³

---

39. Ibid., 254.
40. Ibid., 252.
41. Ibid., 256.
42. Ibid., 257.
43. Ibid.

Expressing her appreciation for Trible's work on the twenty-fifth anniversary of the publication of *God and the Rhetoric of Sexuality*, Jennifer Koosed remarked, "Phyllis Trible taught me to read Genesis 2–3 with new eyes, to strip off thousands of years of interpretation, and to look at the text itself, to ask—is this really there or could the passage be interpreted another way? Is it obvious that Eve is a secondary creature, created inferior to Adam, subject to him for all eternity for her disobedience?"[44] Indeed, one of Trible's most lasting contributions to the study of the second creation story has been her insistence that we need to return to a close reading of the text and be aware of how our own assumptions about a story (deeply shaped by individual and communal readings of the text) can skew our results. This issue strikes at the heart of the current theological debates among the orthodox, liberal, postliberal, and postmodern proponents. Is the tradition a help or a hindrance to our reading? Are some interpretations better than others, and if so, by what standard are they measured? Is there a meaning to a text? If so, is that meaning based on the intention of the author?

Trible's argument does not always fall neatly on either side of many of these questions. First, though clearly critical of many of the traditional readings of the text, Trible develops that critique using the very exegetical tools (e.g., etymology, rhetoric) that have been developed and employed by Jewish and Christian scholars for centuries. In this way, her argument is both revolutionary and traditional. Second, Trible unreservedly holds that some interpretations are better than others. Egalitarian readings of Gen 2–3 are clearly better than patriarchal readings. Reading texts is not like taking a Rorschach test in which we project our own inner world onto the ink blot. Third, on the question of meaning, Trible's argument can go in two possible directions. In another article published in the same year, she argues, "Depatriarchalizing is not an operation which the exegete performs on the text: It is a hermeneutic operating within Scripture itself. We expose it; we do not impose it." Here Trible asserts that there is a meaning embedded in the text that exists prior to readers discovering it. However, she continues, "Tradition history teaches that the meaning and function of biblical materials is fluid. As Scripture moves through history, it is appropriated for new settings."[45] This latter comment could be taken in one of two ways: first, multiple legitimate interpretations can emerge over time. The Christian orthodox tradition has long held that a biblical text can have different spiritual meanings or "senses." For example, the temple can refer to the physical structure in Jerusalem at the time of Jesus ("the literal sense"), the human

---

44. Koosed, "Coming of Age in Phyllis Trible's World," 16.
45. Trible, "Depatriarchalizing in Biblical Interpretation," 48.

soul ("the moral sense"), or heaven ("the anagogic sense"). A second reading of Trible's observation moves in a postmodern direction. The Scripture scholar Dale Martin, for example, argues, "Texts are not containers that hold meaning. The meaning of a text is a result of the interpretive process itself, which is not possible apart from the activities of human interpreters . . . Texts cannot dispense their meaning, and they cannot control their interpretation. These activities are done by human beings."[46]

The Revitalization of the Image of the Second Creation Story

While certainly moving in their own unique direction in their readings of Genesis 2–3, Gregory, Bunyan, and Trible share a deep appreciation for the ways in which the human heart can pursue desires that bring disorder to our personal and social lives. Gregory compared that first step away from the good "like a rock, torn asunder from a mountain ridge, which is driven down headlong by its own weight." The person is "dragged away from his original natural [propensity] to goodness and gravitating with all his weight in the direction of vice . . . and borne away as by a kind of gravitation to the utmost limit of iniquity."[47] Bunyan declares in a similar vein, "Man indeed is the most noble, by creation, of all the creatures in the visual world: but by sin he has made himself the most ignoble."[48] Trible emphasizes the social and interpersonal distortion pictured in Genesis 2–3, yet sees its original vision as a hopeful challenge. "The [second creation story] tells us who we are (creatures of equality and mutuality); it tells us who we have become (creatures of oppression); and so it opens possibilities for change, for a return to our true liberation under God. In other words, the story calls female and male to repent."[49] Just as the seemingly dissimilar theologies of Gregory, Bunyan, and Trible can enrich our appreciation for the many dimensions of the fall, the perspectives of orthodox, liberal, postliberal, and postmodern theologians can revitalize our own thinking about the image of the second creation story.

The Pauline pattern of seeing Adam as a "type" (Rom 5:14) or foreshadowing of Christ pervades orthodox Christian thought. "Therefore just as one man's trespass led to condemnation for all, so one man's act of righteousness leads to justification and life for all. For just as by the one man's disobedience the many were made sinners, so by the one man's obedience

---

46. Martin, *Pedagogy of the Bible*, 30.
47. Gregory of Nyssa, *Great Catechism*, 481.
48. Bunyan, *Grace Abounding*, 25.
49. Trible, "Eve and Adam," 258.

the many will be made righteous" (Rom 5:18–19). In his battle with the Pelagians, Augustine asserted the doctrine of original sin using the Adam-Christ typology. Countering the Pelagian claim that human sin persists because humans imitate the bad example of Adam, Augustine argued,

> Moreover, if Christ alone is He in whom all men are justified, on the ground that it is not simply the imitation of His example which makes men just, but His grace which regenerates men by the Spirit, then also Adam is the only one in whom all have sinned, on the ground that it is not the mere following of his evil example that makes men sinners, but the penalty which generates through the flesh. Hence the terms "all men" and "all men." For [those] who are generated through Adam are actually the very same as those who are regenerated through Christ; but yet the language of the apostle is strictly correct, because as none partakes of carnal generation except through Adam, so no one shares in the spiritual except through Christ.[50]

For Augustine, the concept of a universal flawed human nature ("Adam is the one in whom all have sinned") undergirds the Christian claim that Christ is the savior of all people. If sin is the common malady afflicting all humans, then Christ is the physician who heals their wounded nature. As orthodox theologians dealt with the myriad of questions stemming from the story of the fall, they followed Augustine's lead and understood "the fallen state of Adam" to be the equivalent of "the human condition"—the universal, inescapable state of being in which all humans found themselves. As Augustine wrote regarding Adam in *City of God*, "For, we all existed in that one man, since, taken together, we were the one man who fell into sin ... Although the specific form by which each of us was to live was not yet created and assigned, our nature was already present in the seed from which we were to spring."[51] Only in this light, orthodox thinkers concluded, can we fully understand ourselves as "dead to sin and alive to God in Christ Jesus" (Rom 6:11).

Reinhold Niebuhr's criticism of liberalism, especially in what he regarded as its overly optimistic assessment of human potential and its mistaken belief in the inevitable scientific and moral progress of human history, is well-known. He would, then, seem to be an odd choice to represent the contribution of liberalism to the present discussion. His discussion of myths,

---

50. Augustine, "On the Merits and Forgiveness of Sins," 22.

51. Augustine, *City of God*, 279. See also Rombs, *Saint Augustine and the Fall of the Soul*, 101–6.

CHAPTER TWO: THE SECOND CREATION STORY 35

however, is remarkably liberal in tone.[52] Niebuhr operates with a fundamental distinction between "primitive" and "permanent" myths. In his 1937 article, "The Truth in Myths," he argues that the former "is derived from prescientific thought" while the latter "deals with aspects of reality which are suprascientific rather than prescientific."[53] Primitive myth can be rightly discarded by later generations, but, as the label implies, permanent myth is permanently valid. Referring specifically to the myth of the fall, Niebuhr believes that the orthodox theologians erred by insisting that the story of the fall is actual history, while modern theologians have erred by failing to recognize the crucial distinction between primitive and permanent myth. "It is because man can transcend nature and himself that he is able to conceive of himself as the center of all life and the clue to the meaning of existence. It is this monstrous pretension of his egoism, the root of all imperialism and human cruelty, which is the very essence of sin. To recognize all this is not to accept the story of the fall as history."[54] As Niebuhr noted in his earlier work, *An Interpretation of Christian Ethics*, "It is in its interpretations of the facts of human nature . . . that the myth of the Fall make its profoundest contribution to moral and religious theory."[55] The story of the fall correctly suggests that "the root of man's sin lies in his pretension of being God" and sadly, this "tragic reality of life, is attested by every page of human history."[56]

Bunyan's *Grace Abounding* illustrates in interesting ways many of the themes in postliberal theology: a strong church/world distinction, the formative power of Scripture, and the Christian life as an interiorization of the language of the biblical narrative. Bunyan's sharp distinction between the church at Bedford and the world appears when he offers a description of the physical landscape surrounding the church. The church is in a walled town on the sunny side of a tall mountain which he enters through a straight and narrow gate. "Now, this mountain and wall, etc. was thus made out to me; the mountain signified the church of the living God; the sun that shone thereon, the comfortable shining of his merciful face on them that were therein: the wall I thought was the Word that did make the separation between the Christians and the world: and the gap which was in the wall,

52. See Langdon Gilkey's assessment that "both Bultmann and Niebuhr, so it appears from the vantage point of the present, seemed surprisingly too liberal" on the issue of the primitive versus real or permanent meaning of Christian myths in *On Niebuhr*, 68. For a helpful discussion of Niebuhr on myth, see Dorrien, *Word as True Myth*, 122–26.
53. Niebuhr, "Truth in Myths," 16.
54. Ibid., 25.
55. Niebuhr, *Interpretation*, 46.
56. Ibid., 53–54.

I thought was Jesus Christ, who is the way to God the Father" (John 14:16; Matt 7:14).[57] When he first met the women at Bedford, it seemed as if "they had found a new world, as if they were people that dwelt alone, and were not to be reckoned amongst the nations" (Num 23:9).[58] The "new world" that the women had discovered was in fact an account of the world and human existence in it as narrated in the biblical story. Bunyan's spiritual journey involves learning about this new world and entering into it. After coming into contact with the women of Bedford, he "began to look into the Bible with new eyes."[59] With these new eyes, he sees Esau's sale of his birthright as his own sin and the cities of refuge in Joshua 20 as his own place of refuge. Even Stephen's vision at his stoning becomes Bunyan's own vision (Acts 7:55).[60] The entire arch of story that Bunyan relates in *Grace Abounding* involves his ever-increasing interiorization of the biblical narrative. The postliberal theologian George Lindbeck contends that to "become a Christian involves learning the story of Israel and Jesus well enough to interpret and experience oneself and one's world in its terms."[61] Bunyan's autobiography provides a splendid example of how this very process unfolds in the course of his own life.

The postmodern engagement with the second creation story's imagery of Adam and Eve, the Garden of Eden, and the fall has produced some interesting reflections on the theme of distortion. Postmoderns sees a triad of interrelated forms of distortion described in Genesis 2–3: a distortion of human desire, a distortion of human relations, and a distortion of language and meaning. Gregory's careful examination of the driving force of the emotions and passions and Augustine's claim that our hearts are restless until they rest in God reappears in postmodern reflection. As John Caputo comments in an exchange with the philosopher Edith Wyschogrod, "Our hearts are structurally restless, with the restlessness of this desire [for God], which is as you say 'inherently unfulfillable' and not a desire for 'static eternity,' which is part of its so-called 'post-modernity,' and does not expect rest. This is what interests me, the way this most classical, most biblical, desire, this most Augustinian aspiration, has been rediscovered, refashioned—'repeated,' as Derrida says—in what is popularly called 'postmodernism,' or at least a certain version or voice of

---

57. Bunyan, *Grace Abounding*, 18.
58. Ibid., 14.
59. Ibid., 16.
60. Ibid., 59.
61. Lindbeck, *Nature of Doctrine*, 34.

postmodernism."[62] The story of the fall expresses this fundamental drive within humans, but also recognizes the instability of our desires and our inherent tendency to pursue that which ruptures our friendship with God and neighbor and drains us of the fullness of being.

Following from the discussion of desire and its possible misdirection, the theologian Jan-Olav Henriksen distinguishes between a desire that is accepting of the other and a desire that seeks to control the other. "There is a difference between the desire to control and master reality and the desire to enjoy, participate, and communicate. The first emerges out of concern, worries, and insecurity, the other out of trust and gratitude."[63] The desire to control the other results in various forms and degrees of subjugation of the other. Trible highlighted the distorted relationship that develops between men and women, but the argument could also be applied to issues such as international relations, racial tensions, and income inequality.

The third type of distortion and the one that perpetuates oppressive social structures over time is the distortion of language and meaning. Language requires differentiation and differentiation requires naming: God is not a human; a human is not one of the various birds that fill the sky; the tree of knowledge is not the tree of life, etc. Graham Ward notes that in the rabbinical tradition the story of God blowing the breath of life into Adam is interpreted to mean the giving of speech to humans. In this view, the snake represented the distortion in language and meaning when it asked Eve, "Did God say, 'You shall not eat from any tree in the garden'?" (Gen 3:1). "The snake imitates God and Adam in its ability to speak. But its representation, and repetition of God's instructions to the earthly creature distorts them."[64] Eve's repetition of the divine command not to eat of the tree of knowledge does not dissuade the serpent from offering a distorted reading of the command. In fact, Ward argues, "Even if the woman's words to the serpent had remained the same there would have been a slippage of meaning, because the context of each iteration is different. The woman cannot then repeat what God intended when he first spoke. Reiteration will always be interpretation and misreading."[65] Language in a fallen world can be twisted and misused for ends not intended by the original speaker. Even speech suffers the destabilizing effect of the fall.

Just as Gregory of Nyssa, John Bunyan, and Phyllis Trible opened up new and thought-provoking perspectives on the second creation story,

62. Wyschogrod and Caputo, "Postmodernism and the Desire for God," 301.
63. Henriksen, *Desire, Gift, and Recognition*, 32.
64. Ward, "A Postmodern Version of Paradise," 7.
65. Ibid., 8.

so too contemporary thinkers help us to read the text in a new light. The orthodox correlation of the old Adam (anthropology) and the new Adam (Christology and soteriology), the liberal treatment of the fall as existential estrangement, the postliberal absorption of the biblical narrative into one's own life story, and the postmodern focus on the various forms of distortion suggested by the fall help revitalize our appreciation for Genesis 2–3 as a text that speaks powerfully to the human condition.

Discussion Questions

1. What is your interpretation of the story of the fall?
2. Gregory of Nyssa speaks of the human as positioned between divinity and brutality. Is this an accurate portrayal? If so, how do humans move closer to divinity rather than brutality?
3. Is the persistence of temptation and despair a sign that a person has not made any progress in the Christian life?
4. Does the traditional reading of Genesis 2–3 legitimate patriarchal attitudes and practices? What are some common misreadings of the second creation story?
5. What types of personal and social forms of distortion exist? How does the gospel address these conditions?

Suggested Readings

For background on Gregory of Nyssa's understanding of the creation and fall of humans, see chapter 4 of Johannes Zachhuber, *Human Nature in Gregory of Nyssa* (Boston: Brill, 2000) and chapter 11 of Morwenna Ludlow, *Gregory of Nyssa: Ancient and (Post)modern* (Oxford: Oxford University Press, 2007). For a discussion of Bunyan's theology, see Michael Davies, *Graceful Reading: Theology and Narrative in the Works of John Bunyan* (Oxford: Oxford University Press, 2002). For general background on Bunyan, see Anne Dunan-Page, *The Cambridge Companion to Bunyan* (Cambridge: Cambridge University Press, 2010). For a fuller exposition of Trible's position, see chapter 4 of her *God and the Rhetoric of Sexuality* (Philadelphia: Fortress, 1978).

Chapter Three: Biblical Journeys

THE STORIES OF ABRAHAM setting out for the land of Canaan, Moses leading the Israelites through the wilderness, and Jesus traveling to Jerusalem have long sparked the imagination of Christian writers who discovered a deep resonance between these pivotal events in the biblical narrative and the twists and turns of their own journeys of faith. Both in the life of the community and the life of the individual, the journey stories function as compasses to orient Christians as they navigate their way through time. The elements that comprise the journeys become symbols of the dynamics of the Christian life: the allies who make it possible for the sojourner to advance in the journey become the virtues, the foes who attack under the cover of darkness become our deepest fears, and the destination being sought describes our deepest aspirations. In this chapter we will examine how the image of the biblical journey has been incorporated into the theology of the third-century biblical scholar Origen of Alexandria in his *Homily XVII on Numbers*, the twelfth-century Augustinian canon Achard of St. Victor in his *Sermon XV*, and the contemporary Franciscan Richard Rohr in his recent work, *Falling Upward*. It is hoped that a study of how they employ the image of the biblical journey might help us revitalize the use of the image in our own theological reflection and spiritual reading of the Bible.

Origen, *Homily XVII on Numbers* 33

The common thread that runs throughout all areas of Origen's thought is his deep familiarity with the Bible. This, his supporters contend, enables him to uncover various levels of meaning from the most seemingly insignificant biblical passages. According to his critics, however, he can spin fanciful tales from the simplest biblical details. Origen's exact position on the number of meanings to be found in a biblical passage remains a matter of scholarly dispute. At the heart of the debate is Origen's observation in Book IV of his *On First Principles* (or *Peri archon*):

> One must therefore [portray] the meaning of the sacred writers
> in a threefold way upon one's own soul, so that the simple man

may be edified by what we call the flesh of the scripture, this name being given to the obvious interpretation; while the man who has made some progress may be edified by its soul, as it were; and the man who is perfect and like those mentioned by the apostle: "We speak wisdom among the perfect; yet a wisdom not of this world, nor of the rulers of this world, which are coming to nought; but we speak God's wisdom in mystery, even the mystery that hath been hidden, which God foreordained before the worlds unto our glory"—this man may be edified by the spiritual law, which has "a shadow of the good things to come." For just as man consists of body, soul, and spirit, so in the same way does the scripture, which has been prepared by God to be given for man's salvation (IV, 2, 4).[1]

Many of Origen's interpreters have taken this to mean that each passage has a threefold sense. This position, however, is not without its problems. In his study on the history of biblical interpretation, Henning Graf Reventlow notes that "it is conspicuous that nowhere in his later practice of exegesis does [Origen] carry out this threefold sense."[2] Other scholars believe the three groups mentioned by Origen are not meanings within the text, but rather different strategies (each with its own unique types of emphasis) that preachers and teachers can employ when addressing Christians at various stages of their discipleship: beginners in the faith, the intermediate, and the advanced.[3] Origen more commonly speaks in terms of two types of meanings: of the letter and the spirit, the shadow and the reality, or the surface of a field that is in plain sight and the hidden treasures below that we seek to discover. "There are in Scripture," writes Henri de Lubac, "fundamentally, only two senses: the literal and the spiritual, and these two senses themselves are in continuity, not in opposition. The spirit is in the letter like honey in its honeycomb."[4]

In *Homily XVII on Numbers*, Origen plays the metaphorical role of beekeeper as he extracts the honey (the spiritual meaning) from the honeycomb (the literal meaning) in the summary account of the Israelites' journey from Egypt to the borders of the Promised Land in Numbers 33. Even a passage as seemingly insignificant as one that simply lists the cities on each

---

1. Origen, *On First Principles*, 275–76.

2. Reventlow, *History of Biblical Interpretation*, 181.

3. Torjesen, "'Body,' 'Soul,' and 'Spirit' in Origen's Theory of Exegesis," 17–30. She contends, "Body, soul, and spirit of Scripture do not designate three levels of meaning in the interpretation of texts but a threefold 'usefulness' of Scripture in ordering the doctrines that correspond pedagogically to the soul's progress" (24).

4. De Lubac, *History and Spirit*, 205.

stage of the journey is important, for we "cannot say of the Holy Spirit's writings that there is anything useless or unnecessary in them, however much they appear obscure to some."[5] As Origen asks rhetorically, "Who would dare to say that what is written 'by the Word of God' is of no use and makes no contribution to salvation, but is merely a narrative of what happened and was over and done a long time ago, but pertains in no way to us when it is told?"[6] The Bible is a historical work, literary masterpiece, and for Christians, religious text. How an interpreter relates each of these aspects of the Bible to the other two determines how that person reads the Bible. For Origen, the religious dimension of the text dominates the other two. The various biblical texts have as their author the Holy Spirit. The historical details, in this case the story of Israel's journey from Egypt to the border of the Promised Land, are the means by which the spiritual meaning is conveyed to the reader. The literary features, especially the etymologies of the various cities' names, is given spiritual rather than cultural meaning.

In looking for the spiritual sense of Numbers 33, Origen sees two lines of interpretation emerging from the story that begins with an "exodus" from Egypt and concludes with the Israelites poised to enter the Promised Land. The "exodus" may refer to a person's departure from his or her old life as he or she moves towards Christian perfection, or the "exodus" may refer to one's departure from this life as he or she moves towards union with God in the next life. "Thus, employing a double line of interpretation, we must examine the entire order of stages as it is narrated, so that our soul may make progress by both interpretations, when we learn from them either how we ought to live the life that turns from error and follows the Law of God or how great an expectation that we have of the future hope that is promised on the basis of the resurrection."[7] Origen finds further evidence for this "double line of interpretation" in the fact that the name of each site at which the Israelites stop is mentioned twice. "The stages are repeated twice in order to show two journeys for the soul. One is the means of training the soul in virtues through the Law of God when it is placed in flesh; and by ascending through certain steps it makes progress, as we have said, from virtue to virtue, and uses these progressions as stages. And the other journey is the one by which the soul, in gradually ascending to the heavens after the resurrection, does not reach the highest point unseasonably, but is led through many stages."[8]

5. Origen, *Homily XXVII*, 247.
6. Ibid., 248.
7. Ibid., 253.
8. Ibid.

The key to understanding the journey, according to Origen, is to be found in the biblical delineation of forty-two stages in both the exodus from Egypt (Num 33) and the genealogy of Christ (Matt 1).[9] "Therefore, in descending to the Egypt of this world Christ passed those forty-two generations as stages; and those who ascend from Egypt pass by the same number, forty-two stages . . . And so, the person who ascends, ascends with Him who descended from there to us, so that he may arrive at the place from which He descended . . . ."[10] The first and most obvious theme to arise from this is that Origen is giving a very christological form to his reading of a portion of Old Testament history. The classic descent–ascent Christology expressed, for example, in the Philippians hymn (Phil 2:6–11) is the context for a Christian reading of the Israelites' journey. Second, the journey is an ascent. There is a movement from earthly to heavenly that requires the sojourner to pass through each of the stages in a certain sequence. Origen admonishes his hearers to leave behind the adoration of idols and fix their attention on Christ. "After this," he continues, "let us strive to go forward and to ascend one by one each of the steps of faith and the virtues. If we persist in them until we come to perfection, we shall be said to have made a stage at each of the steps of the virtues until, when we attain the height of our instruction and the summit of our progress, the promised inheritance is fulfilled."[11] Third, the logic of the arduous journey will only be revealed when we reach our destination. Commenting on Origen's *Homily XXVII*, the patristic scholar Rowan Greer notes, "The remarkable feature of his treatment is that the journey does not proceed in a straight line. As for the children of Israel, the Christian's journey to the promised land is not by the easiest or the shortest route (cf. Exod 13:17). The long and convoluted journey has its own logic and is meant to train and prepare the soul for its destiny."[12] Origen assures his audience, "We understand these pilgrimages only dully and darkly so long as the pilgrimage still lasts. But when the soul has returned to its rest, that is, to the fatherland in paradise, it will be taught more truly and will understand more truly what the meaning of its pilgrimage was."[13]

Origen offers a detailed analysis of each of the early stages of the journey, but then realizes that time does not permit him to offer commentary with that level of detail for each of the forty-two stages, so beginning with

9. The chapter may have only forty stages to correspond to the forty years of wandering in the desert.
10. Origen, *Homily XXVII*, 249.
11. Ibid., 250.
12. Greer, "Introduction," 18.
13. Origen, *Homily XXVII*, 250.

the staging site of Alush (Num 13:13) his comments on each stage are much briefer. We will first follow Origen's more extended commentary. The Israelites start out from Ramesse [Rameses], which means "confused agitation" and travel to Sochoth [Succoth]. "Sochoth is interpreted 'tents.' Thus, the first progress of the soul is to be taken away from earthly agitation and to learn that it must dwell in tents like a wanderer, so that it can be, as it were, ready for battle and meet those who lie in wait for it unhindered and free."[14] The Israelites move on to Buthan [Etham] which means "valley." A progress in the life of virtue requires testing and the valley provides that. "And a virtue is not acquired without training and hard work, nor is it tested as much as in prosperity as in adversity. So the soul comes to a valley. For in valleys and in low places the struggle against the devil and the opposing powers takes place."[15] From Buthan they travel to the border of the Iroth [Pi-hahiroth] which means "villages." Symbolically the soul has not yet reached the city, "nor is the perfect already held, but first and for the moment some small places are taken. For progress consists in coming to great things from small ones. So the soul comes to Iroth, that is to the great entrance of a village, which is the beginning of conversion and of a moderate self-control."[16] In the distance to one side is Beelsephon [Baal-zephon] ("the ascent of the watchtower or citadel") and to the other is Magdalum [Migdol] which means "grandeur." Both sites represent the things to come in the journey. Passing through the Red Sea, the Israelites camp at Bitter Waters [Marah]. Here we are reminded that it is not "possible to attain the promised land unless we pass through bitterness." After the temptations comes Helim [Elim], with its twelve springs of water and seventy (or seventy-two) palm trees. God "put some places of refreshment into the midst of toils so that the soul may be refreshed and restored by them," but the soul must not tarry, but once again continue on the way.[17] From Helim, the Israelites camp alongside the Red Sea and then move into the desert of Sin. While this again suggests temptation, the soul has become able to discern between spirits (1 Cor 12:10). After Sin, the Israelites camp at Raphia [Dophkah] which means "health." "You see the order of the progresses, how when the soul is once made spiritual and begins to have the discernment of heavenly visions, it arrives at health."[18] At this point in his homily Origen breaks off his more

14. Ibid., 258.
15. Ibid.
16. Ibid.
17. Ibid., 260.
18. Ibid., 261.

detailed commentary and offers a brief observation about each of the succeeding stages on the journey.

We will confine our attention to a few more stages discussed by Origen. There are later stages which clearly mark progress, but temptations continue to appear. At Ressa [Rissah] Origen comments, "Here it becomes clear that temptations are brought to it as a kind of protection and defense. For just as meat, if it is nor sprinkled with salt, no matter how great and social it is, becomes rotten, so also the soul, unless it is somehow salted with constant temptations immediately becomes feeble and soft."[19] Interestingly, when Origen comes to Oboth, he confesses that its meaning eludes him. "Although we have not found an interpretation of this name, nonetheless we do not doubt that in this name as in all the others the logic of the progresses is preserved."[20] The penultimate stage of Abrarim opposite Nabau [Nebo] suggests "separation" (Nebo). The person at this stage has spiritually "separated" him or herself from the world. The person is in the world, but not of the world. At the final stage, Moab, the soul stands ready for entrance into the promised land. "For the whole journey takes place, the whole course is run for the purpose of arriving at the river of God, so that we may be made neighbors of the flowing Wisdom and may be watered by the waves of divine knowledge, and so that purified by them all we may be made worthy to enter the promised land."[21]

Achard of St. Victor, *Sermon XV*

The monastic communities of both the East and the West employed and expanded the method of biblical interpretation outlined by Origen. In the twelfth century a community of Augustinian canons at the abbey of St. Victor on the outskirts of Paris produced a series of masters (e.g., Hugh, Richard, Andrew, and Achard of St. Victor) who composed an impressive collection of biblical commentaries, sermons, and theological treatises. Because the Augustinian canons were trained with a broad education in the liberal arts and had pastoral responsibilities outside the abbey, they brought both scholarly knowledge and practical wisdom to their theological work. Franklin Harkins and Frans van Liere describe "the Victorine model of scriptural exegesis [as one that] sought to embrace both scientific and spiritual culture, learning and wisdom, *scientia* and *sapientia*. It emphasized the scholarly examination of the biblical text, but always in

19. Ibid., 263.
20. Ibid., 266.
21. Ibid., 268.

the context of the deeper, spiritual formation of the reader."[22] In Achard's *Sermon XV* we have a fine example of the Victorine model of scriptural interpretation in which wisdom and knowledge, theology and spirituality, and scholastic and pastoral concerns converge. There is scholarly debate over whether the text is a sermon or a treatise, but it was most likely a Lenten reflection for his fellow canons which Achard composed during his time as abbot of St. Victor (1155–61).

Sermon XV is a theological and spiritual meditation on Jesus' movement into the desert, "Then Jesus was led up by the Spirit into the wilderness to be tempted by the devil" (Matt 4:1). The sermon is an extended reflection on this "short and modest sentence." Achard continues in his introduction, "It is modest, but only on the surface: in meaning and mystery it goes far beyond my reach. The superficial meaning is modest, but the depth of the understanding and the mysteries is great."[23] As we soon discover, for Achard the mystery of Jesus going into the desert is nothing less than an image of the entire drama of salvation. Humans "deserted" God, but God took on flesh and dwelt among us so that we can be led back to God. In language borrowed from Augustine, Achard speaks of humans having gone into "a region of unlikeness" from God.[24] The soul is like Cain. "Cast away from God's face, and from the face of a certain inner land—that is, its own heart—it became a wanderer from itself and a fugitive from God upon the land the Lord has cursed, seeking outside the peace it had lost and never finding it."[25] By taking on our human condition, the Word makes possible the restoration of our likeness with God. "He was led by his Spirit into our desert, indeed into the desert which we are, where he left us an example so that we may follow in his steps and be led after him and through him into the desert—not by the flesh but by the Spirit, and not by our spirit or any other one, but by his alone."[26] The desert into which Christ was led is the human condition; the desert into which those united with Christ are led involves our "desertion" of all that which separates us from God.

Achard adds one more element of complexity into the *Sermon*: the soul's journey back to God involves passing through not simply one desert, but seven. As Hugh Feiss notes, "Achard is very fond of schemas that map the path of spiritual progress."[27] The particular schema that Achard

22. Harkins and van Lierre, *Interpretation of Scripture*, 31.
23. Achard of St. Victor, *Sermon XV*, 298.
24. Merrill, "Achard of Saint Victor," 57.
25. Achard, *Sermon XV*, 306.
26. Ibid., 301.
27. Feiss, *On Love*, 80.

employs in the *Sermon* is derived from the seven gifts of the Holy Spirit as enumerated in the Vulgate (Douay) rendering of Isa 11:2–3: "And the spirit of the Lord shall rest upon him: the spirit of wisdom, and of understanding, the spirit of counsel, and of fortitude, the spirit of knowledge, and of godliness. And he shall be filled with the spirit of the fear of the Lord." Achard follows these in reverse order in *Sermon XV*. There are seven evil spirits paired with the seven gifts of the Holy Spirit. As Feiss explains, "It was an ancient belief that there were seven evil spirits, each connected with one of the seven basic inclinations towards sin. The Victorines called them seven '*vitia*'; in later times they were known as 'capital sins,' that is, the 'heads' under which many subdivisions of vice and sin can be found. Achard calls the seven gifts of the Holy Spirit seven good spirits, and takes the opportunity to refer to several other scriptural 'sevens.'"[28] For example, in Revelation John sees both "a Lamb standing as if it had been slaughtered, having seven horns and seven eyes, which are the seven spirits of God sent out into all the earth" (5:6), and "a great red dragon, with seven heads" (12:3). Led in succession by each of the seven gifts of the Holy Spirit, the soul passes through the deserts that separate it from the Father.

The first four deserts require the "desertion" of those vices that characterize our unlikeness to God. When humanity deserted itself, the devil calls the seven evil spirits and they enter the vacant house and dwell there (Matt 12: 43–45). The first desert into which the soul enters, therefore, requires the fear of the Lord. "This fear is the starting point, but it is perfected in the chaste fear that lasts forever, and that consists in the perfect love that casts out the initial fear; it is however necessary at the beginning."[29] The spirit of godliness that leads the soul into the second desert generates a reorientation of the heart towards God and away from the earthly allures of power, wealth, and fame. The spirit of knowledge leads the soul into the third desert which cultivates the virtue of temperance as it relates to bodily needs, for example, avoiding the extremes of gluttony and malnutrition. After the first three deserts, the soul arrives at the mountain of God, which is the human spirit. "The spirit is the mountain of God, because in it lies the image and likeness of God: the image in reason, the likeness in will."[30] The fourth spirit of fortitude is needed if we are to "desert" our own will for the will of God.

Achard devotes a great deal of time to the fifth desert. Having treated the will in the previous section, he turns his attention to reason which he associates with the image of God. Because we are commanded to love the

---

28. Feiss, "Introduction," 293.
29. Achard, *Sermon XV*, 307.
30. Ibid., 312.

Lord our God with all our heart, soul, and mind, reason ultimately needs to submit itself to the tribunal of God's eternal truth. We must abide by "the counsels of God's reason." "Accordingly, it is good for people not to be ruled by their own counsel but to be led into this fifth desert by the fifth spirit of God, that is, by the spirit of counsel."[31] Achard next lists ten issues or mysteries that exceed the grasp of human reason and must therefore be accepted on faith alone, including creation *ex nihilo*, the two natures of Christ, and the end of time. "Let them fear a fall who would wish to imitate God's flight in these matters, and, as it were, to fly on wings like God, especially the wings of fallen reason. They will surely fall and, repelled by the light, be enfolded in denser darkness if God does not spread his wings and bear them up."[32]

In the sixth and seventh deserts we reach the final leg of the journey. Like a house that has been emptied of its contents, the soul has been emptied of its clutter and room has been made for God. "In the present too, from the time people leave themselves for God's sake, yielding to God and preparing a home for him in themselves completely and not just partially, God follows after them at once and enters secretly."[33] Echoing Paul, Achard continues, "They no longer live in themselves, but Christ lives in them when they follow God's will and reason, receiving these into themselves, deserting not just their own flesh but also their wills and reason."[34] Those in this sixth desert receive the spirit of understanding, a joyous understanding of divine love and beauty that sets their heart ablaze. "They experience in themselves 'the beauty of God's house' [Ps 26:8] and the great sweetness he hides there for those who fear him and cling to him. Manna rains down on them from heaven."[35] They in effect "desert" their neighbors for the sake of God. Then, in the seventh desert, led by the spirit of wisdom, that is, perfect love, the soul imitates the very act of God in the drama of salvation and "deserts" the sublime joy of the sixth desert to care for humanity. They are like Moses who "deserted" the burning bush and went into Egypt to free his brothers and sisters, or the apostles who set out on dusty roads to carry the gospel to the ends of the earth. The seventh desert, in short, represents a state of conformity to the image of Christ (Rom 8:29) who came not to be served, but to serve (Mark 10:45).

31. Ibid., 319.
32. Ibid., 343.
33. Ibid., 344.
34. Ibid.
35. Ibid., 345.

Richard Rohr, *Falling Upward*

Not only can the entire biblical narrative be understood as a journey from creation to the consummation of the kingdom, journeys are critical elements in the stories of many of the leading biblical figures (Abraham, Moses, Elijah). Christ, of course, journeys into the desert before beginning his public ministry in the Synoptics and in John's Gospel he knows that "he had come from God and was going to God" (13:3), so it is not surprising that spiritual writers so frequently speak of the Christian life as a journey. Richard Rohr, a Franciscan priest and popular spiritual writer, has taken a similar approach in his *Falling Upward*. Drawing on the work of the psychologist Carl Jung, Rohr speaks of the two halves of the spiritual journey. Rohr writes, "The task of the first half of life is to create a proper *container* for one's life and answer the first essential questions: 'What makes me significant?' 'How can I support myself?' and 'Who will go with me?' The task of the second half of life is, quite simply, to find the actual *contents* that this container was meant to hold and deliver."[36] In the first half of life, we are preoccupied with "the big three concerns of identity, security, and sexuality and gender."[37] In the second half of life, these concerns are "included, but transcended." The second half of life is marked by the capacity to hold law and freedom in a creative tension. "Without a contemplative mind, we do not know how to hold creative tensions. We are better at rushing to judgment and demanding a complete resolution to things before we have learned what they have to teach us. This is not the way of wisdom, and it is the way that people operate in the first half of life."[38]

That there are stages in life is not seriously doubted: infants, adolescents, young adults, middle-age persons, and seniors all have their unique set of needs and concerns. The aspect of the literature that speaks of the Christian life as a journey that some readers find troubling is the notion of "spiritual progress" or "spiritual maturation." The expression for some suggests Pelagian self-aggrandizement that claims for itself the very type of knowledge that Paul warns "puffs" up the self rather than builds up the other (1 Cor 8:1). Rohr counters, "*Unless you can chart and encourage both movement and direction, you have no way to name maturity or immaturity.*"[39] For Rohr, spiritual maturity allows those at higher stages on the journey to "see and understand the earlier stages from the wider perspective of the later

---

36. Rohr, *Falling Upward*, 1. Emphasis original.
37. Ibid., 4.
38. Ibid., 36.
39. Ibid., 8–9. Emphasis original.

stages" and in terms of their own journey, it allows the person to "stretch yourself to comprehend people just a bit beyond yourself."[40] At the heart of controversy about "spiritual progress" is the theological question of the relationship between nature and grace. Rohr quotes Paul's teaching that "God's love has been poured into our hearts through the Holy Spirit that has been given to us" (Rom 5:5). He adds, "Our life will be 'done unto us,' just as happened to Mary (Luke 1:38). Although on another level we are doing it too. Both are equally true . . . True spirituality is a kind of *synergy* in which both parties give and both parties receive to create one shared truth and joy."[41] Does "spiritual maturity" exist? If so, is the spiritual progress the sole working of the Holy Spirit, or can humans facilitate or hinder the progress? Rohr would affirm that there is "spiritual maturity" and assert that such progress requires the cooperation of the individual.

How does Rohr conceive of this journey from immaturity to maturity? Borrowing again from Carl Jung and Joseph Campbell, Rohr sees the classic hero or heroine story as the key to the spiritual life. In its skeleton form, the hero or heroine is called to leave home for some greater purpose. The hero or heroine travels to a foreign land and is wounded in some way. He or she suffers hardship and peril, battles powerful forces of opposition, but emerges victorious. There is typically a mentor or sage, companions for the journey, and perhaps a secret of some kind is revealed. The hero or heroine returns home and, transformed by the experience, reassesses what is truly important in life. The hero or heroine's hard-earned wisdom is then used for the good of others. At the center of the spiritual journey, says Rohr, is "the stumbling stone." The stumbling stone is that person or event that causes us to fall, and in that moment of seeming defeat, we find the inner resources to see the journey through to the end. The loss of the "false self" awakens us to the realization of the "true self." "Your false self is your role, title, and personal image that is largely a creation of your own mind and attachments. *It will and must die in exact correlation to how much you want the Real.*"[42] It is here that we can understand Jesus' teaching about hating family and dying to self. The self that develops in the second half of life "emerges gradually as we learn to 'incorporate the negative,' learn from what we used to exclude, or, as Jesus put it, 'forgive the enemies' both within and without."[43] The boundaries that we marked to form our own identities in the first half of life are relativized in the second half of life. Rohr labels this new understanding as "nondualistic think-

---

40. Ibid., 9–10.
41. Ibid., 92. Emphasis original.
42. Ibid., 85. Emphasis original.
43. Ibid., 146.

ing." It is not that evil is now considered good, but rather that many of the lines of demarcation that we drew earlier in life (e.g., along racial, gender, or economic lines) now seem insignificant. We come to appreciate Jesus' teaching that God "makes his sun rise on the evil and the good, and sends rain on the righteous and the unrighteous" (Matt 5:45).

Rohr offers a summary of his vision of the Christian journey with a spiritual reading of Exodus 32–34. Moses shattering the tablets of the Law represents the transition from the first half of life to the second. "People who know how to creatively break the rules also know why the rules were there in the first place."[44] Our understanding of the law must be "shattered" so that a new and creative engagement with the law can emerge. Between the accounts of Moses breaking the tablets and then receiving the second set stand the stories of Moses coming into God's presence in the tent of meeting where "the Lord used to speak to Moses face to face, as one speaks to a friend" (Exod 33:11) and the intriguing passage of Moses being allowed to see the back of God. After receiving the new set of tablets Moses descends Mt. Sinai for a second time and his face shines radiantly. Rohr comments, "Only after breaking the first tablets of the law . . . does he see God's glory (Exodus 33:18 f.), and only afterwards does his face 'shine' (Exodus 34:29 f.). It might just be the difference between the two halves of life!"[45]

Like Origen and Achard, Rohr assumes that there are multiple levels of meaning in the biblical text. Reflecting on his own spiritual journey, he writes, "I totally believe in Adam and Eve now, but on about ten more levels. (*Literalism is usually the lowest and least level of meaning.*)"[46] Rohr mentions the influence that the work of Paul Ricoeur had on his own reading of the Bible. "*Paul Ricoeur's first naiveté was the best way to begin the journey, and a second naiveté was the easiest way to continue that same journey*, without becoming angry, alienated, or ignorant."[47] This movement of thought that Ricoeur described decades ago continues to exert a tremendous amount of influence on thinkers in various academic disciplines. Ricoeur argues that in the history of Western thought, we have reached "an awareness of the myth as myth." Myths such as Adam and Eve, for example, do not and cannot function as explanations of the development of the human race for the vast majority of twenty-first-century Western thinkers as they once did for our ancient forbears. "The dissolution of the myth as explanation is the necessary way to the restoration of

---

44. Ibid., xxviii.
45. Ibid.
46. Ibid., 106. Emphasis original.
47. Ibid., 108. Emphasis original.

the myth as symbol. Thus, the time of restoration is not a different time from that of criticism; we are in every way children of criticism, and we seek to go beyond criticism by means of criticism, by a criticism that is no longer reductive but restorative."[48] We must pass from the first naiveté in which the myth functions as explanation through criticism toward a second naiveté that brackets (in whole or in part) questions of historical truth and allows the myth to function as a symbol expressing a spiritual, psychological, or existential truth. Ricoeur explains,

> Does that mean that we could go back to a primitive naiveté? Not at all. In every way, something has been lost, irremediably lost: immediacy of belief. But if we can no longer live the great symbolisms of the sacred in accordance with the original belief in them, we can, we modern men, aim at a second naiveté in and through criticism. In short, it is by *interpreting* that we can *hear* again.[49]

Rohr echoes this idea when he writes, "Our myths are stories or images that are not always true in particular but entirely true in general. They are usually not historical fact, but invariably they are spiritual genius."[50]

The Revitalization of the Image of the Biblical Journey

Origen, Achard, and Rohr's use of the image of the biblical journey raises two sets of questions: the first concerns the claim that there are multiple levels of meaning in a biblical text and the second focuses on the idea that the spiritual journey consists of certain successive stages. First, are Origen and Achard right to assume that there are multiple levels of meaning in a biblical passage? Could their readings of the biblical texts be regarded as credible in either the church or the academy in the twentieth-first century? Is it possible to employ the historical-critical method of interpretation, yet still offer a spiritual reading of the biblical text?

Second, is there a sufficient degree of commonality in the various accounts of the Christian life to speak of certain "stages" in the Christian journey? If so, are certain earlier stages necessary preparations for later stages? Are the stages that Origen, Achard, and Rohr identify in their writings imposed on the biblical writings or do they emerge out of a reading of the texts themselves? With these issues in mind, we turn our attention

---

48. Ricoeur, *Symbolism of Evil*, 350.
49. Ibid., Emphasis original.
50. Rohr, *Falling Upward*, xxx.

to how orthodox, liberal, postliberal, and postmodern thinkers might respond to some of these questions and in doing so, provide us with insights into how we might revitalize the image of the biblical journey in the life of the church today.

While not all of Origen's teachings have received a warm reception in the orthodox tradition, his positions on the issues of biblical interpretation and spirituality have been deeply influential.[51] In addition to the spiritual itinerary that he offered in *Homily XVII on Numbers*, Origen also provided an account of the spiritual life in his prologue to his *Commentary on the Song of Songs*. After noting a common threefold division of Greek thought into ethics, physics, and enoptics (contemplation), Origen next turns his attention to the canonical order of the writings attributed to Solomon: Proverbs, Ecclesiastes, and Song of Songs. As Peter Martens observes, Origen believed that "these three books were not haphazardly arranged. Solomon inculcated his teachings in a planned series, so that readers would move through his curriculum in a sequential manner."[52] Origen explains,

> Thus, he first taught in Proverbs the subject of morals, setting regulations for life together, as was fitting, in concise and brief maxims. And he included the second subject, which is called the natural discipline, in Ecclesiastes, in which he discussed many natural things. And by distinguishing them as empty and vain from what is useful and necessary, he warns that vanity must be abandoned and what is useful and right must be pursued. He also handed down the subject of contemplation in the book we have in hand, that is, Song of Songs, in which he urges upon the soul the love of the heavenly and the divine under the figure of the bride and the bridegroom, teaching us that we must attain fellowship with God by the paths of loving affection and of love.[53]

This progression through the Solomonic books mirrors the soul's journey to God, and becomes known in the orthodox tradition as the purgative, illuminative, and unitive ways. Andrew Louth notes, "The idea of *successiveness* of the stages is often emphasized. For instance, speaking of Jesus as going before us through these stages, he says: 'We should speak of Him first as a beginner in Proverbs; then as advancing in Ecclesiastes; and lastly as more perfect in

---

51. The Second Council of Constantinople in 533 condemned certain elements of Origen's teaching, especially his views on the preexistence of souls and the possibility that Satan could eventually return to God.

52. Martens, *Origen and Scripture*, 215.

53. Origen, "Prologue to the Commentary," 232.

the Song of Songs.' We clearly have here the beginning of the idea of the three ways of the mystical life, and very nearly the later, familiar language of the way of purification (Origen's *ethike*), the way of illumination (*physike*) and the way of union (*enoptike*)."[54] If this description of the Christian life is accurate, then the revitalization of the image of the biblical journey requires that we consider three questions: Of what must we be purged? By which light should we walk? and With what should we desire to be united? In doing so, we can locate our own journeys in the biblical movement from the creation stories through the Gospels to Revelation.

In the liberal tradition, Schleiermacher's discussion of his "highest intuition" sheds light on the course of the Christian journey. In his *Soliloquies*, written shortly after his addresses *On Religion*, Schleiermacher identifies this intuition as a recognition of each person's unique individuality. Schleiermacher notes his initial attraction to Kant's theory of universal reason. "For a long time I too was content with the discovery of a universal reason; I worshipped the one essential being as the highest, and so believed that there is but a single right way of acting in every situation, that the conduct of all men should be alike, each differing from the other only by reason of his place and station in the world."[55] Schleiermacher does not reject Kant's claim as much as relativize it in light of what he believes to be a higher stage in his thinking. He also sees in the development of his own thinking the key to understanding the emergence of human consciousness over the grand sweep of human history. "Thus is it ever with mankind! When, turning with discontent from the unworthy particularity of a sensuous animal life, man wins a realization of humanity in its universal aspects and submits himself to duty, he is not [straightaway] capable of rising to the still higher level of individuality in growth and in morality, nor to perceive and understand the unique nature which freedom chooses for herself in each individual."[56] As Terrence Tice observes, Schleiermacher's individualism was not of "an ingrown, self-centered variety,"[57] but rather one that flourished in the midst of human friendship and political association. Nevertheless, Schleiermacher viewed human fulfillment as consisting of the full realization of one's own unique personality. "Thus there dawned upon me what is now my highest intuition. I saw clearly that each man is meant to represent humanity in his own way, combining its elements uniquely, so that it may reveal itself in every mode, and all that can issue from its womb be made actual in the

---

54. Louth, *Origins of the Christian Mystical Tradition*, 57–58. Emphasis original.
55. Freiss, *Schleiermacher's Soliloquies*, 30.
56. Ibid., 30–31.
57. Tice, "Schleiermacher's 'Highest Intuition' in Landsberg," 31.

fullness of unending space and time."[58] If the image of the three ways in the orthodox tradition maps the spiritual life as an ascending line, then Schleiermacher's account might be pictured as an ellipsis, with the two foci being the universal features of human existence on the one hand, and the features of the unique individual personality on the other.[59] The spiritual life would be a dynamic movement between social obligations and personal enrichment, universal human reason and one's own individuality, the body politic and one's own inner life.

Hans Frei, one of the pioneering thinkers in postliberalism, clearly would not propose a sequence of stages in the spiritual life, but he would speak in broad terms of the Christian life as a journey in Christ's presence. In *The Identity of Jesus Christ*, Frei argues that we come to an understanding of the presence of Christ through a description of his identity. "In a way, our procedure is simple, perhaps even as naive as this: Inquiry about Jesus' identity establishes that he is to be defined as one who lives. To live is to have presence. Hence, when we think about *who* he is, we must think of him as present."[60] While for the believer, this is true, Frei acknowledges that this may not be the case for those who do not ascribe to the Christian faith. Frei admits that for "the pilgrim, the one who is in transition from belief to unbelief or unbelief to belief," the change in mind-set could be prompted by any number of causes. "Every path must be considered possible for the pilgrim—even the incongruous one that such a transition (in either direction!) occurs in the process of purely circular discourse concerning the unity of Christ's identity and presence."[61] It is this "circular discourse" that represents Frei's understanding of the Christian journey in *Identity*. Where Schleiermacher preferred the ellipsis, Frei pictures the Christian life in circular form. "In our knowledge of Jesus Christ, his presence and his identity are completely one. We cannot properly think of him as not present, as we can think of others without their real presence. Whether, then, we begin by asking about his presence and go on to his identity, or reverse the procedure by beginning with reflection about his identity—only to realize that it involves the affirmation of his presence—we have a circular notion."[62]

Because "it is appropriate to speak of the relationship between Christ and believer as one of *presence to each other*,"[63] this circularity suggests

---

58. Freiss, *Schleiermacher's Soliloquies*, 31.
59. The image of the ellipsis is taken from Lamm, "Introduction," 45–46.
60. Frei, *Identity of Jesus Christ*, 5–6. Emphasis original.
61. Ibid., 8–9.
62. Ibid., 6.
63. Ibid., 3.

that the image of the Christian journey might be the Risen Christ walking side-by-side with the disciples on the road to Emmaus. The story is richly textured with themes of journey, recognition, and presence. In *Identity*, Frei employed the image of the pilgrim, and according to his friend, John Woolverton, "the term pilgrim was a non-heroic one which he liked and used. Seldom was the pilgrim glamorous or 'an aristocrat of the spirit,' but quite ordinary. He 'always followed this Lord at a distance,' much as the disciples followed Jesus to Jerusalem. The pilgrim's track is 'mysterious yet directed' and may involve a single person or a whole people who move toward a promised land or heavenly city."[64] Whether the disciple enters into the narrative world of the Bible and walks next to the Risen Christ or follows the earthly Christ, the image conveys a powerful expression of Frei's postliberal vision of the Christian life.

The postmodern concept of the biblical journey reverses our typical use of the image: it is not our journey to a divinely-appointed destination, but rather our reception of the divine Stranger who arrives at our door. As Richard Kearney notes, the encounter with the stranger provokes one of two responses: hostility or hospitality. In that moment, our response to "the other" is a wager. It is not a blind leap of faith, but a moment of careful discernment. "There is the other who kills and the other who brings life. The other who loves and the other who lies. The knock on the door may be the Lord (qua host) inviting us to a feast or (qua guest) seeking entry to our home; but it may be a psychotic murderer . . . "[65] There are, to be sure, limits to hospitality, but Kearney believes that the "healing potential of religion" can be realized when we allow hospitality, rather than hostility, to shape our imaginative construal of who the stranger is.[66] Kearney cites the example of Abraham who is shocked when three strangers arrive at his tent in Mamre. "Abraham's heartless banishment of Hagar and Ishmael is totally at odds with his hospitable reaction to the three alien nomads from the desert, intruding into his camp out of nowhere. Capable of those cruel acts, Abraham is also capable of welcoming potentially threatening strangers into his home with open arms. And as a result of his radical trust, he opens up for himself and his wife Sarah the possibility of new life, that is, the impossible become possible (Gen 18:14)."[67] In his display of hospitality, Abraham welcomes the Divine. The Abrahamic legacy, contends Kearney,

---

64. Woolverton, "Hans W. Frei in Context," 391.
65. Kearney, *Anatheism*, 45.
66. Kearney, "Imagining the Sacred Stranger," 15.
67. Ibid., 17.

"fosters a radical attentiveness to the Stranger as portal to the Divine."[68] It is a message reiterated by Christ in his teaching on the final judgement: "I was hungry and you gave me food, I was thirsty and you gave me something to drink, I was a stranger and you welcomed me" (Matt 25:35). Those who did not do these things, writes Kearney, "were looking to some metaphysical god: some 'omni-god' of omnipotence, omnipresence, and omniscience—to some metaphysical god in the sky rather than to the flesh and blood presence here on earth. There were looking up, not down. They were looking in the wrong place."[69]

The revitalization of the image of the biblical journey—whether that be in terms of the orthodox notion of the three ways, the liberal ascent to the "highest intuition" of the human spirit, the postliberal circularity of retelling the story of Jesus and experiencing his presence, or the postmodern embrace of the stranger—allows us to see our own journeys reflected in the stories of Moses's trek through the wilderness and Christ's temptation in the desert.

Discussion Questions

1. Do the journeys of Abraham, Moses, or Christ in any way reflect stages of a spiritual journey through which we all must pass?
2. Origen assumes that no detail of Scripture, no matter how insignificant it may seem to us, is without meaning. Do you agree or disagree with Origen?
3. Is Origen's reading into Numbers 33 meanings that simply are not there, or does he offer an exegetically sound, spiritually illuminating commentary on the chapter?
4. Achard interiorizes the biblical language: the "land of promise" is within us, and those in the fifth desert "experience in themselves 'the beauty of God's house'" and "manna rains down on them from heaven." Is this an appropriate application of the biblical language?
5. Is Rohr's account of the two halves of life accurate?
6. Is there "progress" in the spiritual life or successive stages though which we must pass?
7. What is Schleiermacher's "highest intuition"? Do you agree with it?

---

68. Ibid.,18.
69. Ibid., 23.

Suggested Readings

For a discussion of the four senses of Scripture, see Karlfried Froehlich, *Sensing the Scriptures* (Grand Rapids: Eerdmans, 2014). For background on Origen, see Rowan Greer, "Introduction" to *Origen* (New York: Paulist, 1979), Peter W. Martens, *Origen and Scripture* (Oxford: Oxford University Press, 2012), and Henning Graf Reventlow, *History of Biblical Interpretation, Volume One* (Atlanta: Society of Biblical Literature, 2009), 174–99. For an overview of the Victorine school, see Steve Chase, *Contemplation and Compassion* (Maryknoll, NY: Orbis, 2003) and chapter 9 of Bernard McGinn, *The Growth of Mysticism* (New York: Crossroad, 1994). See also the *Victorine Texts in Translation* series edited by Grover A. Zinn that is published by New City Press. For background on Achard, see Hugh Feiss, "Introduction" to *Achard of St. Victor: Works* (Kalamazoo: Cistercian, 2001). For more information regarding Richard Rohr, see the website for the Center for Contemplation and Action in Albuquerque (https://cac.org). Rohr is the Founding Director of the Center.

Chapter Four: Biblical Vision of Jacob's Ladder

THE CLASSIC FORM OF the ladder story appears in Genesis 28. After cheating his brother Esau out of his blessing, Jacob flees Beersheba and travels to Haran. On his way, Jacob stops to rest for the night. Using a stone as a pillow, he falls asleep and dreams of a ladder that stretches from the desert floor up to heaven itself. In his dream, Jacob sees angels ascending and descending on the ladder—it is "the gate of heaven," the very route taken by the messengers of the Lord as they travel from heaven to earth and back again to their heavenly abode. The Lord appears in the dream and promises Jacob the land upon which he now sleeps and multiple descendants who will share in the blessings of the covenant. When Jacob awakes from the dream, he realizes that God has visited him at this very spot and marks the site with a memorial stone. He names the site Bethel ("house of God"). The Jewish and Christian fascination with this episode in the biblical narrative stems in part from its many evocative elements: the encounter with the divine in the world of dreams, the discovery of the gateway from the natural to the supernatural realm, and the ritual marking of the site of the divine encounter. The image of the ladder offers the hope that we might ascend in mind and heart from the temporal to the eternal. We will focus in this chapter on the accounts of the Christian life based on the image of Jacob's Ladder as presented in *The Ladder of Divine Ascent* composed by the sixth-century monk John Climacus, *The Ladder of the Monks* by the twelfth-century Carthusian Guigo II, and *Jacob's Ladder* by the contemporary philosopher Peter Kreeft.

John Climacus, *The Ladder of Divine Ascent*

Little is known about the life of "John of the Ladder" or "John the Scholastic." Probably born around 579, he was sixteen when he entered monastic life at what is now known as St. Catherine's Monastery on the Sinai Peninsula. After about three years, John moved outside the monastery and lived a life of solitude at Tholas, about five miles away from the main monastery. At some point during his time as a hermit he visited the monastery at Alexandria. After forty years as a hermit, John was elected abbot at the main

CHAPTER FOUR: BIBLICAL VISION OF JACOB'S LADDER

monastery at Sinai. At some point during his tenure as abbot, John received a request from an abbot of a nearby monastery to set down in writing the wisdom he had acquired during his time on Sinai. John reluctantly agreed and near the end of his tenure as abbot he composed *The Ladder of Divine Ascent*. Shortly before his death (ca. 649) he stepped down as abbot and returned to the life of solitude.

"I have put together a ladder of ascent," writes John Climacus towards the end of the *Ladder*, and modestly adds, "though my meager knowledge makes me something of a second-rate architect."[1] The ladder that he devised consists of thirty steps—one for each year of Jesus' life prior to his public ministry. In this way, Climacus includes the christological application of Jacob's Ladder found in Christ's response to Nathaniel in John's Gospel, "Very truly, I tell you, you will see heaven opened and the angels of God ascending and descending upon the Son of Man" (John 1:51). There is scholarly debate over the structure of the *Ladder*, but we will follow the outline proposed by the Climacus scholar John Chryssavgis who sees the work falling into three sections of unequal length.[2] The first section (steps 1–3) deals with the break from the world; the second section (steps 4–26) discusses the virtues and the struggle against the passions in the active life, and the third section (steps 27–30) describes the life of contemplation.

The reader does not need to delve far into the first section to be reminded that the *Ladder* is a thoroughly monastic text: its author is a man who lived the solitary life for forty years and his audience is a community of monks living on the arid Sinai Peninsula. The first three steps of the *Ladder* are filled with references to the "denial of the world," "the constant remembrance of death," and the "renunciation of everything in one's familiar surroundings." Modern readers feel like they are eavesdropping on a fiery coach admonishing players during a strenuous practice. Endurance, fortitude, and perseverance are themes constantly preached in both arenas. Climacus even refers to "the spiritual athlete."[3] The novices must break the bonds of attachment that they have with the world. Only with the severing of these ties can the monk begin to ascend the spiritual ladder. "Withdrawal from the world is a willing hatred of all that is materially prized, a denial of nature for the sake of what is above nature."[4] The *Ladder* in many ways is an extended reflection on the admonition to "set

---

1. John Climacus, *Ladder of Divine Ascent*, 265.

2. Chryssavgis, *John Climacus*, 8–29. For a discussion of the various proposals regarding the structure of the *Ladder*, see chapter 1 of Zecher, *Role of Death*.

3. John Climacus, *Ladder of Divine Ascent*, 79.

4. Ibid., 74.

your mind on things that are above, not on things that are on earth" (Col 3:2). In the third step, Climacus begins, "There is such a thing as exile, an irrevocable renunciation of everything in one's familiar surroundings that hinders one from attaining the ideal of holiness. Exile is . . . the longing for what is divine."[5] Only when we are exiles in this world, Climacus suggests, can we realize that "here we have no lasting city, but we are looking for the city that is to come" (Heb 13:14).

Having concluded his preparatory discussion of detachment, Climacus turns his attention to the ascent of the divine ladder (steps 4–26). In this second part of the *Ladder* Climacus draws upon the rich classical and Christian heritage regarding the virtues and vices, especially Evagrius's "eight deadly thoughts" and Gregory the Great's "seven deadly sins."[6] "The holy virtues are like the ladder of Jacob and the unholy vices are like the chains that fell off the chief apostle Peter. The virtues lead from one to another and carry heavenward the man who chooses them."[7] Climacus does not develop a system in which he correlates the various virtues with each of the ascending rungs, but instead insists "that no one can climb a ladder in a single stride."[8] Therefore, while the virtues are the rungs on Jacob's ladder, they are more importantly skills to be honed in a long and protracted battle against the forces within us that restrain our ascent. As Climacus makes clear, the monks are warriors and the virtues are their weapons.

The cultivation of the virtues requires a community whose beliefs and practices can foster the development of moral character. For Climacus's audience, that community is the monastery. "At the beginning of our religious life, we cultivate the virtues, and we do so with toiled difficulty. Progressing a little, we then lose our sense of grief or retain little of it. But when our mortal intelligence turns to zeal and is mastered by it, then we work with full joy, determination, desire, and a holy flame."[9] The monastery is "the school of virtue."[10] Elsewhere Climacus refers to the monastery as "heaven on earth."[11] Nevertheless, he maintains a realistic assessment of life in community. Just as a sharp stone has its edges smoothened when it strikes another stone, the short-tempered monk learns patience in a community

---

5. Ibid., 85.
6. Climacus refers to both figures in the opening sentences in Step 22.
7. John Climacus, *Ladder of Divine Ascent*, 152.
8. Ibid., 225.
9. Ibid., 77.
10. Ibid., 117.
11. Ibid., 111.

of monks.[12] Climacus speaks of three forms of the monastic life. "There is the road of withdrawal and solitude for the spiritual athlete; there is the life of stillness shared with two or three others; there is the practice of living patiently in community."[13] The solitary life is a unique calling and Climacus warns that not all those who have taken up that way of life have preserved their sanity. "My humble advice to them was to abandon solitary living in case they be turned from human beings into devils."[14] For the vast majority of Christians, therefore, the ascent of the soul arising from the training in virtue occurs not in life of hermitical isolation, but rather in the rough and tumble of community life.

The ascent of the divine ladder comes slowly, but over the course of the various battles with vices such as despondency, malice, and vainglory, the monk receives the gift of discernment (1 Cor 12:10). "To put the matter generally, discernment is—and is recognized to be—a solid understanding of the will of God in all times, in all places, in all things; and it is found only among those who are pure in heart, in body, and in speech."[15] Climacus not only describes discernment as "a solid understanding," but also as "pure perception" and "a light to all the mind."[16] The gift of discernment allows the monk to detect the divine in the midst of the human, or for Climacus, even the demonic. "It is characteristic of the perfect that they always know whether a thought comes within themselves, or from God, or from the demons."[17] Without this knowledge, the monk could head down the wrong path. It is for this reason that Climacus warns, "In the matter of actions, words, thoughts, and movements, the monastic life has to be lived with a perceptive heart. Otherwise it will not be monastic or indeed angelic."[18] Furthermore, the gift of discernment is not only of benefit to the individual monk, but also to those who seek spiritual guidance from him/her. "The man who takes the road of monastic life under his own direction may be easily lost, even if he has all the wisdom of the world."[19]

In the third section (steps 27–30) Climacus discusses the stillness experienced during the contemplative union with God, the same stillness that Paul experienced when he "was caught up into Paradise and heard things

12. Ibid., 147.
13. Ibid., 79.
14. Ibid., 148.
15. Ibid., 229.
16. Ibid., 229, 244.
17. Ibid., 255.
18. Ibid., 33.
19. Ibid., 259.

that are not to be told, that no mortal is permitted to repeat" (2 Cor 12:4). "He who has achieved stillness has arrived at the very center of the mysteries ... Paul confirms this. If he had not been caught up into Paradise as into stillness, he would never have heard the unspeakable words (cf. 2 Cor 12:4)."[20] When the waves of passions have been stilled, the soul experiences a state of "dispassion," which Climacus describes as "a heaven of the mind within the heart."[21] "Its effect is to sanctify the mind and to detach it from material things, and it does so in such a way that, after entering the heavenly harbor, a man, for most of his earthly life, is enraptured, like someone already in heaven, and he is lifted up to the contemplation of God."[22]

Stillness and dispassion should not, however, be understood as a disengagement from the love of neighbor or an extinguishing of the love of God. As Climacus puts it, "the man who claims to love the Lord but is angry with his neighbor is like someone who dreams he is running."[23] Furthermore, the love of God stirs a desire to know what awaits the soul when one has stepped off the highest rung of the divine ladder. It might be a state of tranquil stillness, or perhaps there is a "progress of eternity" that awaits the soul.[24] In any event, Climacus ends his treatise on a note of mystical longing.

> I long to know how Jacob saw you fixed above the ladder (cf. Gen 28:12). That climb, how was it? Tell me, for I long to know. What is the mode, what is the law joining together those steps that the lover has set as an ascent in his heart (cf. Ps 83:6). I thirst to know the number of those steps, and the time required to climb them. He who discovered Your struggle and Your vision has spoken to us of the guides. But he would not—perhaps he could not—tell us any more.[25]

The ladder of divine ascent leads the soul into the unfathomable mystery of God, but if the story of Jacob is our spiritual guide, we may also have to wrestle with the thoughts that attack us in the darkness and leave us wounded by the struggle.

20. Ibid., 264.
21. Ibid., 282.
22. Ibid.
23. Ibid., 289.
24. Ibid.
25. Ibid.

Guigo II, *The Ladder of Monks*

Like Climacus, the twelfth-century Carthusian monk Guigo II was fascinated with the image of the ladder. Instead of Climacus's thirty steps, Guigo speaks of only four. This minimalist approach reflects the spirit of the Carthusian Order. Begun by Bruno of Cologne, the Carthusians first gathered as a community in Grenoble in the French Alps. After an avalanche in 1132, they relocated to what is now regarded as their motherhouse, the Grand Chartreuse.[26] In 1180 Guigo II became its ninth prior. The austere Carthusian life is a unique combination of the eremitical and communal monastic traditions. The monks spend the bulk of their day in their individual cells working and praying, gathering together for morning and evening prayer and the celebration of Mass. Their meals are delivered to them in their cells where they are eaten in solitude. Only on Sundays and major feast days does the entire community gather for dinner, take a long walk, and engage in conversation. The historian C. H. Lawrence notes, "The diet was sparser than St. Benedict has allowed: meat was excluded, and on Mondays, Wednesday and Fridays, bread and water was the rule, though wine was permitted with food. Clothes and bedding were of the coarsest materials; and this spirit of poverty was extended to the monastic church—the customs forbade the use of gold or silver ornaments and vessels other than the chalice."[27]

Little is known about the exact date and details of the composition of *The Ladder of Monks*. In the prologue we learn that Guigo is responding to the request of a friend named Gervase who has asked for his thoughts on the spiritual life. The idea for the work, Guigo reports, entered his mind one day while he was working in his cell.

> One day when I was busy working with my hands I began to think about our spiritual work, and all at once four stages in spiritual exercise came into my mind: reading, meditation, prayer and contemplation. These make a ladder for monks by which they are lifted up from earth to heaven. It has few rungs, yet its length is immense and wonderful, for its lower end rests upon the earth, but its top pierces the clouds and touches heavenly secrets.[28]

The entire sweep of the Carthusian spiritual journey is outlined in the four rungs. As Keith Egan notes, "the central emphasis of Guigo's thoughts on the four steps ... [is] the dynamic process of the way to union with God and

---

26. Lawrence, *Medieval Monasticism*, 157.
27. Ibid., 158.
28. Guigo II, *Ladder of Monks*, 67–68.

the interrelationship of the stages on the road to 'tasting the joys of eternal sweetness.'"[29] This tasting of the eternal sweetness refers to the fourth and highest run of contemplation. Guigo writes, "Contemplation is when the mind is in some sort lifted up to God and above itself, so that it tastes the joys of everlasting sweetness."[30] Much reading, meditation, and prayer, however, precedes the contemplative state. "Reading is the careful study of the Scriptures, concentrating all one's power on it. Meditation is the busy application of the mind to seek with the help of one's own reason for knowledge of hidden truth. Prayer is the heart's devoted turning to God to drive away evil and obtain what is good."[31] Again Guigo reminds us, the four steps on the ladder are interrelated and the monk's ascent depends on the sturdiness of each rung. As Guigo warns later in the *Ladder* that, "reading without meditation is sterile, meditation without reading is liable to error, prayer without meditation is lukewarm, meditation without prayer is unfruitful, prayer when it is fervent wins contemplation, but to obtain it without prayer would be rare, even miraculous."[32]

While Guigo employs the image of the ladder for overall structure of his work, he also offers various analogies for the spiritual life throughout his treatise. One of his favorites is the comparison of reading a biblical passage with the process of eating. In order to devour the biblical text, the monk must first practice the art of spiritual reading (*lectio divina*). As Lawrence Cunningham and Keith Egan explain, "*Lectio* does not mean technical study (which is the task of the professional biblical commentator) or the mere scanning of the text for the sake of information or the 'story.' It means a close, prayerful, openness to the text so that one both reads the text and, in patient expectation, is open to the text speaking back to the person."[33] Guigo writes, "Reading, as it were, puts food whole in the mouth, meditation chews it and breaks it up, prayer extracts its flavor, contemplation is the sweetness itself which gladdens and refreshes."[34] Like both Ezekiel and John the Divine who consume scrolls containing the message of the Lord, the monk is nourished by devouring the sacred books. If spiritual reading is the consumption of the biblical text, then the monk eats slowly. Taking as his example the beatitude, "Blessed are the pure in heart, for they will see God" (Matt 5:8), Guigo reflects, "This is a short text of Scripture, but

---

29. Egan, "Guigo II," 109.
30. Guigo II, *Ladder of Monks*, 68.
31. Ibid., 68.
32. Ibid., 82.
33. Cunningham and Egan, *Christian Spirituality*, 38.
34. Guigo II, *Ladder of Monks*, 69.

CHAPTER FOUR: BIBLICAL VISION OF JACOB'S LADDER 65

it is of great sweetness, like a grape that is put into the mouth filled with many senses to feed the soul." Like a food gourmet who savors every flavor in a dish, the monk lingers on a single biblical verse as he or she tastes the goodness of the Lord (Ps 34:8).

Like animals that chew the cud, monks "ruminate" over a biblical passage in the act of meditation. "So, wishing to have a fuller understanding of this [purity of heart], the soul begins to bite and chew upon this grape, as though putting it in a wine press, while it stirs up its power of reasoning to ask what this precious purity may be and how it may be had. When meditation busily applies itself to this work, it does not remain on the outside, is not detained by unimportant things, climbs higher, goes to the heart of the matter, examines each point thoroughly."[35] In this meditative reflection, the reader recalls other verses that might shed light on the passage under consideration. In the case of the beatitude concerning the pure of heart, Guigo recalls the plea of the Psalmist, "Create in me a clean heart, O God, and put a new and right spirit within me" (Ps 51:10) and next reflects on the struggles of Job to maintain his purity. A barrage of verses is brought to bear on the beatitude, each adding a different element or perspective to the meditation. Meditation does not simply enlighten the intellect, it kindles the heart. As Simon Tugwell highlights, "Meditation both indicates what we need to pray for and fires our will so that we shall pray with real eagerness."[36] As Guigo explains, "When the soul is set alight by this kindling, and when its flames are fanned by these desires, it receives a first intimation of the sweetness, not yet by tasting but through its sense of smell, when the alabaster jar is broken; and from this it deduces how sweet it would be to know by experience the purity that meditation has shown to be so full of joy."[37]

The desire for purity of the heart spurs the reader to prayer. "Lord, for long have I meditated in my heart, seeking to see your face. It is the sight of you, Lord, that I have sought; and all the while in my meditation the fire of longing, the desire to know you more fully, has increased."[38] The careful reading of the biblical text and the meditation on its meaning intensifies the heart's desire to experience in one's soul what one understands in the mind. In this way, the life of study and the life of prayer are joined. The deliberations of the mind fuel the desires of the heart which in turn spark the intellect. Reading, meditation, and prayer are rungs on a ladder and all three play a

---

35. Ibid., 69–70.
36. Tugwell, *Ways of Imperfection*, 95.
37. Guigo II, *Ladder of Monks*, 70.
38. Ibid., 73.

vital role in the soul's ascent. But if these first three rungs of the ladder emphasize human effort, the final rung is purely a gift from God.

Like the father who rushes out to embrace his returning prodigal son, God "does not wait until the longing soul has said all its say, but breaks in upon the middle of its prayer, runs to meet it in haste, sprinkled with most heavenly dew, anointed with the most precious perfumes, and restores the weary soul."[39] In this moment of divine embrace during contemplation, the soul savors, in Guigo's words, "the sweetness of the Lord." But, Guigo warns, the experience of contemplation is fleeting. "For a short time He allows us to taste how sweet He is, and before our taste is satisfied He withdraws."[40] Just as the angel that wrestled with Jacob fled at first light, God "gives His blessing, and withers the nerve of the thigh, and changes Jacob's name to Israel, and then for a little while He withdraws . . . He goes, it is true, for this visitation ends, and with it the sweetness of contemplation; but yet He stays, for He directs us, he gives us grace, he joins us to Himself."[41] While these moments of sweetness provide the monk a foretaste of the heavenly banquet, the regular discipline of spiritual reading, meditation, and prayer is the daily bread that nourishes and sustains the soul that longs to taste and see the goodness of the Lord.

Peter Kreeft, *Jacob's Ladder*

While Climacus and Guigo employ the image of the ladder in their spiritual theology, the contemporary Roman Catholic philosopher Peter Kreeft puts it to use in the area of apologetics. Using a ladder with ten rungs, Kreeft argues for the orderly progression in thought beginning with the universal human passion to know the truth to his distinctly Catholic advocacy of episcopal authority and its necessary role in defining orthodox doctrinal and moral positions to be held by the faithful. The ten rungs are presented in the form of a dialogue between Libby Rawls, a skeptical yet open-minded seeker, and "Mother" Maria Kirk, whose voice represents that of the Catholic Church. Their conversation takes place on ten successive days on Nahant Beach outside of Boston. In their first conversation Mother compares a good book with a ladder. "A lot of good books are that way. Like a ladder. You get the view only from the top, but to get to the top you have to climb up the rungs, one at time."[42] That comment

---

39. Ibid., 74.
40. Ibid., 77–78.
41. Ibid., 76.
42. Kreeft, *Jacob's Ladder*, 11.

leads into the ensuing dialogue dealing with passion, truth, meaning, love, principles, God, Jews, Jesus, Catholics, and authority.

The first two rungs deal with what drives and fulfills the human quest for understanding. The indispensable first rung on the ladder is the relentless passion to pursue truth wherever it may be found. Passion alone, however, "is blind power. It's fire without light. It ignites *whatever* it touches, good or evil, truth or lies, unselfishness or selfishness, love or lust."[43] Passion, therefore, needs to be tethered to truth, which is the second rung of the ladder. Kreeft adamantly defends the existence of objective truth and takes aim at skepticism, relativism, and deconstructionism. The character Mother declares, "Simple skepticism says nobody is ever right, and relativism says nobody is ever wrong. And that's just as self-contradictory as saying nobody is ever right. Because if nobody is ever wrong, then the person who says relativism is wrong isn't wrong either."[44] Deconstructionism is similarly rejected on the basis that it "claims that truth is only the hypocritical mask painted on the face of power; that truth is only whatever other people of your class or race or gender or sexual orientation or ideological group let you get away with saying."[45] For Kreeft the restless heart can only find contentment in the truth that is the same yesterday, today, and tomorrow.

The third, fourth, and fifth rungs form a philosophical trilogy: Love stands at the center, while the question of life's meaning precedes it and the principles that direct love to its proper end follow it. The journey of discerning the meaning of life proceeds by testing various life philosophies and seeing if they lead to happiness. Mother Kirk advises Libby, "Your heart is the tester. If something can't satisfy your heart's longing, deep down and long range, after you test that thing by time and experiences, then that thing is not real happiness."[46] The only thing that can fulfill this lofty goal, Mother contends, is love—not a love that is rooted in selfish desire, but a love that is exclusively concerned with the well-being of the other. In the fourth dialogue Mother explains further, "What do you want most from other people? Love. When you're loved, your happy. And everybody wants happiness. So that's how to live: give what you most want to get: love."[47] Just as Mother had earlier argued that passion must be wedded to truth, she now insists that there is an inseparable connection between love and principles such as those found in the Decalogue. "The Commandments are for love, and love

---

43. Ibid., 20. Emphasis original.
44. Ibid., 27.
45. Ibid., 29.
46. Ibid., 37.
47. Ibid., 62.

is for life; that's why the Commandments are for life. They describe love. *Love* does not kill, *love* does not steal, *love* does not bear false witness, *love* does not commit adultery."[48]

The sixth and seventh rungs deal with the existence of God and the covenant with Israel. The topic of love leads Libby and Mother into a consideration of the claim that God is love. Libby proposes that if we accept that God is love, then love is God. The profound experience of human love is what we mean by God. Mother sees in Libby's proposal an unnecessary constriction of our understanding of God. The sun and sunlight at the beach, Mother contends, provides a better analogy for the relationship of God and love. "All this sunlight comes from the sun, whether we see it or not. We can trace all the sunlight back up into the sun. So maybe we can trace all the love light, all the little rays of love we know, back to God who's Absolute Love."[49] In this way, human love is a reflection of the love of God that, in Dante's words, moves the sun and stars. Rather than equating God and love, Mother prefers to speak of love as Godlike, as something that participates in a much greater reality. This, of courses, leaves open the question of whether this God of boundless love does actually exist or is simply the sum total of human projection—a wish fulfillment of the highest order? Seeing reason alone unable to resolve this question, Mother suggests that Libby and other like-minded seekers should consider making the leap of faith. If they do, they will land squarely in the field of Jewish theology. The uncreated God worshipped by Jews, Christians, and Muslims brought all that is created into being. Unlike other religions that presented creation as a battle between two opposing deities, Jews, without compromise, asserted that the one and only God whom they worship is also solely responsible for creation. Unlike the popular image of different roads leading to a mountain summit representing different religions, Mother insists that Judaism makes a far different claim "It's not a road up the mountain—it's a road down. God made it, not man. And it's public, not private. It's a public revelation from the top down, not a private mystical experience from the bottom up."[50]

The final three rungs continue from the contention that Christianity is a "top down" revelation. The first instance of this "top down" view occurs in the eighth dialogue concerning Christ. Mother declares, "[Jesus] *claims* to be much more than a prophet, and either He is or He isn't. If He is, well, then He is. And if He isn't, then he's much *less* than a prophet. He's a liar and a fake."[51]

48. Ibid., 75. Emphasis original.
49. Ibid., 85.
50. Ibid., 96.
51. Ibid., 106.

CHAPTER FOUR: BIBLICAL VISION OF JACOB'S LADDER

Kreeft has described this argument, popularized by C. S. Lewis, as "the most important single argument all of Christian apologetics."[52] Kreeft continues, "it opens all the other doctrinal doors. For most Christians believe all the doctrines of their faith not on the basis of their own reasoning or experience of each separate doctrine (at least at first) but on the basis of the authority of Christ the Teacher of those doctrines—whatever the respective roles of Church and Scripture in channeling that authority down the centuries."[53] The last two rungs of Kreeft's ladder deal precisely with the role of the Church in channeling the authority of Christ. As a Catholic apologist, Kreeft stresses the historical continuity of the Catholic church with the early church and believes that this line of apostolic succession is the theological precondition for the church's authority to determine which books should have been included in the canon. In the final dialogue, Kreeft carries the issue of the Church's authority into the present age and argues in favor of the Catholic prohibition on contraception, divorce, and abortion.

The image of Jacob's Ladder proves to be a fertile image for Christian reflection. For Climacus, it provides the framework for integrating the life of prayer with the life of action in the Christian's spiritual journey. In the hands of Guigo, it becomes an image of the monk's life of spiritual reading, meditation, prayer, and contemplation. Finally, Kreeft sees the ladder as a symbol of the reasoning process that moves from existential concerns about truth and meaning to religious claims about God, Christ, and the church. Given its numinous quality, the image of Jacob's Ladder has unbounded potential to vitalize theological reflection. We now turn our attention to some possible ways in which the image of Jacob's Ladder could be incorporated into present theological positions, ranging from the orthodox to the postmodern.

The Revitalization of the Image of Jacob's Ladder

In the orthodox tradition, there has been a constant stream of commentaries on the passage regarding Jacob's mystical vision at Bethel.[54] As one might expect, the results fall into one of two categories: first, a variety of intriguing theories regarding the various details in the story and second, a general consensus about the christological significance of the passage. The various thinkers have speculated on, among other things, the significance of the text mentioning that Jacob used both multiple stones and a single stone for a

---

52. Kreeft, "Most Important Argument," 243.

53. Ibid.

54. For a brief overview of many of these interpretations, see the entry, "Jacob's Ladder" in Jeffrey, *Dictionary of Biblical Tradition in English Literature*, 388–90.

pillow, the possible location of the incident, and the importance of the pillar of stone that Jacob builds to mark the spot.[55] The christological consensus emerges from the general acceptance of the hermeneutical principle that Christ is the center of all Scripture. In the case of this particular passage, the christological interpretation is expressly stated in John's Gospel, "Very truly, I tell you, you will see heaven opened and the angels of God ascending and descending upon the Son of Man" (1:51). Calvin, for example, in his commentary on Genesis asserts, "It is Christ alone who joins heaven to earth. He alone is Mediator. He it is through whom the fullness of all heavenly gifts flows down to us and through whom we on our part may ascend to God. Therefore, if we say that the ladder is a symbol of Christ, the interpretation is not forced."[56] We will focus our attention on Luther's interpretation of the story of Jacob's Ladder to discover his own unique points of emphasis as well as his widely shared christological interpretation.

Luther's Jacob is the model of faith. Prior to his arrival in Luz, Jacob "traversed that long journey with many tears and with frequent sighs and sobs, for he fled in secret that he might hide himself from the fury of his brother Esau, lest Esau pursue him, seize him on the journey, and do him some violence."[57] Despite his anxiety and unworthiness, God speaks to Jacob. Jacob is, in Luther's estimation, saintly. However, Luther quickly adds that "there are two kinds of saintliness. The first is that by which we are sanctified through the Word. The second is that by which we are saintly on the basis of what we do and how we live."[58] Jacob represents the former form of saintliness, which is "imputed to those who have the Word. And a person is simply accounted saintly, not because of us or because of our works but because of the Word."[59] Luther speaks about ascending and descending the ladder: "It is true that a preacher must first ascend through prayer in order to receive the Word and doctrine from God. He should also study, learn, read, and meditate. Later he should descend and teach others."[60] This ascent, however, must never be confused with works of righteousness. David Steinmetz offers the following assessment of Luther's position: "There is not a hint in his lecture that he disapproves of the idea that Christians ascend and descend Jacob's ladder. The problem is not with

---

55. Steinmetz, "Luther and the Ascent of Jacob's Ladder," 182–86.
56. Calvin, *Genesis*, 249.
57. Luther, *Lectures on Genesis*, 209.
58. Ibid., 213.
59. Ibid., 213–14.
60. Ibid., 217.

CHAPTER FOUR: BIBLICAL VISION OF JACOB'S LADDER

the metaphor of ascent and descent but with the notion that the ascent is helped along by the merit of good works."[61]

Luther stands in the mainstream Christian tradition when he locates the central meaning of Jacob's Ladder in the Incarnation. "We should believe and be content with this explanation of our Savior; for He has a better understanding than all other interpreters, even though they agree properly in this point, that this dream signified that infinite, inexpressible, and wondrous mystery of the incarnation of Christ, who was to descend from the patriarch Jacob . . ."[62] There is, according to Luther, a second meaning to the image of the ladder, an allegorical meaning that refers to our own union with Christ. We "ascend into Him and are carried along through the Word and the Holy Spirit. And through faith we cling to Him, since we become one body with Him and He with us . . . On the other hand, He descends to us through the Word and the sacraments by teaching and by exercising us in the knowledge of Him."[63] The ladder serves as an image for the union of the human and the divine found supremely in the Incarnate Word, but also in the spiritual union of Christ and the church. The revitalization of the image of Jacob's Ladder along orthodox lines would speak in a similar way of one side of the ladder symbolizing God's descent into the world in the Incarnation and the other side symbolizing the Christian elevation of others' concerns over our own expressed in loving service, with the rungs ensuring that the two sides remain securely in place.

Those in the liberal tradition may find in Harrier Beecher Stowe's *The Minster's Wooing* (1859) a use of the image of the ladder that speaks to their theological concerns. On the surface level, *The Minister's Wooing* is a quaint romance novel involving a young Mary Scudder whose beloved James Marvyn has gone off to sea. Mary lives with her widowed mother who operates a boarding house in Newport, Rhode Island. A recent boarder, the minister Samuel Hopkins has fallen in love with Mary.[64] When reports come that James's ship was lost at sea, Mary and James's family are distraught over his presumed death and in the midst of their heartbreak a discussion develops about whether James—a good man who had little interest in religion—could be with the Lord. At this point the reader realizes that not far below the surface is Stowe's participation in a theological debate rooted in New England Calvinist theology. Hopkins eventually proposes marriage to Mary and she

61. Steinmetz, "Luther and the Ascent of Jacob's Ladder," 190.

62. Luther, *Lectures on Genesis*, 217.

63. Ibid., 223.

64. The character is based on the actual Samuel Hopkins, but Stowe alters the events in Hopkins's life. "Hopkins was, in fact, an elderly man during his Newport years, but Mrs. Stowe makes him middle-aged bachelor . . ." (Adams, "Family Influences," 32).

accepts. In her study of Stowe's life, Nancy Koester explains, "Mary cares for Hopkins. She respects his learning and knows him to be a man of integrity, for at the risk of offending a wealthy member of his church, Hopkins denounced the slave trade. Mary knows a good wife could support Hopkins in his ministry and her sense of duty tells her to accept him."[65] However the town is soon shocked to learn that James has survived the shipwreck. Putting Mary's happiness ahead of his own, Hopkins nobly breaks off the engagement and Mary weds her beloved James.

Stowe's depiction of Samuel Hopkins, the colleague of Jonathan Edwards, reveals her ambivalence toward the Calvinism. On the one hand, he is morally upright and has risked alienating the wealthiest member in his congregation with his denunciation of slavery. On the other hand, his theology of predestination has created a rungless ladder from human to divine love.[66]

> There is a ladder to heaven, whose base God has placed in human affections, tender instincts, symbolic feelings, sacraments of love, through which the soul rises, higher and higher, refining as she goes, till she outgrows the human and changes, as she rises, into the image of the divine. At the very top of this ladder, at the threshold of Paradise, blazes dazzling and crystalline that celestial grade where the soul knows self no more, having learned through long experience of devotion, how blest it is to lose herself in that eternal Love and Beauty which all earthly fairness and grandeur are but a dim type, the distant shadow. This highest step, this saintly elevation, which but few selectest spirits ever on earth attain, to raise the soul to which the Eternal Father organized every relation of human existence and strung every cord of human love, for which this world is one long discipline, for which the soul's human education is constantly varied, for which it is now torn by sorrow, now flooded by joy, to which all its multiplied powers tend with upwards hands of dumb and ignorant aspiration,—this Ultima Thule of virtue had been seized upon by our sage [Hopkins] as the *all* of religion. He knocked out every round of the ladder but the highest, and then, pointing to its hopeless splendor, said to the world, "Go up thither and be saved!"[67]

In her study on race and gender in nineteenth-century Protestantism, Carolyn Haynes argues that Stowe "sought to widen the appeal of Reformed

65. Koester, *Harriet Beecher Stowe*, 218.
66. See Foster, *Rungless Ladder*.
67. Stowe, *Minister's Wooing*, 53–54.

Protestantism and its hopeless ladder theology." Rather than focusing on the moment of conversion, ministers should focus on the life-long process of sanctification. "Because of their emphasis on product over process and part over totality, the ministers are not only bolstering a rigid elitism (comprised of the 'few selectest spirits'), they are also denying their very responsibilities as servants of God . . . In other words, according to Stowe, these ministers are tragically oblivious to their obligation to assist church members in mounting the everyday ladder rungs that she believes would inevitably lead them to salvation."[68]

Stowe's alternative ladder theology is found in a letter written by James to Mary that is only delivered after his return to Newport. In this letter James recounts his conversion to Christianity during his time at sea. James had begun to read the Bible that Mary had given him, and he came upon the passage of Jacob's Ladder.

> There was one passage in particular, and that was where Jacob started off from all his friends to go off and seek his fortune in a strange country, and laid down to sleep all alone in the field, with only a stone for his pillow. . . . And so lying with the stone under his head, he saw a ladder in his sleep between him and heaven, and angels going up and down. That was a sight which came to the very point of his necessities. He saw that there was a way between him and God, and that there were those above who did care for him, and who would come to help him. . . .
>
> [Jacob] wanted to know whether [God] cared anything about men, and would do anything to help them. And so, in fact, it was saying, "If there is a God who interests Himself at all in me, and will be my Friend and Protector, I will obey Him, so far as I can find out His will."[69]

James then resolves to undertake the same "great experiment" that Jacob undertook and soon he begins to realize that Someone is guiding his life. "But about this time I began to read the New Testament, and then the idea came to me, that the Same Power that helped me in the lower sphere of life would help me carry out those higher aspirations."[70] James's great experiment is to live as if there is a loving connection between God and himself, and between each and every individual created in the image of God. It is trusting that there is a way between God and humans and that the ladder represents the way not only of angels, but of every human being.

68. Haynes, *Divine Destiny*, 60.
69. Stowe, *Minister's Wooing*, 297–98.
70. Ibid., 299.

The image of the ladder also appears in recent work in the area of postliberal theology. In his work, *Transforming Postliberal Theology*, C. C. Pecknold contends that the advancement of postliberalism requires that its proponents address more specifically the relationship between language and experience, Scripture and church practice, the church and Israel, and the church and the world. Pecknold asserts, "Under all of these issues the category of 'semiotics' has become increasingly critical in the extension and supplementation of postliberal theology because 'semiotics' names a discipline of thinking about the unavoidable mediation of signs."[71] As we will see, it is in this "thinking about the unavoidable mediation of signs" that the image of the ladder arises. Augustine recognized centuries ago that a "sign is a thing which of itself makes some other thing come to mind."[72] A sign bridges two realties. It is this theme of the power of language to mediate that is at the heart of postliberal theology. Referring to the ground-breaking work of the postliberal thinker George Lindbeck, Pecknold argues, "Lindbeck transformed the liberal concern with 'universal' experience by attending to descriptions of concrete 'particular' experience as *mediated* through cultural-linguistic signs. This mediatorial move is extremely significant. *Postliberalism transforms liberal theology by a greater descriptive attentiveness to the mediatorial capacity of signs, that is, to our culturally and linguistically mediated experience of reality* . . . "[73] Lindbeck even speaks in language similar to Augustine when he describes "the semiotic universe paradigmatically encoded in holy writ."[74]

Pecknold develops this critical dialogue between Augustine's semiotics and postliberal theology. According to Augustine, the need for signs developed only after the fall. Prior to the fall, there was unmediated communication between God and humans. This direct knowledge of God will only be restored in the *eschaton*. In his essay on Augustine's theory of signs, David Dawson poses the question that Augustine confronts when he discusses the proper interpretation of the signs in Scripture: "How, then, will one be able to read Scripture in a way which makes its signs an antidote, rather than a catalyst for sin?"[75] Pecknold writes, "What Augustine discovers is that an effective mediation is required, a new reparative relation, a 'third' [a third way] to bridge (like Jacob's ladder) the linguistic gulf between God and human beings after the fall—and it is the mediation of the Word

---

71. Pecknold, *Transforming Postliberal Theology*, 10.
72. Augustine, *On Christian Teaching*, 30.
73. Pecknold, *Transforming Postliberal Theology*, 6. Emphasis original.
74. Lindbeck, *Nature of Doctrine*, 116.
75. Dawson, "Sign Theory," 131.

which makes the scriptures legible as scripture."[76] Scripture, then, is Jacob's Ladder, mediating the divine will to humans through the signs contained in its pages. The strange world of the Bible is where the reader becomes familiar with God's will. The postliberal emphasis on the formative power of Scripture arises from its core conviction that by absorbing our world into the biblical narrative we discover the ladder by which the dis-eased soul experiences the healing touch of the divine Physician.

The image of Jacob's Ladder appears as an element in an often-cited experiment conducted by the postmodern literary critic Stanley Fish. After his first class of the day Fish had left an assignment on the board that read:

Jacobs-Rosenbaum

Levin

Thorne

Hayes

Ohman(?)

The list consisted of various linguists and the question mark after the last name reflected Fish's uncertainty as to whether it was spelled with one "n" or two. Before the next class arrived, Fish drew a frame around the names and wrote on the top of the frame "p. 43." The next class was devoted to the study of seventeenth-century religious poetry. Fish explains, "When the members of the second class filed in I told them that what they saw on the blackboard was a religious poem of the kind they had been studying and I asked them to interpret it."[77] The students began to offer various interpretations. Fish reports, "The first line of the poem (the very order of events assumed the already constituted status of the object) received the most attention: Jacobs was explicated as a reference to Jacob's ladder, traditionally allegorized as a figure for the Christian ascent to heaven. In this poem, however, or so many of my students told me, the means of ascent is not a ladder but a tree, a rose tree or rosenbaum."[78] Fish concludes that the meaning of a poem does not reside in the text, but rather arises out of the expectations of the readers who are members of a specific interpretive community. Each interpretive community has its own set of conventions that shapes the readers' very definition of what constitutes a poem and what range of interpretations are acceptable within that community.

76. Pecknold, *Transforming Postliberal Theology*, 44.
77. Fish, *Is There a Text in This Class?*, 323.
78. Ibid., 324.

"Skilled reading is usually thought to be a matter of discerning what is there, but if the example of my students can be generalized, it is a matter of knowing how to *produce* what can thereafter be said to be there. Interpretation is not the art of construing but the art of constructing. Interpreters do not decode poems; they make them."[79]

Fish's work leaves us considering a host of fundamental questions that have been lurking in the background since we discussed Climacus. Are there *fanciful* interpretations of biblical stories that are *true*? In what sense do we claim the Scriptures to be *true*? Are there *better* and *worse* interpretations of biblical texts? If so, how are they measured? If not, then where does that leave us? Could an interpretive community ever be said to be approaching a text in a thoroughly consistent way that is *incorrect*? Do the rungs laid out by Climacus, Guigo, and Kreeft lead us to God? Answering these questions helps us decide whether we should endorse the orthodox, liberal, postliberal, or postmodern strategy for the revitalization of the image of Jacob's Ladder.

Discussion Questions

1. In your view, what is the meaning of the story of Jacob's Ladder?
2. Climacus refers to the monastery as "the school virtues." In what way does this description apply to the church?
3. What is your evaluation of the spiritual interpretations offered by Climacus and Guigo II?
4. What role should apologetics play in Christian theology?
5. Is a christological reading of a story found in Genesis appropriate?
6. What is your evaluation of Fish's position?
7. Has the story of Jacob's Ladder appeared in any works of literature that you have read or movies that you have seen?

Suggested Readings

For background on Climacus, see John Chryssavgis, *Ascent to Heaven* (Brookline, MA: Holy Cross, 1989). For background on the *Ladder*, see chapter one of John Chryssavgis, *John Climacus* (Burlington: Ashgate, 2004) and Kallistos Ware, "Introduction" to *John Climacus* (Mahwah, NJ: Paulist,

---

79. Ibid., 327. Emphasis original.

1982). For background on the Carthusians, see Tim Peeters, *When Silence Speaks* (London: Darton, Longman, and Todd, 2015). See also Keith Egan, "Guigo II: The Theology of the Contemplative Life" in *The Spirituality of Western Christendom*, edited by Roxanne Elder (Kalamazoo: Cistercian, 1976). For a study of Catholic apologetics, see Peter Huff, "New Apologists in America's Conservative Catholic Subculture," *Horizons* 23 (1996) 242–60.

Chapter Five: Biblical Longings for the Future

IN OUR MOST ARDENT hopes for the future we find our deepest motivations for living as we do in the present. This intimate relation between the present and the future takes various forms in the New Testament. In apocalyptic writings, faithfulness during the present evil age will be rewarded in the new age to come. "Be faithful until death, and I will give you the crown of life" (Rev 2:10). The present state of persecution bears no resemblance to the future state of glory. In Paul's First Letter to the Corinthians, we can catch a fleeting glimpse of our future state. "For now we see in a mirror, dimly, but then we will see face to face" (1 Cor 13:12). We can detect a glimmer of what will be fully revealed at the end of time. Finally, in the "realized eschatology" of the Johannine writings, the individual's response of faith determines his or her standing before God. "Beloved, we are God's children now; what we will be has yet to be revealed. What we do know is this: when he is revealed, we will be like him, for we will see him as he is. And all who have this hope in him purify themselves, just as he is pure" (1 John 3:2-3). While there is still a future transformation to be awaited, the emphasis shifts to one's present status as a child of God. Given the breadth of positions in the New Testament, it is not surprising that in the Christian tradition we find a wide array of works that spark the imagination of those seeking to revitalize the classic language of the biblical visions of the future in our own day and age. In this chapter we turn our attention to three thinkers who theologically relate their own aspirations and expectations regarding the future with the biblical images associated with the *eschaton*. The first two theologians wrote in the fourth century. Ephrem the Syrian (ca. 306-73) expressed his hope for the future in his *Hymns of Paradise*, and we look once again at a work by Ambrose (ca. 340-97), "On Belief in the Resurrection," written on the occasion of his brother's death. Our third work comes from the contemporary theologian Maria Pilar Aquino in her 2007 work, "Feminist Intercultural Theology: Toward a Shared Future of Justice."

Ephrem the Syrian's *Hymns on Paradise*

Ephrem the Syrian brought his unique set of skills as a poet, hymnist, and theologian to bear on his *Hymns on Paradise*, a lyrical description of the eschatological restoration of humanity's relationship with God won by the victory of Christ.[1] Weaving together various strands of the biblical narrative (e.g., the creation stories, the design of the temple, and the parable of the wise and foolish bridesmaids), Ephrem produces a series of fifteen hymns celebrating the biblical drama of salvation. Ephrem further includes a wide array of biblical characters (e.g., Uzziah), images (e.g., the tree of life) and events (e.g., the crucifixion of the thieves alongside Jesus) into the poems. One of the overarching images running throughout the fifteen hymns is Paradise. Ephrem begins with the original Paradise in Genesis and carries the image through Christ to the present liturgical life of his church and finally carries it out to the end of time. The image of Paradise can therefore refer to a number of realities throughout the hymns: the original state of humanity, the sacraments of Baptism and Eucharist, and the eternal life that awaits the righteous on the Last Day. Ephrem's *Hymns* beautifully illustrate the practice of creatively incorporating Scripture into the life of a specific Christian community as they express in song their deepest religious aspirations and hopes. In this way, our fourth-century counterparts might provide us with a model for the use of Scripture in our present communities of faith.

Before we begin our examination of Ephrem's use of the image of Paradise, we need to first situate it within his broader understanding of the Bible as God's symbolic revelation to humanity. For Ephrem, our knowledge of God comes from God's condescension down to our level of understanding. We learn about God through the natural world, but more importantly in the symbols found in Scripture and of course through Christ himself. As he writes in the *Hymns of Paradise*, "If someone concentrates his attention solely on the metaphors used of God's majesty, he abuses and misrepresents that majesty and thus errs by means of those metaphors with which God clothed Himself for his benefit, and he is ungrateful to that Grace which stooped low to the level of his childishness . . ."[2] (XI, 6). Elsewhere in his *Diatessaron Commentary*, Ephrem counsels, "Do not (merely) ask the meaning of the words [of the Bible], which taken in their outward sense can impede the (real) point; but search out their (true) sense and what they refer to."[3] Because of the symbolic character of the biblical language, it would be

---

1. Though he is known as Ephrem the Syrian and did write in Syraic, he lived in Turkey. Kitchen, "Ephrem the Syrian," 201.

2. Ephrem the Syrian, *Hymns on Paradise*, 156.

3. Quoted in Murray, "Theory of Symbolism," 6.

a mistake in Ephrem's eyes to read all Scripture solely for its literal meaning. Sebastian Brock concludes, "Any true understanding of Scripture accordingly [for Ephrem] needs to preserve a proper balance: the literal meaning of the Biblical text has its own validity, but at the same time the text has an inner meaning (the 'hidden power' in Ephrem's terminology) which belongs to a different mode of reality."[4]

Ephrem's lyrical reflections on the biblical image of Paradise illustrates how he enters into the symbolic world of the Bible and allows the imagery to give form and content to his hopes regarding the end of time. In the first *Hymn*, Ephrem tells us, "Joyfully did I embark on the tale of Paradise—a tale that is short to read but rich to explore. My tongue read the story's outward narrative, while my intellect took wing and soared upward in awe as it perceived the splendor of paradise—not indeed as it really is, but insofar as humanity is granted to comprehend it" (I, 3). Ephrem's image of Paradise combines elements of Eden, Sinai, Noah's ark, and the temple. Paradise is pictured as a mountain. Halfway up the mountain is the tree of knowledge. In a blending of Eden and temple imagery, Ephrem describes the tree as a gate and the fruit that hangs from it is like the curtain in the temple separating the holy of holies.[5] An angel stands alongside the fence that separates the upper and lower regions. At the peak of the mountain is the Shekinah of God's presence as well as the tree of life.[6] Below the tree of knowledge the base of the mountain sits in a valley. Adam and Eve after the fall are exiled to the foothills of the mountain, and so like the three decks in Noah's ark, the mountain has the repentant at its base, the righteous halfway up the mountain, and the victorious at the summit (II, 11). It is into this symbolic world that Ephrem carries his readers, and it is in this world that Ephrem situates humanity's exile and return to Paradise.

The image of "clothing" serves many purposes in Syriac theology and it figures prominently in Ephrem's works. In keeping with the theme of revelation as grounded in God's condescension, Ephrem writes of how God "puts on" names in Scripture (e.g., Shepherd, Rock, King) so that we can come to a knowledge of God. Likewise, thinkers in the Syriac tradition speak of Christ "putting on" a body at the Incarnation (see VI, 23). When Christ entered the waters of the Jordan he made available "the robe of glory" that each Christian assumes when he or she enters into the baptismal waters.[7] We will examine a bit further three instances of Ephrem

---

4. Brock, "Introduction," 49.
5. Here I am relying on the fine scholarship of Maier, *Poetry as Exegesis*, 165.
6. Buchan, "Paradise as the Landscape of Salvation," 150.
7. Brock, "Introduction," 67.

describing Paradise in terms of "putting on" the robe of life, the crown and the wedding garment.

Ephrem speaks of Adam and Eve before the fall as wearing robes of glory.[8] After the fall they are stripped of these robes. Comparing Adam with Uzziah, the king who fraudulently attempted to assume the role of a priest (2 Chron 27:16–21), Ephrem sees both biblical characters as overstepping their divinely imposed limits. "Two people did the evil one beguile and captivate with his blandishments—promising to make Adam into a god and Uzziah into a priest, whereas in reality he stripped the one of his glory and clothed the other in leprosy" (XV, 9). After the final resurrection at the end of time, the faithful receive their eternal robe of glory. "Among the saints none is naked, for they have put on glory, nor is any clad in those leaves or standing shame, for they have found, through our Lord, the robe that belongs to Adam and Eve" (VI, 9). In his *Commentary on Genesis*, Ephrem associates Adam and Eve's robes of glory with "reason, thought, and an awareness of the Majesty" (II, 4).[9] In Paradise, then, these powers are restored to their original heightened state. All thoughts turn towards God which in turn becomes praise of God (V, 11, see also Rev 7:9–10). It is for this reason that Baby Varghese argues that according to Ephrem, worship is humanity's true vocation. As Varghese notes, humanity "has been created as a liturgical being, to live in communion with God. For the poet-theologian, as well as for the Eastern fathers, the sole intent of communion with God is praise and adoration."[10] Paradise at the summit of the mountain is filled not with silence, but rather with the "thunderous sound" of a heavenly choir.

A second image that appears in Ephrem's *Hymns* is the crown of victory. Its prominence in the *Hymns* arises out of Ephrem's strong emphasis on free will. In Ephrem's thought, Adam and Eve were created in an intermediate position. "For when God created Adam, He did not make him mortal, nor did he fashion him as immortal; this was so that Adam himself, either through keeping the commandment, or by transgressing it, might acquire from this one of the trees whichever outcome he wanted."[11] Adam and Eve possessed the capacity to obey God, but were not compelled to do so. If they overcame the temptation, they would be awarded the crown. "The Just One did not wish to give Adam the crown quite free, even though He had allowed him to enjoy Paradise without toil; God knew that if Adam wanted he could win the prize. The Just One ardently wished to enhance

---

8. Brock, "Clothing Metaphors," 12.
9. *Commentary on Genesis* II is included in Ephrem, *Hymns on Paradise*.
10. Varghese, "Saint Ephrem and the Early Syriac Liturgical Traditions," 19.
11. Ephrem, *Hymns on Paradise*, 208–9.

him, for, although the rank of supernal beings is great through grace, the crown for the proper use of free will is by no means paltry" (XII, 18). The crown signifies, then, the victory that those in Paradise secured by persevering through the trials that they confronted in their lives. This is especially true of the martyrs. "Those who have been crowned for our Lord's sake with the martyr's death by the sword shine out in glory there with their crowns because their bodies despised the persecutors' fire" (VII, 19). While not all Christians will face the prospect of martyrdom, they are nonetheless tested, and it is this essential element of the Christian life that Ephrem correlates with his vision of Paradise. "They count themselves blessed unendingly, for their warfare is over; they have taken up their crowns and found rest in their new abode (VII, 23) and "in his glorious Paradise He who is Good will sweeten their bitter trials, their crowns He will make great; because they have borne their crosses He will escort them into Eden" (IX, 2).

A third image employed by Ephrem is the garment associated with the wise and foolish virgins of Matt 25:1–13 who eagerly await their entrance into the wedding banquet (see also Matt 22:1–14). In *Hymn* 1 when Ephrem tells us, "Joyfully did I embark on the tale of Paradise—a tale that is short to read but rich to explore. My tongue read the story's outward narrative, while my intellect took wing and soared upward in awe as it perceived the splendor of Paradise (I, 3). He sees the "children of light" "on high in their bridal chambers" (I, 6). In his "Letter to Publius," we learn that the garment worn by the virgins symbolizes moral goodness. "I saw there pure virgins whose virginity, because it was not adorned with the precious ointment of desirable deeds was rejected. They implored their fellow virgins to give them some assistance, but they received no mercy and [they asked] that they might be given the opportunity to go and purchase some deeds, but this was not permitted them because their end, their departure from this life, was quickly coming."[12] While modern readers cannot help but read this passage in light of Reformation debates over justification, it illustrates how Ephrem transposes the eschatological images found in the Revelation and Matthew into spiritual and moral exhortation. Elsewhere in his "Letter to Publius" he overlays the imagery of the robe of glory (sometimes called a "robe of light"), the crown, and the wedding garment.[13]

> I saw their bridal chamber on the opposite side into which no one who did not have a lamp was allowed to enter.

---

12. Ephrem, "Letter to Publius," 350.
13. Brock, *Luminous Eye*, 86.

> I saw their joy and I sat mourning the fact that I possess none of the deeds that were worthy of that bridal chamber.
>
> I saw that they were arrayed in a garment of light, and I was distressed that no noble garments had been prepared for me.
>
> I saw their crowns, which were adorned with victory, and I was grieved that I had no victorious deeds with which I might be crowned.[14]

Ephrem revitalizes biblical images by entering into the "outward narrative" of Paradise and composing hymns that allow the splendor of that world to radiate through the worship of his community.

Ambrose's *On the Death of His Brother Satyrus* and *On Faith in the Resurrection*

When his brother Satyrus died in 378, Ambrose, bishop of Milan, delivered the homily at his funeral. Following the custom of the day, Ambrose offered a second, more formal oration seven days after the funeral. In their introduction to this second oration, John Sullivan and Martin McGuire note that this second address was more formal and "more definitely related to the pagan literary genre known as the consolation. While drawing freely from pagan models, and especially the lost *De consolatione* of Cicero, St. Ambrose naturally lays greater emphasis on the consolation to be derived from basic Christian ideas on death and resurrection."[15] These two orations, typically entitled *On the Death of His Brother Satyrus* and *On Faith in the Resurrection* respectively, provide us with examples of Ambrose's pastoral writings that attempt to offer consolation to both himself and his congregation. In doing so, he may have also contributed to our present attempt to revitalize biblical imagery.

Some of the most compelling passages in *On the Death of His Brother Satyrus* come when Ambrose speaks as a man who has lost his brother rather than a bishop addressing his congregation. Especially poignant is his account of his beloved brother dying in his arms. "How sorrowful those embraces, in the midst of which your dying body grew tense and your last breath vanished! I tightened my arms about you, but, as I took the last breath from your mouth that I might share in your death, I had already lost you as I held you . . . What, therefore, shall I do, now that I have lost all the

---

14. Ephrem, "Letter to Publius," 349.
15. Sullivan and McGuire, "Introduction," 160.

sweetness, all the consolations . . . all the charm of this life?"[16] Toward the end of the oration, Ambrose pleads, "So, once again, O sacred Scripture, I seek your consolations, for I like to dwell upon your precepts and your sayings."[17] Here we are reminded once again of a simple truth. Images do not function in a purely intellectual way. Consolation is not a matter of academic persuasion as much as it is touching the heart or comforting the soul. There is, of course, an inherent danger in every attempt to comfort those who are grieving. We can say too much or little, choose the right word or say the wrong thing, but Ambrose's work reminds us yet again that our words above all need to be genuine.

In his second oration, *On Faith in the Resurrection*, Ambrose expounds upon "our hope in the resurrection and the sweetness of future glory"[18] that awaits those who die in Christ. Throughout the address Ambrose offers a good deal of moral exhortation, especially on the virtue of perseverance during times of trial. Toward the end of the oration, however, Ambrose goes down a different road and offers a spiritual interpretation of the biblical image of the trumpet. He begins with the various references to trumpets in Revelation. The angels are given trumpets (8:2); God's voice is described as being like a trumpet (4:1); and God's imminent victory over evil is heralded by a trumpet (11:15). He then expands his search to include all the books of the Bible, from Paul (1 Cor 15:22) to Numbers (10:1–10). Ambrose concludes, "We should, therefore, observe as carefully as possible the signification which the trumpets have, so as not to run the risk of looking upon this matter as an old wives' tale, and of thinking of it as unworthy of spiritual teaching and out of accord with the dignity of the Scripture. For when we read that our warfare is not against flesh and blood, but against spiritual forces of wickedness on high, we ought not to think of carnal weapons, of course, but such as are powerful before God. It is not enough that we see a trumpet or hear its sound, unless we understand the meaning of its sound."[19]

In order to discern the meaning of trumpet's sound, argues Ambrose, we must read the biblical passages allegorically. For example, a trumpet sound may announce the start of the Sabbath. "The seventh trumpet, then, seems to signify the weekly day of rest,"[20] writes Ambrose. The earthly Sabbath observance and the New Year celebration observance (Lev 23:24) foreshadows what Ambrose calls "the Sabbath of the world." "That is why

16. Ambrose, *On the Death of His Brother Satyrus*, 170.
17. Ibid., 189.
18. Ibid., 198.
19. Ambrose, *On Faith in the Resurrection*, 245.
20. Ibid., 247.

Moses gave the children of Israel a commandment that in the seventh month, on the first day of the month, rest should be observed by all, a memorial of the blowing of trumpets, and that no servile work should be done, but sacrifice should be offered to God, because at the end of the week, the Sabbath of the world, as it were, spiritual, and not bodily, work will be required of us."[21] Second, a trumpet functioned as the means by which troops were summoned for battle (2 Chr 13:14). Our battle is with spiritual forces and so the trumpets here might be taken allegorically to refer to proclamations of truth. Referring to the command to create two silver trumpets (Num 10:1), Ambrose writes, "If anyone, therefore, desires to behold this image of God, he must love God so as to be loved by Him, no longer as a servant but as a friend who observes His commandments, that he may enter the cloud where God is. Let him fashion for himself two spiritual trumpets of pure and beaten silver, that is, composed of and adorned with precious speech. And let them not emit harsh and raucous tones inspiring fear, but let them pour forth thanks in the highest to God in continuous exultation."[22] If it is true, as Tertullian once wrote, that we should imitate what we will one day become, then our present "precious speech" will be expressions of gratitude to God.[23]

Third, the earthly trumpet is sounded as a command to break camp and travel to a new land. "These are also salutary trumpets, if we believe with the heart and confess with the mouth, 'For with the heart a man believes unto justice, and with the mouth confession is made unto salvation.' Accordingly, with these two twin trumpets we arrive at that holy land, namely, the grace of resurrection."[24] The image of the Christian life as a journey to God, a return to the homeland, and a place of rest for the restless appears commonly in Christian literature. And so, for Ambrose, the trumpets represent an eternal life of worship, a share in the victory won by Christ, and a return to the land for which our hearts deeply yearn.

Ambrose's multi-layered interpretation of the trumpets is in the final analysis an extension of the general hermeneutical principle that all Scripture should be interpreted in the light of Christ. Commenting on Ambrose's interpretation of the fall, the patristics scholar J. Patout Burns observes that for Ambrose the "true life of humanity is not something which can be seen and touched, something which can be plucked from a tree, even

---

21. Ibid.
22. Ibid., 248.
23. See Pelikan, *Christian Tradition*, 145.
24. Ambrose, *On Faith in the Resurrection*, 249.

in the garden of paradise. Instead, true life is hidden with Christ in God."[25] Ambrose's vision of the future is, therefore, deeply christological. "Shall we, then, think of festival days in terms of eating and drinking? On the contrary, let no one call us to account in respect to eating, 'For we know that the Law is spiritual.' Let no one, therefore, call you to account for what you eat or drink in regard to a festival or a new moon or a Sabbath. These are a shadow of things to come, but the body is of Christ. So let us seek the body of Christ which is the voice of the Father from heaven, the last trumpet, as it were, showed to you on that occasion when the Jews said that it thundered for Him. Let us seek, I repeat, the body of Christ which the last trumpet will again reveal to us."[26] Before the sounding of the final trumpet at the end of time Christians are to announce by word and deed the good news to the world. "Let us, therefore, be preachers of the Lord and let us praise Him with sound of trumpet."[27]

Maria Pilar Aquino, "Feminist Intercultural Theology"

The Latina theologian Maria Pilar Aquino brings her unique life-story to bear on her theological work. The daughter of a migrant farmworker, Aquino was born in Nayarit, Mexico, and at a young age moved with her parents to San Luis, Arizona. Her early memories of seeing Cesar Chavez in the fields near her home and her experience with the Society of Helpers, a religious order of nuns who work with the poor, have shaped her understanding of the role that theology should play in fulfilling the fundamental human and Christian aspirations for greater justice and peace in the world.[28] She exclaims, "With my theological world I am attempting to reclaim, for myself and for women of similar background, a place in the world as builders of knowledge. I learned early enough that theology is not the concern of an individual or a mere academic 'career,' as I suspect it's often perceived in the United States. For me, theology is the process of faith lived with the Christian community with which I share joy and suffering, company and loneliness, and with which I often spend 'days of mourning in hope.'"[29] It is this very concrete lived experience of the Latino/a community (comprising persons "born or raised in the United

---

25. Burns, "Creation and Fall according to Ambrose of Milan," 76.
26. Ambrose, *On Faith in the Resurrection*, 246–47.
27. Ibid., 250.
28. Jones, "'No time for glorifying and exalting,'" para. 1.
29. Aquino, "Theological Method in U.S. Latino/a Theology," 41.

States of Latin American ancestry"³⁰) that is the starting point for understanding Aquino's theological method as well as her vision for the future state of humanity as described in the biblical writings.

Aquino sees systematic theology as "an attempt to coherently and in an orderly fashion examine and explain the lived and reflected faith of the Christian community."³¹ Given the particularity of the lived experience of each community, Aquino acknowledges the deep pluralism that exists within the church. In developing her own strategy for dealing with this pluralism, she rejects two options: modern liberal individualism and postmodern deconstructionism. Quoting with approval the work of Roberto Goizueta, she writes, "Both traditions operate with notions of reason and of the human person which are unacceptable to theologies linked to the faith of marginalized groups and are impediments to any possibility of theological pluralism."³² Liberal individualism restricts what is of value to what can be quantified and confines truth to what can be known by all persons regardless of the conditions of their existence. In its drive to create a single world order, the proponents of liberal individualism steamroll over marginalized communities, with the result being greater conflict within the world. While the liberal individualists emphasize the universal to the exclusion of the particular, the postmodern deconstructionists make the opposite mistake, according to Aquino. She insists that "this second tradition represents a radical break in the conditions that would permit any possible basic consensus on the fundamental truths that ground human dignity, justice, or the integrity of the world."³³ The third option, which Aquino promotes, is intercultural dialogue. Unlike liberal individualism, it does not assume that one community's way of seeing the world is the same for each and every community without neglecting the hard work of resolving conflicts, creating and sustaining economic and social justice, and exercising proper stewardship of the Earth's natural resources.

Intercultural dialogue has as one of its goals the construction of a vision of a shared future of justice. Aquino asserts the Western European Christian tradition with its monocultural emphasis and its endemic patriarchy "appears to be obsolete and incapable of offering visions that are convergent with the values and aspirations of the social, intellectual, and religious movements that seek answers to the growing problems of social injustice."³⁴

30. Espin and Diaz, *From the Heart of Our People*, 262.
31. Aquino, "Theological Method in U.S. Latino/a Theology," 8.
32. Ibid., 11.
33. Ibid., 12.
34. Aquino, "Feminist Intercultural Theology," 10.

By contrast, intercultural dialogue "offers alternatives for deliberating about our common commitment to forging, out of our diverse cultural contexts, a world free of violence and injustice."³⁵ In order to enter into fruitful dialogue, according to Aquino, we need to recognize the deep influence that a community's understanding of its place in the world has on its thinking. In doing so, we realize that communities with a much different history than our own hold quite divergent views of what is "rational," "just," and "possible." This awareness then allows us to enter into a genuine dialogue with our neighbors. "Thus, the intercultural theological approaches seek to make universal a proposal for discourse that affirms the dignity and human rights of every person and promotes the integrity of creation in all parts of the world."³⁶ Aquino argues that intercultural dialogue promotes the framework for a theology that best addresses the concerns of women, Latino/a communities, and the wider Christian community. "From the viewpoint of Christian tradition, feminist theologies of liberation imagine and visualize a new world, and they use their interpretive resources to create religious languages that sustain every effort to establish the social conditions most compatible with that world of justice and liberation desired by God. The redeeming and creative presence of God in the world is truly expressed only by the historical reality of justice, solidarity, peaceful living together (*convivencia*), and human fulfillment."³⁷

When Aquino expounds on the content of the shared vision that she envisions, she stands firmly in the liberal theological tradition with her identification of a principle by which all biblical writings are to be measured. "For the Christian community, the duty of working for justice emanates from the biblical affirmation that all of humankind—men and women alike—has been created in the image of God and that the equality and dignity of each person as a child of God, is affirmed in Christ Jesus (Gal 3:26-28). For that reason, no person has reason or is permitted to subordinate another person or to destroy God's creation. According to this biblical affirmation, everything that harms the world or degrades humanity is contrary to God's liberating purpose and so formally constitutes a sinful reality that must be eradicated."³⁸ In a similar vein, Aquino asserts in *Our Cry for Life* that "the Bible's central message" is "intrinsically liberating."³⁹ She argues that "there is a growing awareness that forms of *machismo* are

---

35. Ibid., 13.
36. Ibid., 18.
37. Ibid., 21.
38. Ibid.
39. Aquino, *Our Cry for Life*, 127.

CHAPTER FIVE: BIBLICAL LONGINGS FOR THE FUTURE

also to be found in the Bible; it contains negative remarks about women and is couched in andocentric language. These texts and traditions cannot be divinely inspired, especially when through Jesus' life and ministry we discover that God does not condone any discrimination against women."[40]

In language that Ambrose might appreciate, Aquino speaks of this shared future as humanity's true home. "For feminist intercultural theology, a new world of justice is the only world that we can call our home."[41] This eschatological impulse in Aquino's theology is decidedly, though not exclusively, this-worldly. When she speaks of "widespread aspirations for a new world of well-being and justice," Aquino is speaking of social and political realities, but Christian hope extends beyond that. She notes, "[Hope] is a force that gives the liberation struggles energy and has at its heart the certainty that God is on the side of the oppressed, that their cause is just, and that what is at stake is not only the historical destiny of the poor and oppressed but also that of the whole of humanity. From those without power, from the strength of those considered to be insignificant, women from oppressed peoples know that although the sacrifice is immense, life must triumph over death, truth over lies, good over evil, love over hate, justice over injustice, solidarity over selfishness, grace over sin."[42]

The Revitalization of the Biblical Longings for the Future

In the final two sections of his *Systematic Theology*, the Lutheran scholar Robert Jenson turns his eye to the "Great Transformation" promised in the Bible and the life of "The Saints." In these chapters Jenson defends the orthodox positions on questions relating to the end of time. In fact, Carl Braaten claims, "It might not be an exaggeration to say that the chief concern and contribution of Jenson's theology is to get eschatology right."[43] Of the many questions that Jenson tackles regarding the end of time, he will focus on three. First, the visions of Revelation 21 and 1 Corinthians 15 find resonance with Jenson's discussion of the "The Great Transformation." "The great transformation, in all its aspects, has this at its center: the dialectic of Christ's presence to and by the church will end, the people of God will directly be Christ's availability also for her members, and Christ will be directly our availability to each other."[44] Whereas in the Western tradition we

40. Ibid., 121.
41. Aquino, "Feminist Intercultural Theology," 22.
42. Aquino, *Our Cry for Life*, 107.
43. Braaten, "Eschatology and Mission in the Theology of Robert Jenson," 307.
44. Jenson, *Systematic Theology*, 340.

speak of heaven in terms of seeing God face to face (1 Cor 13:12), Eastern theologians (e.g., Ephrem) rely on the principle that "God became human so that humans could become God," and therefore speak of the goal of the Christian life as deification. Language about "seeing" suggests separation, slight though it may be, between God and the holy ones in heaven. Deification language suggests unity, though not annihilation, with God. In both traditions, however, there is a fundamental agreement that even those in the afterlife cannot grasp the very essence of God.

Jenson's vision of the afterlife of the saints in heaven rests on Paul's claim that we will receive "spiritual bodies" (1 Cor 15:44), the exact nature of which Paul himself does not claim to know. What both Paul and Jenson reject, however, is the notion that those who are saved will be disembodied spirits who can cast aside their bodies as we discard a coat upon entering the house.

> We have made one small step toward understanding "the resurrection of the body" as the creeds confess it and as it applies to the redeemed individually. The personal body, we have seen, is the presence of the past. In the *perichoresis* [mutual indwelling] of triune time the saints past will be there for them, to interpret with Christ and together as that for which Christ died. Just so the redeemed will live with and in Christ.
>
> And we can make a second step: the redeemed will therefore be available to one another; they will be able to intend one another in love . . . And then a third step: to intend one another they must be able to locate one another. The personal body is personal location. Somehow the redeemed will have their space.[45]

The most important dimension of Jenson's theology is that the afterlife is characterized by love: the love shared by the three persons of the Trinity, the love of Christ for the redeemed, and the love shared among the redeemed. It is in this context that Jenson grounds his speculation about the nature of the life of the saints.

Third, Christ is the exclusive means of salvation for Jenson. This affirmation does not exclude the possibility that all people will be saved, but simply that "if followers of other religions enter the Kingdom proposed by the gospel, this is not because they have arrived at the salvations proposed by their religions."[46] Jenson speaks of the end-time as incorporation in

---

45. Ibid., 355.
46. Ibid., 363.

Christ.⁴⁷ That is the promise of the gospel. To develop this theme, Jenson draws upon the work of Jonathan Edwards and his use of musical imagery to describe heaven. Edwards writes, "The best . . . way that we have of expressing a sweet concord of mind to each other, is music. When I would form an idea of a society in the highest degree happy, I think of them . . . sweetly singing to each other."⁴⁸ Fittingly, then, Jenson ends his *Systematic Theology* on a musical note. "The point of identity, infinitely approachable and infinitely to be approached, the enlivening telos of the Kingdom's own life, is perfect harmony between the conversation of the redeemed and the conversation that God is. In the conversation God is, meaning and melody are one. The end is music."⁴⁹

For Rudolf Bultmann, the musical metaphor might be one of discerning the lyric in the midst of the distorted sound. Despite his rejection of many of the tenets of liberalism, Bultmann does retain at least one key element of liberalism in his biblical theology. Bultmann's project of demythologizing the New Testament *kerygma* relies on the liberal belief that there is a central message that can be recovered from the mythological elements that appear in the biblical writings concerning the end-time. The eternally valid truth (the kernel) remains valid, while the mythological trappings (the husk) present a series of obstacles to the modern reader. What is the biblical interpreter to do? Bultmann famously proposes that we extract the central message from the mythological framework in which it is couched and express the message in language that is relevant to a contemporary audience.

Bultmann makes the historical argument that such demythologizing can be detected within the canon of the New Testament itself. "The problem of Eschatology grew out of the fact that the expected end of the world failed to arrive, that the 'Son of Man' did not appear on the clouds of heaven, that history went on, and that the eschatological community could not fail to recognize that it had become a historical phenomenon and that the Christian faith had taken on the shape of a new religion."⁵⁰ The apocalyptic, mythological eschatology held by the earliest Christians became increasingly difficult to maintain. Paul alters, but does not entirely abandon, the apocalyptic belief in the *parousia*. He speaks of Christians presently being a new creation (2 Cor 5:17) and believes that in some sense history has reached its end (Rom 10:4). The Christian experiences a freedom from the Law. In John's Gospel, this process picks up more steam. Judgement shifts

---

47. Ibid., 364.
48. Edwards, "Miscellanies," no. 188. Quoted in Jenson, "End is Music," 169–70.
49. Jenson, *Systematic Theology*, 369.
50. Bultmann, *History and Eschatology*, 38.

from being a universal, future event to becoming a moment of decision in each individual's life. "Those who believe in him are not condemned; but those who do not believe are condemned already, because they have not believed in the name of the only Son of God" (John 3:18).

Bultmann claims that his project of demythologizing continues along the trajectory begun by Paul and John. "According to the New Testament, *Jesus Christ is the eschatological event*, the action of God by which God has set an end to the old world. In the preaching of the Christian Church the eschatological event will ever again become present and does become present ever and again in faith."[51] The person living in the twenty-first century who hears the *kerygma* preached faces an eschatological decision to either be open to God's future or to reject that divine offer. "This means that the eschatological existence of the believer is not a worldly phenomenon, but is realized in the new self-understanding."[52] Borrowing language from Martin Heidegger, Bultmann speaks of this new self-understanding as "authentic existence." "If the authentic life of man is one of self-commitment, then that life is missed not only by the blatantly self-assertive but also by those who try to achieve self-commitment by their own efforts. They fail to see that self-commitment can be received only as a gift from God."[53] In accepting that gift from God, "the age of salvation has already dawned for the believer and the life of the future has become a present reality."[54]

For the postliberal ethicist Stanley Hauerwas, the end of history has been revealed to us in the life, death, and resurrection of Jesus Christ. Christ is the decisive eschatological frame of reference for understanding all Christian belief and action. According to Hauerwas, "Christians are a people who believe that we have in fact seen the end; that the world has for all time experienced its decisive crisis in the life and death of Jesus of Nazareth. For in his death we believe that the history of the universe reached its turning point. At that moment in history, when the decisive conflict between God and the powers took place, our end was resolved in favor of God's lordship over this existence."[55] This understanding of the events of human history—this story—is not shared by all humans, so the Christian thinker is not presuming that Christian belief and action will be intelligible to those who make sense of their own lives through the lens of a different story. Christian ethics, then, is an account of a particular way of life for a particular group of

---

51. Ibid., 151. Emphasis original.
52. Bultmann, *Jesus Christ and Mythology*, 81.
53. Bultmann, *Kerygma and Myth*, 29.
54. Ibid., 20.
55. Hauerwas, *Against the Nations*, 165.

people, and for Hauerwas what should be most apparent about Christians is their commitment to peace.

According to Hauerwas, because Christians believe that we have seen the end of history in the resurrection of Christ, we walk by faith that the future end-time in which God's kingdom will be fully realized has been revealed to us. "God's kingdom, God's peace, is a movement of those who have found the confidence through the life of Jesus to make their lives a constant worship of God. We can rest in God because we are no longer driven by the assumption that we must be in control of history, that it is up to us to make things come out right."[56] Christians furthermore believe that in a sense we live in that new age. Hauerwas contends that "the Christian commitment to the protection of life is an eschatological commitment. Our concern to protect and enhance life is a sign of our confidence that in fact we live in a new age in which it is possible to see the other as God's creation."[57] Such a commitment puts the Christian at odds with the world. "Though we continue to live in a time when the world does not dwell in peace, when the wolf cannot dwell with the lamb and a child cannot play over the hole of the asp [cf. Isa 11:6–9], we believe nonetheless that peace has been made possible by the resurrection."[58]

The Christian community's commitment to peace allows us to enjoy "the trivial." As Hauerwas puts it, "there is nothing more important for us to do in face of the threat of nuclear war than to go on living—that is, to take time to enjoy a walk with a friend, to read of all of Trollope's novels, to maintain universities, to have and care for children, and most importantly, to worship God."[59] Our freedom to enjoy the present rather than fear its annihilation stems from our conviction that in Christ God has revealed the end to us. "In the Sermon [on the Mount] we see the end of history, an ending made most explicit and visible in the crucifixion and resurrection of Jesus. Therefore, Christians begin our ethics, not with anxious, self-serving questions of what we ought to do as individuals to make history come out right, because, in Christ, God has already made history come out right."[60] In the space that this peacefulness creates we can enjoy "trivial" matters such as planting flowers, watching children at play, or writing poetry. In sustaining a peaceful present, we anticipate the future

---

56. Hauerwas, *Peaceable Kingdom*, 87.
57. Ibid., 88.
58. Ibid.
59. Hauerwas, *Christian Existence Today*, 256–57.
60. Hauerwas and Willimon, *Resident Aliens*, 87.

age of peace that was revealed to us in the life, death, and resurrection of Christ and which will be fully realized at the end of time.

Postmodern thinkers appreciate the destabilizing quality of apocalyptic thinking. In the world of apocalyptic thinking, a persecuted minority group believes that God has revealed in coded, symbolic language the events leading up to the imminent overturning of the present social, political, and religious order. The meaning of that code has been revealed to a single visionary or small group of visionaries who in turn offer hope and a promise of deliverance to those being oppressed for their religious beliefs. In Catherine Keller's language, the concept of "the Empire" represents the collective power of the world's power-brokers and ideologues. The visions of Ezekiel and John of the Apocalypse undermine the totalizing claims of the dominant ruling class of their own times. Keller notes, "Both prophets would adjudicate between destruction by and accommodation to the Empire."[61] Keller outlines two paths commonly used by contemporary writers in the appropriation of the apocalyptic tradition. Liberation theologians relate their struggles against injustice and imperialism (e.g., apartheid, economic exploitation) to the drama being played out in apocalyptic writings. Feminists often criticize the misogynistic tendency to associate the offending party with women (e.g., whore of Babylon, Jezebel).

Keller offers a postmodern reading of the four living creatures described in the Book of Revelation (Rev 4:6–11). She is struck by the image of the four living creatures having eyes covering both their front and back. While a traditional interpretation might associate omniscience with the symbol of multiple eyes, Keller sees an image of the deep pluralism of the contemporary theological and philosophical scene ("the polyperspectival view").[62] In her own approach, Keller does not allow any single interpretation to bring the act of interpretation to a close. Instead she advocates for "the proliferation of visions and truths that becomes possible when the 'last' is subtracted from the judgment, when the single, the One, the Only, the Final is taken away from the truth."[63] Later she comments, "We are only denying the text's—this text, any text's—claim to an ultimate or certain truth, for a revelation of the one and only good."[64] Keller's vision of the four living creatures, then, enshrines the deep pluralism treasured by postmodern thinkers. She cryptically remarks, "Perhaps as word-free creatures, dangerously inaudible to Christians and postmodernists, they incarnate nonetheless the

---

61. Keller, "Eyeing the Apocalypse," 267.
62. Ibid., 275.
63. Ibid., 272.
64. Ibid., 274.

sacred sentences of all creatures." Perhaps language fails when we consider the end, and as Wittgenstein noted, what we cannot speak about we must pass over in silence.

Do we revitalize the biblical imagery regarding the *eschaton* by impressing upon students, congregations, and ourselves the beauty of the end as affirmed by Christian orthodoxy or by focusing all our energies on the present existential crisis that the eschatological language presents? Is the effect of a consideration of the eschatological passages of the Bible a commitment to pacifism or is it the destabilization of the prevailing social and political structures of our own time? Which biblical images convey most powerfully our deepest hope for the future? In answering these and other questions, we join with Ephrem, Ambrose, and Aquino in allowing the biblical imagery to shape our own theology, preaching, and spirituality regarding the end of time.

Discussion Questions

1. What do you believe happens when we die or when the end of the world comes?

2. Ephrem speaks of "the hidden power of Scripture." What do you think he means by that? Do you believe that such a power exists?

3. How does the biblical image of the trumpet function in Ambrose's eschatology? How might it be used effectively today?

4. Does eschatology relate in a positive way to work on behalf of the poor and oppressed? If so, what is the connection between the two?

5. Do you agree or disagree with Jenson's description of the afterlife?

6. Is demythologizing the best strategy for revitalizing the apocalyptic imagery in the Bible?

7. Is Hauerwas right? Does the eschatology that Christians hold commit us to being pacifists? Why? Why not?

Suggested Readings

For background on Ephrem the Syrian, see Sebastian Brock, *The Luminous Eye* (Kalamazoo: Cistercian, 1992) as well as his Introduction to *Hymns on Paradise* (Crestwood, NY: St. Vladimir's Seminary Press, 1990). See also Kathleen E. McVey, "Introduction" to Ephrem the Syrian, *Hymns* (Mahwah, NJ: Paulist, 1989). For Maria Pilar Aquino, see her work *Our Cry for Life*

(Maryknoll, NY: Orbis, 1993) and chapter 7 of Maria Pilar Aquino, Daisy L. Machado, and Jeanette Rodriguez, eds., *A Reader in Latina Feminist Theology* (Austin: University of Texas Press, 2002). For the role of eschatology in Latino/a theology, see Luis G. Pedtaja, "Eschatology and Hope," chapter 13 of Orlando O. Espin, *The Wiley Blackwell Companion to Latino/a Theology* (Malden, MA: Wiley Blackwell, 2015). For a helpful overview of Bultmann's theology, see David W. Congdon, *Rudolf Bultmann* (Eugene, OR: Cascade, 2015). For an anthology of Hauerwas's writings, see John Berkman and Michael Cartwright, eds., *The Hauerwas Reader* (Durham, NC: Duke University Press, 2001). For an interesting overview of eschatological beliefs held throughout Christian history, see Jeffrey Burton Russell, *A History of Heaven* (Princeton: Princeton University Press, 1997).

Chapter Six: Biblical Numbers

NUMEROLOGY IS AN INTEGRAL element of the biblical narrative. Certain numbers are associated with various qualities or conditions (e.g., holiness, imperfection). Three, seven, twelve, and forty are among the most common. Seven, most likely because it is the number of days in creation and the day on which God rests, symbolizes completion or wholeness. In this chapter we examine how the number seven plays a central role in the understanding of the Christian life presented by the fourteenth-century Flemish thinker John Ruusbroec (1293–1381) in his *The Seven Steps of the Ladder of Spiritual Love*, the thirteenth-century Franciscan theologian Bonaventure (1220–74) in *The Soul's Journey into God*, and the influential theorist on faith development, James Fowler (1940–2015), in his work *Stages of Faith*. In the work of all three thinkers, the number seven is used to symbolize the contours of the lifelong relationship that humans have with their Creator.

John Ruusbroec, *The Seven Steps of the Ladder of Spiritual Love*

John Ruusbroec (also spelled Jan Van Ruysbroeck) was born in 1293 in a village near Brussels. At a young age, he lived with his uncle who was a priest in Brussels and Ruusbroec himself was ordained to the priesthood in 1317. During his time in Brussels, he published *The Spiritual Espousals*, which is perhaps his best known work. In 1343, Ruusbroec and some others left Brussels and formed a community in the forest in the town of Groenendaal where they in 1350 adopted the Rule of St. Augustine. The work, *The Seven Steps of the Ladder of Spiritual Love*, comes from his time in Groenendaal.[1] *Seven Steps* draws upon the image of the first creation story and Jacob's ladder that we have discussed in earlier chapters, but it is also a concise treatment of the spiritual movement from the initial desire to do God's will (the first rung of the ladder) to the final unity of one's own will with that of God's (the seventh rung).

---

1. For biographical information, I am relying on Davies, "Ruysbroeck"; Jones et al., *Study of Spirituality*, 322; and Maesen, "John Ruusbroec," 64–73.

Ruusbroec begins, "Grace and the holy fear of the Lord be with us all. *Whatsoever is born of God overcometh the world*, says St. John, and indeed true holiness is born of God. The holy life is a ladder of love with seven steps, by which we may climb up into the kingdom of heaven."[2] He moves fairly quickly through the first four steps. The first of the seven rungs is the desire to have our own will correspond with the will of God. This requires detachment from material possessions (the second rung). Like the wise merchant, we must exchange the earthly goods for the pearl of greatest value, heaven itself. The third rung is the purity of the soul and body, which for Ruusbroec's monastic community involved separation from one's family. "Think upon John the Baptist: he was sanctified even before he was born, yet from the days of his youth he left father, mother, honors, and worldly riches; and to avoid every occasion of sin, betook himself to the wilderness."[3] Humility, one of great virtues emphasized in the monastic life by luminaries such as Benedict and John Cassian, is the fourth step on the spiritual ladder. "Humility is a certain lowliness of spirit, wherein God lives in true peace with us, and we with God; in it abides the living ground of all holiness."[4]

When turning his attention to the fifth rung on the ladder, Ruusbroec offers extended and intricate commentary. Much of his time is spent on an allegorical reading of the celestial hierarchy, the angels, archangels, principalities, powers, virtues, dominations, thrones, cherubim, and seraphim mentioned in the Bible and discussed at length by Pseudo-Dionysius. Each of the nine elements in the celestial hierarchy corresponds to a form of spiritual worship (e.g., adoration, petition, and thanksgiving). Near the end of the fifth section, Ruusbroec switches to a consideration of "the heavenly melodies," that is, the "reverence and external veneration" of God. "This is the beginning of all songs, whether of angels or of men, which never more shall cease."[5] Ruusbroec lists four forms of song in praise of God. "The love of God and of our neighbor is the first mode of the chant; wherefore God the Father sent His Son to teach it [to] us. He who knows not this song cannot enter the celestial choirs; and having neither the art nor the choir-dress, will remain shut out for ever."[6] The second type of song is humility, which is the "key of all heavenly singing, and dwells in harmony with all the other virtues, for that it is the dress and adornment of charity itself, and the most sweet voice that can sing in the

2. Ruysbroeck, *Seven Steps of the Ladder*, 17.
3. Ibid., 23.
4. Ibid., 24.
5. Ibid., 47.
6. Ibid., 47–48.

presence of God."[7] The third form of song is the renunciation of our own will in order to do the will of God. Here Christ's struggle in the Garden of Gethsemane is our model. "And Christ, our cantor, shall be the first to sing it, for He is the Prince and King of all suffering willingly borne for the love and honor of God."[8] In the fourth type of song, we "faint in the praise of God" and experience a unity with God, "for we cannot become God, but are united to Him."[9] It is this experience of unity that occupies Ruusbroec's attention in the sixth and seventh rungs.

The sixth and seventh rungs on the ladder deal with union with the Trinity. The sixth step "is a clear intuition or gaze, in purity of spirit, and of thought, which are the three properties of the soul in contemplation . . . This purity is the dwelling-place of God within us, nor can any but God alone act upon it. It is eternal, and in it is neither time nor place, neither before nor after: but it is ever-present, ready and manifest to such pure minds as may be raised up into it."[10] The timelessness that characterizes this experience becomes a sensation of annihilation in the seventh step, which "comes about, when above all conception and knowledge we find in ourselves a certain infinite or abyssal unknowing; when, transcending every name which has been given to God or to any created thing, we expire into the eternal namelessness, wherein we are lost; when beyond any practice of virtue we contemplate and find within us an eternal repose, in which no man can work."[11] The language of the first creation story echoes throughout Ruusbroec's description of the seventh rung: it consists of an eternal Sabbath on which no work is to be done. This state of being is a pure gift from God and far exceeds the capacity of human language to express it.

Ruusbroec's language regarding the seventh step can be misleading in two ways. First, while Ruusbroec employs language that suggests the seventh step is an absorption into God that destroys our individuality, he repeatedly stresses that this is not the case. He does indeed speak of the contemplative state as one in which we are "lost, drowned and liquefied into an unknown darkness,"[12] but, as Rik Van Nieuwenhove notes, "When Ruusbroec talks of union with God (as he does very often) he always points out that we never can shed our creaturely status."[13] Second, while Ruusbroec

7. Ibid., 48–49.
8. Ibid., 50.
9. Ibid., 50–51.
10. Ibid., 55–56.
11. Ibid., 57.
12. Ibid., 63.
13. Van Nieuwenhove, "Experience and Mystical Theology," 420.

speaks of the perpetual rest of the seventh step, there is also a going forth in love, just as there is in the Trinity. "And so, to enter into a restful fruition and go forth again in good works, but ever remain united to the Spirit of God; this is the life of which I wish to tell you."[14] In *The Spiritual Espousals*, Ruusbroec offers this interesting comparison of God with the movements of a sea: "God is a flowing and ebbing sea, which ceaselessly flows back again into all his beloved according to their needs and merits and which flows back with all those upon whom he has bestowed his gifts in heaven and on earth, together with all that they possess or are capable of."[15] On both of these points we see that language ultimately fails Ruusbroec; however, the failure is not without its benefit. Paul Mummers offers his assessment: "No doubt Ruusbroec's descriptions of unity in dividedness represent most strikingly his achievement as a mystical author. Fail as they might, his words seem to be gaining significance through that very failure. As language is pressed to do everything it can, somehow it communicates the core of his original contemplative experience and the heart of his doctrine."[16]

Bonaventure, *The Soul's Journey Into God*

Two years into his tenure as Minister General of the Franciscan Order, Bonaventure went on retreat at Mt. La Verna, the very site at which Francis of Assisi had by tradition received the stigmata some thirty-five years earlier. In meditating on Francis's life and his vision of a seraph, a six-winged angel (see Isa 6:2) in the form of the Crucified, Bonaventure began to compose an itinerary for the soul's pilgrimage back to God. The six wings represented for Bonaventure six stages on a journey that would begin with a consideration of the world outside the self, then move into the depths of the person, and finally turn upward into God. The result of Bonaventure's meditation is the spiritual classic, *The Soul's Journey into God*. Comprised of seven chapters, *Soul's Journey* devotes two chapters to each of the three movements (external world, internal world, ascent) and concludes with a seventh chapter on ecstatic union with God.

The first two chapters of *Soul's Journey* deal with the material world and our perception of it. Bonaventure writes, "In relation to our position in creation, the universe itself is a ladder by which we can ascend into God. Some created things are vestiges, others images; some are material, others spiritual; some are temporal, others everlasting; some are outside us,

14. Ruysbroeck, *Seven Steps of the Ladder*, 60.
15. Ruusbroec, *Spiritual Espousals*, 103.
16. Mommaers, *Jan van Ruusbroec*, 124.

others within us. In order to contemplate the first Principle, who is the most spiritual, eternal and above us, we must pass through his vestiges, which are material, temporal, and outside us."[17] The material world—the clouds that move across the sky, the majestic redwoods that seem to dwarf the distant mountains, and the seashells scattered on our beaches—are "vestiges" or "footprints" of God. Their presence and beauty testify to the power and knowledge of God. As Ewert Cousins explains, "Seen with the eyes of contemplation, creatures are vestiges, that is, the very footprints of God; they are roads leading to God, ladders on which we can climb to God; they are signs divinely given so that we can see God—shadows, echoes, pictures, statues, representations of God; creation is a book in which we can read God, a mirror in which the divine light shines in various colors."[18] God endowed humans with the senses to perceive the vestiges found in the material world and the rational powers to form judgments about the harmonious elements that comprise the beauty and intricacy of creation.

In chapters 3 and 4 Bonaventure turns his attention to the interior of the person. Bonaventure begins, "The two previous stages, by leading us into God through his vestiges, through which he shines forth in all creatures, have led us to the point of reentering into ourselves, that is, into our mind, where the divine image shines forth. Here it is, now in the third stage, we enter into our very selves; and, as it were, leaving the outer court, we should strive to see God through a mirror in the sanctuary, that is, in the forward area of the tabernacle."[19] Like a priest leaving the outer courtyard of the temple and entering the sanctuary, the soul's journey turns inward. Bonaventure follows Augustine's lead in seeing the imprint of the Trinity on human nature in that we have the capacity for memory, intellect, and choice. Because of the effects of sin, all three capacities do not function perfectly: memories can be distorted, reasoning can be faulty, and the will can be misdirected. In the fourth stage, however, Bonaventure focuses on the reparation of the human person through Christ. "So our soul could not rise completely from these things of sense to see itself and the Eternal Truth in itself unless Truth, assuming human nature in Christ, had become a ladder, restoring the first ladder that had been broken in Adam."[20] For Bonaventure, Christ is "like the tree of life in the middle of paradise."[21] Through Christ's healing touch, the soul's "spiritual senses"

17. Bonaventure, *Soul's Journey*, 60.
18. Cousins, "Introduction" to *Soul's Journey*, 30.
19. Bonaventure, *Soul's Journey*, 79.
20. Ibid., 88.
21. Ibid., 88.

(e.g., hearing the Word of God properly, seeing the truth) function in the human person as God intended. "Having recovered these senses, when [the soul] sees its Spouse and hears, smells, tastes and embraces him, the soul can sing like the bride the Canticle of Canticles, which was composed for the exercise of contemplation in this fourth stage."[22]

In the fifth and sixth stages the soul moves inward and upward into God. In both stages, the soul contemplates God, but in the fifth stage the language is more philosophical (i.e., the soul contemplates Being) and in the sixth stage the language is more theological (i.e., the soul contemplates the Trinity). The two approaches are symbolized by the two cherubim standing to each side of the mercy seat of the ark in the holy of holies. In the first approach Bonaventure declares that Being, the source of all that exists, is "most present" to all things because it is eternal. "It is most present precisely because it is eternal. For because it is eternal, it does not flow from another nor of itself cease to be, nor pass from one state to another; therefore it has neither past nor future, but only present being."[23] In the second approach Bonaventure's focus turns to the Trinity with special attention given to the Crucified Christ. "The fact that [the two Cherubim] faced each other, *with their faces turned toward the Mercy Seat*, is not without a mystical meaning, so that what Our Lord said in John might be verified: *This is eternal life, that they may know you, the only true God, and Jesus Christ, whom you have sent.*"[24] In Christ divinity and humanity, eternity and temporality, the Alpha and the Omega are united (VI, 7). Just as the sixth day marked the completion of creation, so too Christ is the goal of creation.

At the completion of the six stages, the soul rests in the peace of the Lord. "We have, therefore, passed through these six considerations. They are like the six steps of the true Solomon's throne, by which we arrive at peace, where the true man of peace rests in a peaceful mind as in the interior Jerusalem."[25] This rest following the six stages is in a passing over into a spiritual exodus. "By the staff of the cross he passes over the Red Sea, going from Egypt into the desert, where he will taste the *hidden manna*; and with Christ he rests in the tomb, as if dead to the outer world, but experiencing, as far as is possible in this wayfarer's state, what was said on the cross to the thief who adhered to Christ; *Today you shall be with me in paradise.*"[26] Bonaventure offers one piece of advice in the closing

22. Ibid., 89.
23. Ibid., 98–99.
24. Ibid. Emphasis original.
25. Ibid., 110.
26. Ibid., 112.

section: "But if you wish to know how these things come about, ask grace not instruction, desire not understanding, the groaning of prayer not diligent reading, the Spouse not the teacher, God not man, darkness not clarity, not light but the fire that totally inflames and carries us into God by ecstatic unctions and burning affections."[27]

James Fowler's *Stages of Faith*

The late James Fowler's *Stages of Faith* is the most influential work in the area of faith development in the last forty years. Drawing on the work of developmental psychologists Erik Erikson, Lawrence Kohlberg, and Jean Piaget, Fowler produced a theory of how faith develops over the course of a person's life. For Fowler, faith is not confined to being "religious," but is a dimension of all human experience. "The persons, causes and institutions we really love and trust, the images of good and evil, of possibility and probability to which we are committed—these form the pattern of our faith."[28] Faith, in other words, is far more concerned with trust than belief. It also has a great deal to do with imagination. "Faith forms a way of seeing our everyday life in relation to holistic images of what we may call the *ultimate environment* . . . Faith, as imagination, grasps the ultimate conditions of our existence, unifying them into a comprehensive image in light of which we shape our responses and initiatives, our actions."[29] Human faith, then, is our deepest level of trust in the very ideas by which we orient ourselves in the world. The images that both shape and give expression to this faith are central to our understanding of the world and our very selves, as well as in a religious sense, of God.

Early in the text Fowler announces, "At the heart of [*Stages of Faith*] you will find an account of a theory of seven stagelike, developmentally related styles of faith that we have identified."[30] Fowler leaves the first of the seven stages unnumbered, simply labeling it "infancy and undifferentiated faith." The chief issue, Fowler surmises, being worked out in this unnumbered stage is the issue of trust. Yet importantly, Fowler adds, "Those observers are correct, I believe, who tell us that our first *pre-images* of God have their origins here . . . I call these *pre-images* because they are largely formed prior to language, prior to concepts and coincident with the

---

27. Ibid., 115.
28. Fowler, *Stages of Faith*, 4.
29. Ibid., 24–25.
30. Ibid., xiii.

emergence of consciousness."[31] The notion of stages appears in the work of Kohlberg, Piaget, and Erikson. The transition from one stage to the next is marked by the acquisition of a new cognitive ability or the resolution of some crisis (e.g., trust vs. mistrust). According to Piaget, "around seven or eight months babies begin to search for objects they have seen and handled when they are removed from them and hidden by researchers in experiments. At four months, typically, they do not search for the hidden objects."[32] Piaget concluded that the four-month-old child has not yet developed a cognitive skill or "structure of thought" that we can see is present in the eight-month-old child. Fowler contends that developments in faith (again, understood broadly to be an indispensable element of human experience rather than simply religious faith) accompany these shifts in the "structure of thought" through which the person understands the world.

The first stage of faith ("intuitive-projective") begins with the development of speech around age two. Children at this stage "combine fragments of stories and images given by their cultures into their clusters of significant associations dealing with God and the sacred."[33] With some exceptions, "only concrete symbols and images really address the child's ways of knowing."[34] In the second ("mythic-literal") stage, the child "works hard at sorting out the real from the make-believe."[35] The child does not yet possess the ability to step outside the stories that guide their lives and reflect upon their general meaning. In the third ("synthetic-conventional") stage, a person identifies the values of the group to which he or she belongs, "defends them and feels deep emotional investments in them, but typically has not made the value system *as a system,* the object of reflection."[36]

In the fourth stage ("individuative-reflective") the reliance on external authority is interrupted. The symbols and their meaning are separated. "If a symbol or symbolic act is truly meaningful, Stage 4 believes, its meanings can be translated into propositions, definitions and/or conceptual foundations."[37] When one's own traditional religious act or image is seen as a symbol, its power to mediate the transcendent might be lost. "Instead of the symbol or symbolic act having the initiative and exerting its power on the participant,

---

31. Ibid., 121. Emphasis original.
32. Ibid., 53.
33. Ibid., 128.
34. Ibid., 129.
35. Ibid., 135.
36. Ibid., 162. Emphasis original.
37. Ibid., 180.

now the participant-questioner has the initiative over the symbol."[38] In the fifth ("conjunctive") stage, the person accepts "as axiomatic that truth is more multidimensional and organically interdependent than most theories or accounts of truth can grasp."[39] While having confidence in one's own religious tradition, the person "assumes that each genuine perspective will augment and correct aspects of the other, in a mutual movement toward the real and the true."[40] Images and symbols are no longer separated from their meaning. The images found in the various religious traditions are treasured for their uniqueness and there is no attempt to reduce them all to a single concept or proposition. In the sixth ("universalizing") stage the persons have a "radical commitment to justice and love and [a] selfless passion for a transformed world, a world made over not in their images, but in accordance with an intentionality both divine and transcendent."[41] The most distinctive quality exhibited by the rare individuals who see the world this way is their "heedlessness to self-preservation."

The Revitalization of the Image of Biblical Numbers

One of the many uses of the number seven in orthodox Christian teaching is the designation of the seven gifts of the Holy Spirit. The teaching is based on Isaiah 11:2–3a. "The spirit of the Lord shall rest on him, the spirit of wisdom and understanding, the spirit of counsel and might, the spirit of the knowledge and the fear of the Lord. His delight shall be in the fear of the Lord." The Septuagint translates the first occurrence of "fear of the Lord" as piety, resulting in the traditional list of the seven gifts of the Holy Spirit. The fourteenth-century Dominican Johannes Tauler (who met with John Ruusbroec) was a popular preacher, and in one of his sermons on the feast of Pentecost he develops the theme of the seven gifts of the Holy Spirit. The events of Pentecost, remarkable as they are, pale in comparison with "the spiritual reality" hidden in the story, contends Tauler.[42] The "whole house" could represent either the church or the many faculties of the individual. Like the disciples gathered together in unity, we must collect our thoughts and prepare ourselves for the reception of the Holy Spirit for "if we wish to feel His action, if we desire to savor His presence, then we must bring ourselves to a focus, shut out eternal matters, and allow the Holy Spirit to

38. Ibid.
39. Ibid., 186.
40. Ibid., 187.
41. Ibid., 201.
42. Tauler, Sermon 26, 91.

unfold within us in stillness and repose."[43] Just as the disciples were seated, we must rest our own wills in the hands of God. "So you, too, must have your seat in the truth and assign all created things, joys and sorrows, willing and surrendering, their seat in God's will. This counsel is binding to all who wish to lead a spiritual life. For what is meant by spirituality except to be one with God's will, in harmony and union with Him?"[44]

For Tauler, there is a progression in the order of the seven gifts bestowed by the Spirit that leads the soul to ever greater heights. "Thus the Holy Spirit always leads us from one gift to the other in such a way that each one opens up paths that run closer to perfection than did the previous one."[45] Tauler compares the first gift, the fear of God, to the natural instinct of wild animals to flee from danger. "Due to the perfection of this holy fear it is able to shield us from the world, from the devil, from ourselves, and all the ways and works by which we lose spiritual repose and that interior peace which is the place where God truly dwells."[46] Piety, the second gift, "brings about a heavenly ease . . . in all circumstances."[47] This ease applies to both our inner state of being and our relations with our neighbors. The following gift of knowledge attunes us to the workings of the Holy Spirit within our soul and the fourth gift of fortitude gives us the same strength and determination that allowed the martyrs to die rather than forsake their faith.

The Holy Spirit's first four gifts bring great comfort and joy to the soul, though with the fifth gift the situation becomes more complex. "For at this point God will remove all His previous favors and will leave us to our own resources in order to see, and allow us to see, how we bear ourselves in such trial. God now lets us sink to the very depth, so that no knowledge of Him remains, no grace, no comfort, nor anything that we or any good person may have ever gained."[48] The abandonment that the soul experiences allows the soul to surrender any remaining sense of self-sufficiency. The assaults upon the soul drive it into the arms of God. "It is a noble and good thing to confess one's weakness and then always return to God. In this as in everything else we must follow the counsel to renounce everything, to overcome everything, and to return to the source, the ground which is God's will."[49] Here Tauler speaks of God as the ground and elsewhere as the abyss,

43. Ibid., 92.
44. Ibid., 93.
45. Ibid., 94.
46. Ibid.
47. Ibid.
48. Ibid., 95–96.
49. Ibid., 96.

language that modern readers will most likely associate with Paul Tillich. The last two gifts, understanding and wisdom, are "a taste of God." "Now God grants the soul by grace that which He is by nature, uniting it with His nameless, unchartered, warless Being. Here everything that is done in the soul God Himself performs: acting, knowing, loving, praising, enjoying. And the soul let it be, in a divine passivity."[50] The soul's surrender into God is complete and the seven gifts of the Holy Spirit have effected a change in the very soul of the person.

Those in the liberal tradition might contend that the references to "the seven ages" of the human person in Shakespeare and poets such as W. H. Auden shed valuable light on the human condition. In Shakespeare's *As You Like It* (Act II, Scene VII), the character Jaques famously declares, "All the world's a stage / And all the men and women merely players: They have their exits and their entrances / And one man in his time plays many parts, His acts being seven ages."[51] The seven ages are infancy, school-age child, lover, soldier, the justice, the pantaloon, and old age. Auden borrows the seven-age sequence in the second part of his lengthy 1947 poem, "The Age of Anxiety."[52] Set in a New York City barroom on the night of All Souls' Day, the poem involves the conversations of four characters. Reflecting his interest in Jungian psychology, Auden has each of the four characters represent a dimension of the human personality: thinking, feeling, intuition, and sensation. The character Malin, a medical officer in the Canadian Air Force, represents thinking, and directs the conversation in the second part of the poem, "The Seven Ages."

As the title of Auden's poem suggests, he believes that the human condition is marked by anxiety. His focus on anxiety testifies to his interest in Kierkegaard's writings as well as his friendship with Reinhold and Ursula Niebuhr. As the Auden scholar John Fuller notes, "The 'anxiety' of the title (according to such Protestant theologians as Niebuhr, by whom Auden was much influenced at the time) is itself a characteristic of the human condition indicating an awareness of the need for God, a characteristic identifiable with the 'dread' of Kierkegaard or the 'angst' of Heidegger."[53] In his study of the influence of Augustine's theology on Auden's thought, Stephen Schuler echoes Fuller's assessment. "Niebuhr's influence is perhaps clearest in Auden's "Age of Anxiety," as the premise of the poem is largely drawn from Niebuhr's explication of the restless heart of Augustine's *Con-*

---

50. Ibid., 97.
51. Shakespeare, *As You Like It*, 165.
52. Auden, "The Seven Ages."
53. Fuller, *W.H. Auden*, 373.

fessions. The very title, which is usually taken as referring to the historical modern age, also refers to the age of an individual who has emerged into self-consciousness and thus into anxiety, and Auden is indebted to Niebuhr for the use of the term in this sense."[54] Anxiety is therefore both a personal state of being arising from the possibilities presented by our free will and a cultural mood and dread and uncertainty about the future.[55]

The anxiety of the four characters in "The Seven Ages" is reflected in their consideration of the meaning of life in light of the certain fact of human mortality. Malin begins by reflecting on the scary dreams experienced by infants. The infants are innocent, yet their dreams are filled with dread. In the second age, youth, life is brimming with boundless possibility.[56] The third age is marked by sexual awakening. Circus imagery fills the fourth age as the character Quant confronts the possibility of life's meaninglessness. In the fifth age of adulthood, according to Malin, the person gains social recognition, but time is fleeting. In the sixth age, with advanced age, the person yearns for a bygone era that may in fact never have existed. In the seventh age, the person is tired and waits for death.

Auden's description of the anxious human condition impressed Tillich. In *The Courage to Be*, Tillich identifies three forms of anxiety (i.e., the threat of non-being): the anxiety of death, the anxiety of meaninglessness, and the anxiety of condemnation.[57] Referring to his own age, Tillich claims that "one must say that the anxiety which determines our period is the anxiety of doubt and meaninglessness. One is afraid of having lost or having to lose the meaning of one's existence."[58] In the face of this challenge, the "courage of despair" affirms the power of being in the face of non-being. Tillich credits Auden with a brilliant poetic diagnosis of what ails the human spirit. "In Auden's the *Age of Anxiety* the courage to take unto oneself the anxiety in a world which has lost the meaning is as obvious as the profound experience of this loss: the two poles which are united in the phrase 'the courage of despair' receive equal emphasis."[59] As Tillich explains, "We have defined courage as the self-affirmation of being in spite of non-being. The power of this self-affirmation is the power of being which is effective in every act of courage. Faith is the experience of this power."[60] In an essay written the year

---

54. Schuler, *Augustinian Theology of W. H. Auden*, 146.
55. See Leiva, "Age of Anxiety."
56. Nelson, *Changes of Heart*, 119.
57. Tillich, *Courage to Be*, 41.
58. Ibid., 173.
59. Ibid., 144.
60. Ibid., 172.

before he began working on "The Age of Anxiety," Auden writes, "I wake into my existence to find myself and the world that is not myself already there, and simultaneously feel responsible for my discovery. I can and must ask myself: 'Who am I? Do I want to be? Who do I want and who ought I to become?' I am, in fact, an anxious subject."[61] In terms of their analysis of the human condition, Tillich's *The Courage to Be* and Auden's "The Age of Anxiety" offer remarkably similar assessments.

Stanley Hauerwas's *Cross-Shattered Christ* is a collection of meditations on the seven last words of Christ on the cross. Not only do the meditations offer Hauerwas's own profound reflections on the death of Christ, they also illustrate some of the dominant themes in the wider movement of postliberalism. Since the sixteenth century, it has been a custom in the Christian community during Lent to reflect on a numbered series of seven sayings that Christ makes from the cross. Hauerwas allows that communal practice to shape his own consideration of the meaning of the crucifixion. In the course of offering his reflections he describes what he takes to be common misinterpretations of what the cross entails. Chief among these is "sentimentality." "I think nothing is more destructive for our ability to confess that the crucified Jesus is Lord than the sentimentality that grips so much that passes for Christianity in our day."[62] The cross is not "about us"; rather, it is an event in the inner life of the Trinity that brings salvation to the world.

We find in his meditation on "My God, my God, why have you forsaken me?" a postliberal emphasis on the power of language to shape religious experience. "It is not by accident that the Psalms are for Jews and Christians our prayer book. We pray the Psalms not because they give expression to our religious experience—though they sometimes may do that—but because our lives are given form by praying the Psalms."[63] Barth, one of the most influential theologians on the development of postliberal theology, warned that the liberal anchoring of our language about God in human experience runs headlong into the charge of Feuerbach that we create God in our own image. Hauerwas makes a similar charge. "'My God, my God, Why have you forsaken me?' shatters all our attempts to understand God in human terms. We try, for example, to compliment God by saying that God is transcendent, but ironically our very notion of transcendence can make a creature after our own hearts."[64]

---

61. Auden, "Purely Subjective," 184.
62. Hauerwas, *Cross-Shattered Christ*, 16.
63. Ibid., 61.
64. Ibid., 64.

In his meditation on, "Father, into your hands I commend my spirit", Hauerwas focuses on the particularity of Christ's story. The Gospels are not four examples of a general universal pattern, but the unique unrepeatable accounts of the life, death, and resurrection of Jesus. "Jesus is the Christ, but the Christ is known only in the one called Jesus. Jesus is not a 'Christ-figure' if by Christ-figure we mean the exemplification of a universal pattern of sacrifice for the goods of others. Jesus is no 'Christ-figure' if we mean that his death is an exemplification of how we should all die, that is, we should die with the confidence that we have nothing to fear from death."[65] Again the Psalms play an integral role in the account of Christ's death. For Christians, "Jesus has become the Father's Psalm for the world, fulfilling Israel's undying hope that death, and the judgment death must be and always is, is not the last word."[66] In this singular life of Jesus the hopes of Israel find fulfillment. "Like Israel, like the Jews, we will be persecuted, we will suffer, we will die. But because of what Jesus has done on this cross, we will be able to die confidently praying: 'Father, into your hands I commit my spirit.'"[67]

The third postliberal emphasis that appears in Hauerwas's meditations is the contrast between the church and the world. Christ's words, "It is finished," are not the words of defeat, but rather of victory. The crucifixion, for John's Gospel, is the moment of exaltation. "Time is now redeemed through the raising up of Jesus on this cross. A new age has begun. The kingdom is here aborn, a new regime is inaugurated, creating a new way of life for those who worship and follow Jesus."[68] For Hauerwas the new way of life is one characterized by a life of nonviolence. "What wonderful news: '"It is finished." But it is not over.' We are made witnesses so the world—a world with no time for a crucified God—may know we have all the time of God's kingdom to live in peace with one another."

Postmodern thinkers would look with a great deal of skepticism upon the claims of thinkers who identify the specific number of steps along the spiritual journey that all persons travel on their way to God or the highest level of faith development. Jean-Francois Lyotard's often repeated definition of postmodernism as "incredulity towards metanarratives"[69] reminds us that postmoderns are suspicious of grand overarching accounts of "the way things are." Among the many reasons postmodern thinkers would give for their disbelief is their rejection of the understanding of the mind as a

65. Ibid., 96.
66. Ibid., 101.
67. Ibid., 102.
68. Ibid., 85.
69. Lyotard, *Postmodern Condition*, xxiv.

mirror that reflects the reality that exists independently of the mind—an image employed by both Ruusbroec and Bonaventure, and one that Fowler in his own way would support. As Ruusbroec argues, "When God manifests Himself to our intellectual eyes with infused light, He gives us the power to know Him under similitudes, as in a mirror, in which we see forms, images and likenesses of God."[70] Because of the illumination provided by God, the mind, for Ruusbroec, has the ability to "see" the truth. Bonaventure makes even greater use of the image of the mirror. The material world is a mirror of God's wisdom and beauty, but the mirror of the soul needs to be purified in order to perceive it correctly. He suggests that "the mirror presented by the external world is of little to no value unless the mirror of our soul has been cleaned and polished."[71] Fowler, while not explicitly employing the image of the mirror, does nonetheless assert that his theory corresponds to the actual stages in faith development. Fowler argues,

> In the way I believe all postmodern scholarship and intellectual production must proceed, FDT [faith development theory] established an acknowledgedly convictional set of starting points. It conducted several waves of qualitative research with increasingly diverse populations. On the basis of those data it refined and reformed a developmental framework whose initial formulations selectively drew on a combination of stage theories shaped by other acute observers and the interpretative efforts of the theory-laden practitioner. Within those limits, and with those strengths, FDT has maintained the claim that *the formally desirable stages it identifies are sequential, invariant, and hierarchical* [emphasis added].[72]

Fowler insists that the theory mirrors the actual stages of faith development through which human beings pass.

Postmodern thinkers operate with a set of philosophical assumptions that renders the image of the mind as a mirror untenable. The late Richard Rorty is most commonly associated with the rejection of this classic image. "The picture which holds traditional philosophy captive is that of the mind as a great mirror, containing various representations—some accurate, some not—and capable of being studied by pure, nonempirical methods. Without the notion of the mind as mirror, the notion of knowledge as accuracy of representation would not have suggested itself."[73] If

---

70. Ruysbroeck, *Seven Steps of the Ladder*, 31.
71. Bonaventure, *Soul's Journey*, Prologue, IV, 56.
72. Fowler, "Faith Development Theory," 167.
73. Rorty, *Philosophy and the Mirror of Nature*, 12.

the mind is a mirror, knowledge results when there is a correspondence between what our mind sees and what actually exists independently of the mind. In his review of Rorty's *Philosophy and the Mirror of Nature*, Cornel West explains that for Rorty "the theory-laden character of observations relativizes talk about the world such that realist appeals to 'the world' as a final court of appeal to determine what is true can only be viciously circular. We cannot isolate 'the world' from theories of the world, then compare these theories of the world with a theory-free world. We cannot compare theories with anything that is not a product of another theory."[74] The separation between the mind and the world that is presupposed by the image of mirror, for Rorty, does not exist.

How can we draw upon the multiple examples of sacred numbers within the biblical tradition in a way that is credible to twenty-first-century Christians? Is there some mystical connection between the number seven and the stages of human life? Is seven a useful symbol of completion and wholeness for those shaped by the biblical narrative, but no more than that? Is the idea of stages of any number in the course of human or spiritual development a construct of the human imagination? These are but a few of the questions that arise when considering how Christian thinkers both past and present have incorporated the number seven into their work. Orthodox writers draw upon one of the many uses of "seven" found in traditional Christian thought and practice. Liberals turn to literary and poetic sources using "seven" in their accounts of the human condition and correlate what they find there with the Christian engagements with the same existential concerns. Postliberals reflect on the distinctive way of life generated by the Christian community's particular use of the number seven to organize its beliefs and practices. Postmoderns are generally suspicious of grand theories of human development with a set number of stages. In deciding which approach to take in the course of one's own theological reflections, the person is considering, among other things, what role the seven gifts of the Holy Spirit, the seven deadly sins, and the seven corporal works of mercy play in his or her understanding of what it means to be a Christian.

Discussion Questions

1. What association do you make with the number seven in the Bible?
2. If you had to offer your reflections on the image of the ladder of various forms of spiritual love, what would each rung represent?

74. West, "Review of *Philosophy and the Mirror of Nature*," 181.

3. Does the material world contain vestiges of God?
4. Are there stages in life? Are there stages in our faith development? If so, what are they?
5. Is there a progression to the gifts given by the Holy Spirit?
6. What do Tillich and Auden mean by "anxiety"? Do you agree with their assessment of the human condition?
7. Which of Christ's sayings from the cross are most powerful to you?

Suggested Readings

For background on Ruusbroec, see Paul Verdeyen, *Ruusbroec and His Mysticism* (Collegeville, MN: Liturgical, 1994), Paul Mommaers, *Jan van Ruusbroec: Mystical Union with God* (Leuven: Peeters, 2009), and John Arblaster and Rob Maesen, eds., *A Companion to John of Ruusbroec* (Leiden: Brill, 2014). For an introduction to Bonaventure, see Ilia Delio, *Simply Bonaventure* (Hyde Park, NY: New City, 2013), Christopher M. Culllen, *Bonaventure* (Oxford: Oxford University Press, 2006), and Jay M. Hammond, J. A. Wayne Hellman, and Jared Goff, *A Companion to Bonaventure* (Leiden: Brill, 2014). For background on Fowler's work in faith development, see Craig Dykstra and Sharon Parks, eds., *Faith Development and Fowler* (Birmingham, AL: Religious Education, 1986), and Jeff Astley and Leslie J. Francis, *Christian Perspectives on Faith Development* (Grand Rapids: Eerdmans, 1992).

Chapter Seven: Music and Art in the Bible

THERE IS NO DIFFERENCE more fundamental to the Christian faith than the one between artistry and idolatry. To mistake the creation for the Creator is a catastrophic theological error, yet to fail to appreciate the beauty of the natural world as well as the music and art created by humans would lead to a terribly impoverished view of the world. From the lyrical praise of the God who created the heavens above (Ps 19:1) to the vision of the bejeweled walls of the heavenly city (Rev 21:15–21), the biblical writers saw in natural and created beauty a reflection of God's own glory. It is for this reason that such care has gone into subsequent theological discussions of beauty and art. The debate found classic expression in the iconoclast controversy of the eighth and ninth centuries, and so we begin with John of Damascus (ca. 675–749) and his influential work *On the Divine Images*, then turn our attention to *The Fire of Love* by the fourteenth-century English hermit Richard Rolle (ca. 1290–1349), and conclude with the contemporary theologian Richard Viladesau's work, *Theology and the Arts* (2000).

John of Damascus, *On the Divine Images*

The iconoclastic controversy erupted in 726 when the Byzantine emperor Leo III ordered the destruction of icons throughout the empire. In 730 Leo issued a formal edict mandating his policy be carried out, and Germanius the patriarch of Constantinople was forced to resign. The policy was formally rejected by the Second Council of Nicaea in 787. The iconoclastic movement found renewed vigor in 815 when the Emperor Leo V came to its defense. This second phase of the controversy continued until 843 when the Empress Theodora reaffirmed the teachings of Nicaea.[1] The controversy dealt not only with icons, but religious imagery in general. As Andrew Louth notes, "the term 'icon' is not, in the context of Byzantine iconography, to be restricted to panel icons (as in current art-historical usage), but includes mosaics, frescos, manuscript illustrations, images woven

---

1. Louth, "Introduction," John of Damascus, *Three Treatises on the Divine Images*, 7. All citations of the treatises are taken from this translation unless otherwise noted.

into cloth, engraved on metal, carved in ivory or wood, and probably also statues, though there is little evidence for religious statues in Byzantium."[2]

The iconoclastic controversy pitted two interesting theological arguments against each other. Those favoring the destruction of the images (iconoclast = "image breaker") argued that their use in communal and personal worship violated the commandment prohibiting graven images (Exod 20:4-5). Those supporting the use of icons (iconodules or iconophiles = "one who serves images") argued that the iconoclasts failed to understand the crucial difference between adoration (or absolute worship) and veneration (or relative worship). Adoration is the worship that only God deserves; veneration or a "bowing down before" is the respect properly given to persons, places, or objects of honor. Scripture, argues the Damascene, is filled with acceptable examples of persons bowing down to persons and objects. "Jacob venerated Esau his brother and Pharaoh the Egyptian, bowing in veneration over the head of his staff. They venerated, they did not worship. Jesus [Joshua] the Son of Nave and Daniel venerated the angel of God, but they did not worship. The veneration of worship is one thing, veneration offered to those who excel on account of something worthy is another."[3] In addition to this, God commanded the carving of images of cherubim for the holy of holies in the temple, so it is clear that God did not oppose all forms of religious imagery. John argues, "Why then does he [God] prescribe carved cherubim fashioned by human hands to overshadow the mercy seat? It is clear that it is impossible to make an image of God or of anything like God, since he is uncircumscribable and unimaginable, lest the creation be venerated in worship as God. Since the cherubim are circumscribable, He prescribes the making of an image of them prostrate before the divine throne, to overshadow the mercy seat; for it was fitting that the image of the divine mysteries should shadow the image of the heavenly servants."[4]

John's christological argument for the use of icons follows from his scriptural argument. "In former times God, who is without form or body, could never be depicted. But now when God is seen in the flesh conversing with men, I make an image of the God whom I see. I do not worship matter, I worship the Creator of matter who became matter for my sake, who willed to take His abode in matter; who worked out my salvation through matter."[5] The Incarnation—the joining of the divine with the material—is the decisive moment in the history of salvation and the ultimate basis for the

---

2. Louth, *St. John Damascene*, 194-95.
3. John of Damascus, *Three Treatises on the Divine Images*, 25.
4. Ibid., 28.
5. John of Damascus, *On the Divine Images*, 23.

veneration of icons. "For it is clear that when you see the bodiless become human for your sake, then you may accomplish the figure of a human form; when the invisible becomes visible in the flesh, then you may depict the likeness of something seen; whence who, by transcending his own nature, is bodiless, formless, incommensurable, without magnitude or size, that is, one who is in the form of God, taking the form of a slave, by this reduction to quantity and magnitude put on the characteristics of a body, then depict him on a board and set up to view the One who has accepted to be seen."[6] The Incarnation therefore makes a larger theological point about the material world. "I do not venerate matter, I venerate the fashioner of matter, who became matter for my sake and accepted to dwell in matter and through matter worked my salvation, and I will not cease from reverencing matter, through which my salvation was worked."[7]

John of Damascus touts the pedagogical benefits of images. "What the book does for those who understand letters, the image does for the illiterate; the word appeals to hearing, the image appeals to sight; it conveys understanding."[8] We can only understand what we can in one way or another conceptualize. This applies to all human cognition, but it is especially true of religious knowledge. "Since the creation of the world the invisible things of God are clearly seen by means of images. We see images in the creation which, although they are only dim lights, still remind us of God. For instance, when we speak of the holy and eternal Trinity, we use the images of the sun, light, and burning rays; or a running fountain; or an overflowing river; or the mind, speech, and spirit within us; or a rose tree, a flower, and a sweet fragrance."[9] Images in nature are not the only ones that teach us about divine realities. Scripture of course has numerous examples of imagery that both remind us of past events and has us anticipate future ones, but the saints also model Christian virtue and share in the glory of the Risen Lord. "For if you make an image of Christ, but in no wise of the saints, it is clear that you do no prohibit the image, but rather the honor due to the saints, something that no one has ever dared to do or undertake with such brazenness. For to make an image of Christ as glorified and yet spurn the image of the saints as without glory is to endeavor to show that the truth is false. 'For I live,' says the Lord, 'and I shall glorify those who glorify me,' and the divine apostle, 'So you are no longer a slave, but a son,

---

6. John of Damascus, *Three Treatises on the Divine Images*, 24.
7. Ibid., 29.
8. Ibid., 31.
9. John of Damascus, *On the Divine Images*, 20.

and if a son, an heir of God through Christ,' and 'we suffer together [with him], so that we are glorified together.'"[10]

John Damascene's treatises regarding the propriety of venerating icons can be studied from a variety of angles. Is the central issue a question of how to interpret Scripture properly? Is Christology at the heart of the iconoclastic controversy, or is it the relationship between the sacred and the profane or the material and the spiritual? The patristics scholar Patrick Henry suggests that worship provides a lens through which to view the battle between the iconoclasts and the iconodules.

> For both the Iconoclast and the Iconodule, worship is an activity in which man gets closer to the divine. The Iconoclast believes that in order to do that, it is necessary to relegate humanity to the background. We can be assured of our kinship with God only in so far as we leave our humanity behind. The Iconodule, on the contrary, believes that our approach to God is specifically through our humanity. *Man* was made in the image and likeness of God; not the soul (*psyche*) or the mind (*nous*) but man (*anthropos*). Worship is the activity not of the man who has transcended his humanity, but of the man whose humanity is restored.[11]

Worship involves one's entire being, not simply the intellect, but the body and soul as well—the entire human personality that the Word assumed in the Incarnation. Worship touches on the issues of Scripture, Christology, and the sacred and the profane, as does iconography. John followed the lead of Basil of Caesarea in insisting that "the honor given to the image passes to the archetype,"[12] and in doing so, advocated for the inclusion of religious imagery in the Christian community's proper worship of the triune God.

Richard Rolle, *The Fire of Love*

At the age of nineteen while home on break from Oxford University, Richard Rolle asked his sister to meet him in the woods and bring two of her frocks and their father's rain-hood.[13] When she arrived, Rolle tore the sleeves from

---

10. John of Damascus, *Three Treatises on the Divine Images*, 32–33.

11. Henry, "What was the Iconoclastic Controversy," 27. Emphasis original.

12. John of Damascus, *Three Treatises on the Divine Images*, 35. Citation is from Basil, *Exegetic Homilies*, 18.45.

13. For biographical information I am relying on Wolters, "Introduction," and Allen, "Introduction." All citations from *The Fire of Love* are taken from the Wolters edition unless otherwise noted.

the gray frock and the buttons from the white one. He fashioned for himself a rough version of a hermit's garb—a white tunic covered by a sleeveless gray one with the rain-hood as a cowl. Richard then set out on his life's journey, which he spent largely as a hermit. Because he never completed his studies at Oxford, he was prohibited from entering into the clerical state. Furthermore, he would have been required to ask permission from the local bishop to be designated as a hermit. In order to receive that permission, he would have been required to demonstrate that he had the ability to support himself financially, for example, by working a plot of land or serving as a keeper of a lighthouse. It does not seem, however, that Rolle ever sought such permission. He was supported by a series of patrons and was serving as a spiritual guide to an anchoress, Margaret Kirkby, and a community of Cistercian nuns in Hampole, England, at the time of his death in 1349.

When recounting his own spiritual experiences, Rolle has three preferred images: heat, music, and sweetness. We find all three in his account of the years following his conversion that he offers in chapter 15 of his *Fire of Love (Incendium Amoris)*, written approximately twenty years after the events took place (ca. 1340).

> I was sitting in a certain chapel, delighting in the sweetness of prayer or meditation, when suddenly I felt within myself an unusually pleasant heat. At first I wondered where it came from, but it was not long before I realized that it was from none of his creatures but from the Creator himself. It was, I found, more fervent and pleasant than I had ever known. But it was just over nine months before a conscious and incredible sweet warmth kindled me, and I knew the infusion and understanding of heavenly, spiritual sounds, sounds which pertain to the song of eternal praise, and to the sweetness of unheard melody; sounds which cannot be known or heard save by him who has received it.[14]

At first Rolle must determine whether the "unusually pleasant heat" that he experiences during the "sweetness of prayer" is of human or divine origin. He soon realizes that it is the latter. The third element becomes apparent nine months later when he receives the "infusion and understanding of heavenly, spiritual sounds." From these experiences and his study of Scripture, Rolle determines the three marks of genuine religious experience. "As far as my study of Scripture goes, I have found that to love Christ above all else will involve three things: warmth and song and sweetness. And these

---

14. Rolle, *Fire of Love*, 93.

three, as I know from personal experience, cannot exist for long without there being great quiet."[15]

If we focus exclusively on the image of music in Rolle's thought, we find that he puts it to use in different ways: there is heavenly song; there is music in the mind; and there is a resonance of that heavenly song within the mind during prayer and meditation. The first element in Rolle's thought that deserves close attention is his association of heaven with music as we find in his repeated references to "heavenly song" and "celestial music." This feature recalls the ancient notion of the "music of the spheres"—the sound produced by the heavenly bodies as they passed by each other in their circular orbits around the Earth. This could be understood as either a metaphorical expression of the perfect harmony of planetary motion or literally as a tone. Rolle makes it clear that the "heavenly symphony" is not audible to the human ear. "It is not an affair of those outward cadences which are used in church and elsewhere; nor does it blend much with the audible sounds made by the human voice and heard by physical ears; but among angel melodies it has its own acceptable harmony, and those who have known it speak of it with wonder and approval."[16] In addition to the music of the spheres, the most obvious source for Rolle's thought is the biblical description of the angelic choirs (Isa 6:3) and the heavenly chant and musical instruments referenced in Revelation (4:8, 5:8). More important than the question of background, however, is the significance of the image in Rolle's thought. The pairing of music and heaven suggests that they both represent a harmony or proper relation among various elements. In terms of music, its structure is mathematical with ratios and intervals underlying the entire work. In terms of heaven, the complete conformity to the will of God and the joy that such conformity brings to those experiencing it is at the heart of the biblical hope for the end-time.

If heaven's music stands at one pole in Rolle's thinking, the music of the human mind stands at the other. This aspect of Rolle's thought provides another avenue by which we can consider the power of song. "Very sweet indeed is the quiet which the spirit experiences. Music, divine, delectable, comes to rejoice it; the mind is rapt in sublime and gay melody and sings the delights of everlasting love."[17] Elsewhere Rolle mentions that "thought turns into song" when "the mind is in thrall to sweetest harmony."[18] Just as the soul has the capacity to receive God, the mind has the faculty of memory

15. Ibid., 88–89.
16. Ibid., 147.
17. Ibid., 76.
18. Ibid., 89.

which allows us to recollect an enormous catalogue of songs. These songs can be retrieved at the sound of the first few notes of the melody or even at the mere mention of the song's title. Recalling a song is usually unlike the recalling of a bit of information such as a mathematical formula memorized years ago, but temporarily forgotten. Song transports us back to an emotional time and place much like the power of smell can evoke memories of our childhood. Music involves both our "right brain" and our "left brain." Furthermore, the precision of our recall is often staggering. If a song comes on the radio while we are driving in our car and we pass through a tunnel which causes the loss of the signal, yet we continue to sing the song, we often find that as we leave the tunnel and reacquire the signal, we have not missed a beat in the song. When a community's "thoughts turn into song," according to Rolle, the transformation is far-reaching.

> Their mind is changed and passes into lasting melody. From now on their meditations become song. Melancholy has been driven out of the mansion of their spirit, and it now resounds with wondrous melody. The one-time torment of their soul has vanished, and now in glowing health they dwell in the heights of harmony, in the wonderful rhythm of sweet and melodious meditation.[19]

While Rolle speaks in exalted terms of the healing power of having thought turned into song, *how* this transformation occurs remains a great mystery. "Some would add to this and say that there sounds in their heart something sweet and tuneful, by which the thirsty soul is ravished and gladdened. But they do not explain, as far as I can make out, how it is that their thought is changed into song, or how the melody remains in the mind, or with what joy it is that he sings his prayers."[20]

If the "music of heaven" and the "music of the mind" are the two poles in Rolle's thought, then his spirituality consists in bringing the two into harmony with each other. This process of harmonization is an arduous one,[21] and the experiences of the divine are fleeting. "Rarely in fact have we found a man who is so holy or ever perfect in this earthly life endowed with love so great as to be raised up to contemplation to the level of jubilant song. This would mean that he would receive within himself the sound that is sung in heaven, and that he would echo back the praises of God as it were

---

19. Ibid., 60.
20. Ibid., 164.
21. The issue of free will and grace once again lurks in the background. Rolle asserts that humans are free (ch. 20) and that salvation is a gift that no human has the power to achieve (ch. 31).

in harmony, pouring forth sweet notes of music and composing spiritual songs as he offers heavenly praises . . . "[22] Rolle relates his own experience of the divine in terms of musical harmony. "In my prayer I was reaching out to heaven with heartfelt longing when I became aware, in a way I cannot explain, of a symphony of song, and in myself I sensed a corresponding harmony at once wholly delectable and heavenly, which persisted in my mind. Then and there my thinking turned into melodious song, and my meditation became a poem, and my very prayers and psalms took up the same sound."[23] If we take the idea of harmonization between "the song of heaven" and "the song of the mind" and extend it over the course of a lifetime, then each person's life is metaphorically an exercise in musical composition. There are different movements, tempos, and styles that blend over time. Christians live in hope that the songs that we compose not only chronicle our own unique experience and enliven the lives of others, but also contribute in some small way to the praise of the Creator.

Richard Viladesau, *Theology and the Arts*

Richard Viladesau is one of the growing number of contemporary theologians interested in the role that aesthetics plays in theology. Viladesau takes as one of his themes the idea that artistic beauty is "a medium of divine self-revelation."[24] While we might immediately think of great works of pictorial art, sculpture, and sacred music, Viladesau reminds us that rhetoric too should enjoy a place of prominence in our theological discussions of beauty. Through the art of preaching, ministers of the gospel convey in Viladesau's words, the "intrinsic beauty [of God's revelation]—its attractiveness and its promise of joy."[25] Viladesau frankly acknowledges, however, that much preaching fails to meet this lofty ideal. He adds, "A major reason has been the failure to recognize that the church's teaching and proclaiming must also constitute a form of art."[26] This, however, was not always was the case. In *On Christian Doctrine*, Augustine draws upon Aristotle and Cicero when he identifies three goals of preaching: "So the speaker endeavouring to give conviction to something that is good should despise none of these three aims—of instructing, delighting, and moving [persuading] his hearers—and should make it his prayerful aim to be

22. Rolle, *Fire of Love*, 51.
23. Ibid., 93.
24. Viladesau, *Theology and the Arts*, 4.
25. Ibid., 170.
26. Ibid., 177.

listened to with understanding, with pleasure, and with obedience... If he does this properly and appropriately he can fairly be called eloquent, even if he does not meet with his audience's assent."[27]

Viladesau draws a parallel between the three goals of preaching outlined by Augustine—to teach, to persuade, and to delight—and Bernard Lonergan's technical description of preaching as the sharing of one's cognitive, effective, and constitutive meanings. Lonergan's "cognitive meaning" corresponds to the purpose of teaching while preaching. The "effective" meaning "involves not only the contemplative knowing but also the active making of the world and of human life itself in accord with our ideas and values, hopes, and plans. To share one's effective meaning with others is to invite them to act in accord with one's insights and values, that is, rhetorically to 'touch' their minds and hearts and persuade them to a certain course of behavior."[28] While teaching and persuading are obvious elements of preaching, the third goal of "pleasing" or "delighting" (the constitutive meaning) the audience also plays a vital role in the revitalization of biblical imagery. "Meaning is 'constitutive' when human insights, judgments, and values in themselves create a new reality, that is, create the human world, the world constituted by meaning," writes Viladesau. The one who preaches ideally casts the familiar in a new light and in doing so creates a new world of meaning. This activity is as much art as putting the brush to the canvas. "The sharing of constitutive meaning is necessarily a work of art (in the wider sense of *creativity*): not the creation of beautiful objects, but of ourselves and our communities as embodiments of moral and spiritual beauty." Viladesau adds, "Crucial to the preacher is the poetic liberation of the imagination."[29]

Viladesau next draws a parallel between Augustine's three goals of preaching and the three types of theology outlined by David Tracy. Tracy categorizes three theologies based on the principal audience envisioned in each approach. Foundational theologies are geared for the academy. Here arguments are advanced on the basis of shared canons of rationality. Systematic theologies are aimed at a church audience. The theological tradition and its religious classics are the source of authority in the positions espoused here. Practical theologies are aimed at the wider society. Social transformation and human flourishing are the central concerns in this approach. According to Viladesau, "Tracy's three specialities represent not so much three different theological sources for preaching or three different methods it may pursue, but rather three theological elements that may

---

27. Augustine, *On Christian Teaching* 4.96 (Green, 123).
28. Viladesau, *Theology and the Arts*, 182.
29. Ibid., 189. Emphasis original.

be present to varying degrees in any homily or sermon, depending on its context, audience, and purpose."[30]

The shape of the sermon would shift considerably depending on how much weight is given to each of Tracy's three theological specialties. If the foundational takes the lead, then the category of shared human experience (e.g., hope) would provide the framework of the sermon. A systematic theology would yield an intertextual reading of the scriptural stories and theological masterpieces. A practical sermon would identify shared goals of justice and peace and specify how Christian convictions mesh with the wider concerns for the welfare of the poor and oppressed. Noting that a shift in perspective yields a different type of sermon is certainly not a new idea. In fact, it sheds some valuable light on past controversies. For example, years ago the religious education scholar Gabriel Moran observed that "Barth's theology is written from the viewpoint of the preacher while Bultmann's theology is developed from the situation of the listener to the preaching."[31] The great twentieth-century theological debates between the Barthians and the Bultmannians was in many ways a battle over the art of preaching.

Viladesau's own proposals for preaching rely heavily on foundational theology. While systematic, intertextual readings are well suited to sermons or homilies delivered during a specific liturgical season (e.g., typological reading of Old Testament stories in relation to the Passion during Lent), Viladesau questions whether even church congregations have an unambiguous experience of the holy in their everyday lives. Viladesau insists that "it must be acknowledged that preaching must take account of the difficulties inherent in presenting the Christian message in the contemporary context in which most Western believers live. That context is marked by pluralism, secularity, and the absence of a Christian or even religious context for daily existence."[32] Even the most faithful of Christians live in a world that has lost contact with the divine. "In this context, the essential challenge to preaching is to find a point of contact for the Christian message in the lives and consciousness of its hearers. It can no longer be assumed that the intrinsic beauty of the message (whether biblical, dogmatic, or ethical) immediately resonates either with contemporary people's experience or with an unquestioned acceptance of traditional views."[33]

Viladesau promotes David Tracy's "revised method of correlation" as the key theological strategy for effective preaching. "In Tracy's formulation

---

30. Ibid., 199.
31. Moran, *Present Revelation*, 23. Moran quotes N. A. Dahl in support.
32. Viladesau, *Theology and the Arts*, 200–201.
33. Ibid., 202.

of a 'revised method of correlation,' Christian theology is seen as the attempt to establish mutually critical correlations between an interpretation of the Christian tradition and an interpretation of contemporary experience."[34] For correlational theologians, there is a theological connection between the existential questions raised by thoughtful humans in all cultures and the specific answers offered in the Christian tradition. According to Viladesau, this dynamic interplay between the human question and the theological answer must animate one's preaching. The sermon may begin with a concrete example of seeing the beautiful in the midst of human degradation and then follow up with a series of questions and theological responses: What innate capacities must be present in the human person in order to recognize the beautiful in art, nature, and human experience (theological anthropology)? What obstacles in the human personality prevent us from seeing beauty (sin)? How does the possibility of experiencing the beautiful alter our present understanding of the world (social justice)?[35]

The Revitalization of the Biblical Imagery of Art and Music

The orthodox position on questions of beauty firmly rejects the notion that "beauty is in the eye of the beholder." One of the twentieth century's greatest proponents of the orthodox view was Jacques Maritain (1882–1973). In his work *Art and Scholasticism*, Maritain presents the medieval conception of beauty as expounded by Thomas Aquinas. "St. Thomas, who was as simple as he was wise, defined the beautiful as what gives pleasure on sight, *id quod visum placet*. The four words say all that is necessary: a vision, that is to say an *intuitive knowledge* and a *joy*. The beautiful is what gives joy, not all joy, but joy in knowledge; not the joy peculiar to the act of knowing, but a joy super-abounding and overflowing from such as act because of the object known."[36] The experience of beauty is therefore a form of knowledge involving the correspondence of the mind with the objective reality that exists separate and apart from the self. The mind apprehends the beauty that radiates from the object and rejoices in the perception of the beautiful. "If beauty delights the mind, it is because beauty is essentially a certain excellence or perfection in the proportion of things to the mind. Hence the three conditions assigned to it by St. Thomas: integrity, because the mind likes being;

---

34. Ibid., 207.
35. Ibid., 216.
36. Maritain, *Art and Scholasticism*, 19. Emphasis original.

proportion, because the mind likes order and likes unity; lastly and above all brightness or clarity, because the mind likes light and intelligibility."[37]

For the medieval thinkers, God is the source of all beauty. "God is beautiful. He is the most beautiful of beings, because as Denys the Areopagite and St. Thomas explain, His beauty is without alteration or vicissitude, without increase or diminution: and because it is not like the beauty of things, which have all a particularised beauty. . . He is beautiful by Himself and in Himself, absolutely beautiful. . . He is beauty itself, because He imparts beauty to all created beings, according to the peculiar nature of each, and because He is the cause of all harmony and brightness."[38] Beauty, then, is a pathway to God because God is the "fountain of all beauty." On this point, there is a deep similarity between the medieval thinkers and Basil the Great's principle that "honor given to the image passes to the archetype."[39] The beauty found in nature and the beauty that is produced in human works of art reflect through a glass darkly the beauty that is God's nature.

The artist's creative act in creating a painting, a poem, or a sculpture mirrors God's original act of creation. It is important to note that the medieval discussions of beauty were not confined to the fine arts, but included as well the practical arts such as shipbuilding and woodworking. "Art, then, is fundamentally constructive and creative. It is the faculty of producing, not of course *ex nihilo*, but out of a pre-existing matter, a new creature, an original being capable in its turn of moving a human soul . . . [The artist] is as it were an associate of God in the making of works of beauty; by developing the faculties with which the Creator has endowed him—'for every perfect gift cometh from on high and down from the Father of light' [Jas 1:17]—and making use of created matter, he creates as it were in the second degree."[40]

Not only is the production of art in a sense a spiritual activity—"the artist, whether he knows it or not, is consulting God when he looks at things"[41]—the admiration of art draws us into the love of God. "The beautiful is essentially delightful. Therefore by its very nature, by its very beauty, it stirs desire and produces love . . . Love in its turn produces ecstasy, that is to say, makes the lover beside himself: an ecstasy of which the soul experiences a lesser form when it is gripped by the beauty of a work of art, and the fullness when it is absorbed, like dew, by the beauty of God."[42] Beauty and love

---

37. Ibid., 20.
38. Ibid., 25.
39. Quoted in John of Damascus, *Three Treatise on the Divine Images,* II, 21.
40. Maritain, *Art and Scholasticism,* 49.
41. Ibid., 50.
42. Ibid., 21–22.

meet in the appreciation of art. Maritain continues, "And of God Himself, according to Denys the Areopagite, one must be bold enough to say that He suffers as it were an ecstasy of love, because of the abundance of His goodness which makes Him give all things a share of His magnificence. But His love causes the beauty of what He loves, whereas our love is caused by the beauty of what we love."[43] The medieval vision of things going out from God and returning to God is displayed in the relationship between love and beauty: God's love issues forth in the beauty of the world and when humans observe and admire beauty either in nature or artistic works they are drawn back to the God who is the source of all beauty.

Edward Farley's discussion of beauty in his *Faith and Beauty* stands squarely within the liberal tradition in two significant respects. First, Farley gives theological priority to experience, not doctrine. "*Theology's route to beauty should be determined initially by the way in which beauty appears in the life of faith*. In this axiom, 'faith' is an inclusive term for the individual and social existence that comes about as the result of divine redemptive activity. The faith of first-century Christians does not mean a list of discrete beliefs expressible in doctrines, but rather an individual, interhuman and social existence affected by redemptive transformation."[44] Second, Farley shares the liberal willingness to translate the traditional doctrine into contemporary categories of thought. "The fact of redemptive transformation (involving liberation, forgiveness, grace, creativity and social/political transformation) presupposes and addresses radical and pervasive evil. Eden and the symbols of primordial innocence know nothing of redemptive existence. Only with the 'Fall,' expulsion and Babel does redemption enter the story."[45]

Farley interprets the central symbols of creation, fall, and redemption though the lens of beauty. By virtue of being created in the image of God, humans enjoy certain capacities that are reflective of the divine nature. What capacity is being assumed in this theological anthropology? "Any adequate answer to this question must meet two requirements; first, the presupposed structure must be something about the human being which sin is able to distort and redemption transform; and second, this distortable and transformable something must be what bears a resemblance to God."[46] For Farley the answer lies ultimately in ethical transcendence, which he defines as "all the ways in which human beings are drawn beyond external and internal determinations into meaning, language, trust, subjectivity,

---

43. Ibid., 22.
44. Farley, *Faith and Beauty*, 83. Emphasis original.
45. Ibid., 34.
46. Ibid., 86.

creativity, self-making and futurity."[47] Humans by virtue of their creation in the image of God have the freedom to reach out in love to the vulnerable and oppressed in the same way that God does. "And if we follow Jonathan Edwards, we will agree that this compassionate going-beyond, this ethical self-transcendence of consent, is the primordial instance and meaning of beauty."[48]

Farley's treatment of the Fall follows from his association of the image of God with the capacity for ethical self-transcendence. According to Farley, "ethical self-transcendence calls forth a human way of being together—an ethical mutuality."[49] This innate capacity for ethical mutuality, however, can be misdirected. This misdirection results in what traditionally has been called idolatry. "We human beings open ourselves to evil when, trying to secure ourselves against the scary, dangerous, unpredictable (chaotic) aspects of the world, we form absolute attachments to the attractive and powerful goods of the world. The evil things we do are almost always done in the name of these goods: religions, races, governments, tribes, heroes, causes, cult figures, territories, ideologies, and world-views. In idolatrous mood, we expect these idols of the tribe to protect us against the very things that constitute our finitude: anxiety, boredom, ambiguity, uncertainty, and tragedy."[50]

Farley carries the concept of beauty forward into his reading of redemption. "Because the *imago Dei* possesses primordial beauty, human evil is a fractured beauty, and redemptive remaking into a new, compassionate, self-transcendence is a restored beauty."[51] According to Farley, "the fundamental event that begins these remakings—the older theologies called it conversion, regeneration or justification—is a 'founding' in and by God that undermines the anxious need for idols and their security. The fundamental effect of this 'founding' is to draw the human being out of the self-preoccupied immanence that cripples its capacity to engage a genuine other."[52] It is in this reorientation that we discover "the other's beauty."[53] It is the process of restoring the beauty grounded in our status as creatures created in the image of God that we discover the beauty of the other. In this redemptive remaking, our selfish, idolatrous tendencies are re-directed towards the concerns of others. In addition to the ethical dimension of

47. Ibid.
48. Ibid., 89.
49. Ibid.
50. Ibid., 90.
51. Ibid., 85.
52. Ibid., 93–94.
53. Ibid., 95.

redemptive existence, Farley insists that such a life increases within the person "a sensibility to the beautiful" and an awareness of "the unpredictable newness of the flow of things."[54] It is a birth to newness of life, to a life that perceives and embodies grace and beauty.

If the focus in orthodox and liberal theologies is on the perception of beauty, the postliberal emphasis is on the beauty expressed in the performance of the Christian story. For the ethicist Samuel Wells this story is best classified as a drama. Relying on the work of Hans Urs von Balthasar (who in turn is drawing on Hegel's discussion), Wells outlines three forms that a telling of a story may take: epic, lyric, and drama. In the epic perspective a person assembles a narrative about an event, but the storyteller tries as best as one can to bracket one's own judgements on the events. In the lyric perspective the storyteller acknowledges his/her emotional involvement in the narrative of events. Neither, according to Balthasar, is the perspective that best serves Christian theology. "The *dramatic* perspective synthesizes the strengths of the epic and lyric dimensions. Like the lyric, it does justice to the role of the subject, the way that events arise from the hearts and minds and actions of people, rather than external impersonal forces. Like the epic, it perceives an object that has reason and validity beyond the subjectivity of the involved observer."[55] The theologian is deeply involved in the events recounted in the narrative, but does not fail to remember that the subject of the story is God, not the storyteller.

Wells divides the Christian drama into five acts: creation, Israel, Jesus, church, and *eschaton*. Wells warns against two dangers that theologians must avoid. The first is to think that we are in a one-act play. When we commit this error we discount all that has preceded us and mistakenly believe that all must be accomplished in our own lifetime. This theme strikes the common postliberal note that the task of Christians is to be faithful disciples, not guarantors that human history comes out right. The second danger to be avoided is thinking that we are in a different act than we actually are. For example, if "one assumes one is in Act One, one places oneself, rather than God, in the role of creator. There have been no significant events before one's appearance in the drama. There is no experience to learn from, no story to join, no drama to enter."[56] The postliberal emphasis falls on the idea that we place our own life stories within the larger story of God's interaction with humanity beginning at creation and

---

54. Ibid., 97 and 98.
55. Wells, *Improvisation*, 47. Emphasis original.
56. Ibid., 55.

CHAPTER SEVEN: MUSIC AND ART IN THE BIBLE

stretching out towards the *eschaton*. As Wells writes, "Humans are not the creators, nor the finishers, of God's story."[57]

Within the performance of the five-act drama there is a lot of improvisation by the church. "Performance does justice to the embodied, communal way in which the church tries to involve itself in the life enjoined by the Scriptures while remaining faithful to the character of God that emerges from the biblical witness."[58] The idea of performing a drama, however, gives the impression that the script covers all eventualities and offers answers to any and all questions that might arise. For this reason, argues Wells, there is a tendency among some thinkers to dismiss the script or to seek to translate it into contemporary language. Wells believes that the issues involved in the performance are handled much more effectively through improvisation. "When improvisers are trained to work in the theatre, they are schooled in a tradition so thoroughly that they learn to act from habit in ways appropriate to the circumstance."[59] The church is called to be a community so profoundly shaped by the scriptural narrative that through participation in its life disciples acquire the skills that are required for the proper improvisation of the drama that is the Christian life.

The distinction between an idol and an icon figures prominently in the work of the postmodern thinker Jean-Luc Marion. He argues in *God Without Being* that the difference between the idol and the icon is not found in the object itself, but rather in the gaze of the one whose eyes fall upon it. In the case of the idol, the gaze stops at the figure. "In this stop, the gaze ceases to overshoot and transpierce itself, hence it ceases to transpierce visible things, in order to pause in the splendor of one of them. No longer transpiercing itself, the gaze no longer pierces things, no longer sees them in transparency; at a certain point, it no longer experiences things as transparent—insufficiently weighted down by light and glory—and a last one finally presents itself as visible, splendid, and luminous enough to be the first to attract, capture, and fill it."[60] The idol functions as "a mirror that reflects the gaze's image, or more exactly, the image of its aim and the scope of that aim."[61] The idol of our creation is, as Feuerbach argued, an idealized version of the self. The icon, by contrast, "summons the gaze to surpass itself by never freezing on a visible, since the visible only presents itself here in

---

57. Ibid., 56.
58. Ibid., 62.
59. Ibid., 65.
60. Marion, *God Without Being*, 11.
61. Ibid., 12.

view of the invisible."⁶² The icon "opens in a face that gazes at our gazes."⁶³ The icon faces us. It expresses the essence of revelation—God reaching out to humanity. "The gaze can never rest or settle if it looks at an icon; it always must rebound upon the visible, in order to go back in it up the infinite stream of the invisible. In this sense, the icon makes visible only by giving rise to an infinite gaze."⁶⁴

Marion's treatment of the idol-icon distinction sets the stage for his thought concerning God. The traditional equivalence drawn between God and Being is, in Marion's view, "idolatrous." "When a philosophical thought expresses a concept of what it names 'God,' this concept functions exactly as an idol."⁶⁵ Thought about God becomes frozen, fixed in place by its own intellectual limitations. In order to guard against this idolatrous domestication of God, Marion emphasizes the three related "iconic" ideas of love, gift, and distance. "God can give himself to be thought without idolatry only starting from himself alone: to give himself to be thought as love, hence as gift . . ."⁶⁶ Love that is freely bestowed on the recipient as a gift requires a distance. As Christina Gschwandtner explains,

> God must always be thought in terms of distance. Marion defines this as a kind of crossing, in which God's coming toward us is crossed by our worship/praise/prayer toward him, although the two are never identified or confused with each other. God is never subject to our thoughts or definitions, but always escapes them. God remains at a distance: a distance that recedes with our approaching it and that can only be traversed or crossed, but never eliminated.⁶⁷

Marion compares the experience of this divine distance to that of pushing against a powerful river current. "In the distance, only *agape* can put everything on earth, in heaven, and in hell, in giving, because *agape* alone, by definition, is not known, is not—but gives (itself). At the heart of *agape*, following its flux as one follows a current that is too violent to go back up, too profound for one to know its source or valley, everything flows along the giving, and, by the wake traced in the water, but without grasping anything of it, everything indicates the direction and meaning of distance."⁶⁸ God's

62. Ibid., 18.
63. Ibid., 19.
64. Ibid., 18.
65. Ibid., 16.
66. Ibid., 49.
67. Gschwandtner, *Reading Jean-Luc Marion*, 131.
68. Marion, *God Without Being*, 106.

love is the gift that pours forth from an unseen source, and in the sound of its torrent we hear what Rolle so beautifully calls "the heavenly symphony."

Discussion Questions

1. Are icons, statues, or images in stained glass a violation of the First Commandment? Why? Why not?
2. How is living the Christian life like the act of (a) creating a musical composition or (b) enjoying a piece of music?
3. What does the Rolle mean by "celestial music"? Why is musical imagery associated with heaven?
4. What is the best style of preaching to reach the members of your church?
5. Is beauty in the eye of the beholder or is it an objective property perceived by the mind? Does it make sense to say that God is beautiful? Why? Why not?
6. Do you find Farley's association of "ethical self-transcendence" with beauty a useful way to think of traditional Christian claims about redemption and idolatry?
7. In what sense is the Christian life a drama? What role does improvisation play in the life of discipleship?

Suggested Readings

For a helpful discussion of the relationship between beauty and theology, see John Navone, *Enjoying God's Beauty* (Collegeville, MN: Liturgical, 1999) and William A. Dyrness, "The Arts" in John Webster, Kathryn Tanner, and Iain Torrance, eds., *The Oxford Handbook of Systematic Theology* (Oxford: Oxford University Press, 2007). For an interesting discussion of the relationship between theology and music, see Jeremy Begbie, *Resounding Truth* (Grand Rapids: Baker, 2007). For John Damascene, see Andrew Louth, *St. John Damascene: Tradition and Originality in Byzantine Theology* (Oxford: Oxford University Press, 2002). For Richard Rolle, see Nicholas Watson, *Richard Rolle and the Invention of Authority* (Cambridge: Cambridge University Press, 1991). For a second work by Richard Viladesau, see his *Theological Aesthetics: God in Imagination, Beauty, and Art* (New York: Oxford University Press, 1999).

Chapter Eight: Elements of Nature in the Bible (Fire, Wind, Water)

GIVEN THE DEEP IMPRESSION that the power of nature makes on the human psyche, it comes as no surprise that the biblical writers used the imagery of massive waves, devastating whirlwinds, and booming thunder to describe the power and majesty of God. For example, the imagery of natural elements (e.g., thunder and lightning, heavy clouds, and earthquake) abounds in the story of the Sinai covenant. In this chapter we examine works by three thinkers who incorporate the imagery of the elements of nature into their theological reflection: Oration 39 of Gregory of Nazianzus (329–90) in which he discusses baptism in terms of light, *Hymn 30* of Symeon the New Theologian (949–1022) in which he describes the Holy Spirit in terms of fire, and *We Drink From Our Own Wells* by the contemporary liberation theologian Gustavo Gutiérrez (b. 1928) in which he reflects on the material and spiritual importance of water in the life of the poor.

Gregory of Nazianzus, Oration 39

Soon after his appointment as archbishop of Constantinople by the Emperor Theodosius in November, 380, Gregory of Nazianzus offered a series of three orations at the Basilica of the Holy Apostles on the liturgical celebrations of the birth of Christ, the visit of the Magi, and John's baptism of Jesus. While scholars debate the dates of these liturgical celebrations in the fourth-century church at Constantinople, the three orations have come down to us as *On the Theophany* (Oration 38), *On the Holy Lights* (Oration 39), and *On Baptism* (Oration 40).[1] Of the various themes developed throughout this trilogy we will focus on Gregory's use of the imagery of light as he reflects upon the theological significance of the events described in the nativity and baptism of Christ.

---

1. Hofer, *Christ in the Life*, 161–62. Because Gregory was the bishop of Sasima, his opponents soon challenged his legitimacy on the grounds that the Council of Nicaea prohibited the transfer of a bishop from one see to another. For historical background see also Daley, "Introduction," esp. 3–26, and McGuckin, *St. Gregory of Nazianzus*.

According to Andrew Hofer, Gregory's overarching concern in Oration 38 is to situate Christ's birth "within a greater biblical context: once again darkness is put to flight, and light comes into being. This hearkening back to the creation account is applied, first to Exodus, where Egypt is darkened and Israel illumined by a pillar of fire (cf. Exod 10:20-21, 13:21–22), then to the prophetic actualization of those sitting in darkness seeing a great light (cf. Isa 9:1, Matt 4:16), then to the shadows disappearing in the Law and the coming of the truth in the Spirit (cf. 2 Cor 3:6, Rom 13:12).[2] For Gregory, the light is sent to guide the people back to God. "This is our feast, this is what we celebrate today: God's coming to the human race, so that we might make our way to him, or return to him (to put it more precisely), so that we might put off the old humanity and put on the new, and that as we have died in Adam so we might live in Christ, being born with Christ and crucified with him and buried with him and raised with him."[3] God's earliest rescue attempts were rejected by humanity and their condition grew worse, so "stronger medicine" was required. "Since all these things required a greater help, they received one that was greater! This was the Word of God himself, who is before the ages, invisible, beyond comprehension, bodiless; cause from cause, light from light, the spring of life and immortality, the impress of the original beauty, the unquestionable seal, the unchangeable image, the Father's definition and Word" (38.13). The coming of the Light of the World was heralded by John whom Gregory calls "the lamp" (38.14). John baptized in water and Christ in the Holy Spirit, but both figures played a role in God's "plan of restoration" for humanity (38.14). Christ "lit a lamp—his own flesh—and 'swept the house,' cleaning the world of sin, and searched for the coin, that royal image caked with the mud of passions, and called together all the powers friendly to him when he found the coin, and let them share his joy" (38.14).

Gregory probably delivered Oration 39 on the vigil of Epiphany. Epiphany was also known as "The Day of Lights," because, as Brian Daley notes, it "seems to have been focused on the baptism of Jesus as the revelation of the divine light in the world and the full manifestation of God in history, as Father, Son, and Holy Spirit."[4] In his opening remarks, Gregory announces, "For the holy Day of Lights, to which we have come and which we are judged worthy to celebrate today, begins with the baptism of my Christ, 'the true light, which enlightens every man and woman coming into

---

2. Hofer, *Christ in the Life*, 163.

3. Gregory of Nazianzus, Oration 38, 118. All citations from Oration 38 are from Daley unless otherwise noted.

4. Daley, *Gregory of Nazianzus*, 127.

the world,' and it sets in motion my own purification and comes to the aid of that light which we received from him as a gift from above, in the beginning, and which we darkened and confused by sin."[5] In this opening section Gregory associates purification, illumination, and baptism, a theme that he will develop over the course of the oration. All three concepts unite in Gregory's initial call to return to our prelapsarian state.[6] "It is the time of new creation: let us take up the first Adam once again; let us not remain what we are, but let us become what we were! 'The light shines in the darkness,' in the darkness of this life and of this poor flesh, and is pursued but not captured by the darkness: by the hostile power, I mean, which sprang shamelessly upon the visible Adam, but was defeated when it encountered God. His purpose was that we might put off our garments of darkness and draw near the light, and then become perfect light, begotten of perfect light."[7]

Putting off our garments of darkness and drawing near to the light, which is at the heart of purification, begins with the fear of the Lord. "Where there is fear, there is observation of the commandments; where the commandments are observed, there is a cleansing of the flesh, that cloud that blocks the soul's vision and keeps it from seeing clearly the rays of divine illumination; but where there is cleansing, there is also illumination, and illumination is the fulfillment of desire for those eager to share in the greatest things—or in the greatest Thing, or in That which is beyond the great!"[8] Purification and illumination dispose the person to enter properly into the sacrament or mystery of baptism the next day. As Brian Matz explains, "Grace is given to initiate the process of drawing near to God; purification is the response of a person to that grace and involves conscious efforts to cultivate virtues and repel vices. Purification, in other words, facilitates proper reception of baptism, together with the enlightenment Christ intends to give through it."[9]

Gregory offers an expansive understanding of baptism by presenting not one, but five types of baptism found in Scripture. All five contribute to the process of purification. The first form of baptism is found in Paul's mystical reading of the Exodus account (1 Cor 10:1–5). Gregory preaches, "Moses baptized, but in water, and before that, in the cloud and the sea. This was by way of figure, as Paul realized. The Sea was a type of the water; the cloud, of the Spirit, the manna, of the bread of life; the drink, of the drink given by

---

5. Gregory of Nazianzus, Oration 39, 128.
6. Matz, "Baptism as Theological Intersection," 42.
7. Gregory of Nazianzus Oration 39, 128.
8. Ibid., 131.
9. Matz, "Baptism as Theological Intersection," 47.

CHAPTER EIGHT: ELEMENTS OF NATURE IN THE BIBLE   135

God."[10] The second baptism is given by John, which though it was aimed at conversion, in Gregory's estimation, "was not completely spiritual, for he does not add the phrase, 'in the Spirit.'"[11] The third baptism, which is given by Christ, includes the giving of the Spirit. "Jesus also baptizes, but in the Spirit; the Spirit is baptism's perfect completion! And can he [i.e., the Spirit] not be God—if I might add a little speculation on this side—if you become God by his gift?"[12] Gregory's aside refers to the theological debates concerning the divinity of the Holy Spirit and the Eastern spiritual emphasis on divinization (*theosis*). The fourth form of baptism involves martyrdom. "And I know of a fourth kind of baptism: that conferred by witness and blood, by which Christ himself was baptized; it is all the more venerable than the other kinds, since it is not soiled by further stains."[13] The fifth form of baptism is the ongoing process of repentance as expressed in the "baptism of tears." "That is more laborious, since the one baptized 'washes his bed and his mattress each night with tears,'" and imitates the example of countless biblical figures such as the Ninevites who donned sackcloth, the tax collector who beat his breast in prayer alongside the Pharisee, and the Canaanite woman who sought the crumbs from the master's table. Later in the oration, Gregory mentions a sixth baptism in connection with the rigorist followers of Novatus who had denied the possibility of those who lapsed during times of persecution being readmitted to the church. "If they wish, these people may follow our way and the way of Christ; but if not, let them pursue their own path. Perhaps in the next world they will be baptized with fire, that final baptism, greater and more severe, which will consume matter like straw, and annihilate the insubstantiality of all that is evil."[14]

In Oration 40, Gregory turns his attention to Christian baptism. He begins by outlining three types of births found in Scripture. "The word of Scripture recognizes three births for us: one from the body, one from baptism, and one from resurrection."[15] Focusing on the second birth, Gregory offers a list of names by which baptism is described: gift, grace, anointing, robe of incorruption, bath of rebirth, etc. Included in the list is illumination. Here Gregory is following the custom of his day. Not only was baptism commonly called illumination or enlightenment, but the baptistery was the

---

10 Gregory of Nazianzus, Oration 39, 136.
11. Ibid.
12. Ibid., 136.
13. Ibid.
14. Ibid., 138.
15. Gregory of Nazianzus, Oration 40, 99.

"place of enlightenment."[16] In the earliest sections of this extended Oration, Gregory devotes a great deal of his attention to the role of illumination in baptism and in the wider Christian life. Gregory declares, "This illumination [i.e., baptism] is radiance of souls, transformation of life, engagement of the conscience toward God. Illumination is help for our weakness, illumination is renunciation of the flesh, following of the Spirit, communion in the Word, setting right of the creature, a flood overwhelming sin, participation in light, dissolution of darkness." In short, baptism is "the most beautiful and most magnificent of the gifts of God."[17]

Gregory does not regard baptism as an isolated event of illumination, but rather as a single instance of a much wider relationship between God and humanity that is often expressed in terms of illumination. As Hofer notes, "Gregory sees light: in the first commandment at the time of creation, in the written Law, the burning bush, in the pillar of fire, in Elijah's flaming chariot, around the shepherds when the Eternal Light was mingled with the temporal light, in the star that guided the magi, on the mount of the transfiguration, in the vision of Saul on the road to Damascus, in those purified now, and in the illumination of baptism."[18] The illumination of baptism is not only a manifestation of the same light that burst forth at creation but is also a foretaste of heaven when the blessed will be with God who is Light for all eternity. Donald Winslow observes, "The images which Gregory employs to depict the quality of the new heavenly life are already familiar to us, especially the image of light. God is light, and those who approach God and become increasingly 'godlike' are themselves then called light, because they reflect the first uncreated light. To be in heaven, says Gregory, is to be filled with the light that streams from God; it is to be enlightened by the rays of Christ."[19]

Symeon the New Theologian, *Hymn 30*

As a boy, Symeon the New Theologian (949–1022) was being groomed for a life in the imperial court in Constantinople, but following a series of political upheavals and his own powerful religious experiences, at age twenty-seven he entered the Stoudios monastery located near the walls of Constantinople. He was drawn in part to Stoudios by the charismatic appeal of the monk Symeon Eulabes whom the younger Symeon regarded as his spiritual father.

16. Ferguson, "Gregory's Baptismal Theology," 70.
17. Gregory of Nazianzus, Oration 40, 100.
18. Hofer, *Christ in the Life*, 170.
19. Winslow, *Dynamics of Salvation*, 172.

His unwavering loyalty to Symeon the Elder put him at odds with his fellow monks, so he transferred to the monastery of St. Mamas where after three years he was elected abbot. Symeon soon began both a renovation of the physical structure as well as the spiritual life of the monastery. At St. Mamas he began the composition of his *Hymns of Divine Love*. Not all were happy with Symeon's changes at St. Mamas and a revolt broke out among the monks against Symeon. Symeon also had opponents in the imperial court and in 1005 he was exiled to St. Marina at Paloukiton, a short distance from the capital. It was during his time at St. Marina that he composed the bulk of his *Hymns*. In 1022 Symeon contracted dysentery and died at the age of seventy-three.[20] Our exploration of Symeon's theology will be narrowly focused on his use of the traditional image of the Holy Spirit as fire as he describes God, the human person, and the spiritual life in Hymn 30.

In the opening verse of Hymn 30 Symeon alludes to the cryptic saying of Christ, "I came to bring fire to the earth, and how I wish it were already kindled!" (Luke 12:49). In his *Seventh Ethical Discourse*, Symeon quotes the same passage. "God is a fire, and has come as fire, and has cast fire on the earth. The same Fire goes about looking for kindling to seize upon, for a ready disposition and will, in order to fall upon it and ignite it. And in those in whom it is kindled, it rises up into a great flame and reaches to the heavens, and it allows the one so enflamed neither delay nor rest."[21] The image of fire includes the fire itself (the Holy Spirit), that which is ignited by the fire (the human soul), and the effects of the blaze (the spiritual life). In the more than six hundred lines that comprise Hymn 30, Symeon moves seamlessly among the three areas.

The earth that Christ wanted to set ablaze is, according to Symeon, the collection of "souls who have the most abundant mercy . . . The Master casts fire into these souls (Matt 25:1ff) as though upon a lamp full of oil and hemp."[22] Symeon frequently refers throughout Hymn 30 to the soul as a lamp. "Understand that the lamp is my soul, and the oil is virtues, and my mind is the wick, and in it the divine fire shines and illuminates the whole house of my whole soul, and all thoughts and considerations in this house (Matt 5:15)." The illumination brought about by the divine fire pervades the entire soul, including the spiritual and moral life of the person. Symeon declares to his monks that when the fire burns, it consumes perverse thoughts

---

20. For biographical information, I am relying on McGuckin, "Symeon the New Theologian's *Hymns of Divine Eros*" and Griggs, "Introduction."

21. Symeon the New Theologian, *Seventh Ethical Discourse*, 98–99.

22. Symeon the New Theologian, Hymn 30, 231. All citations of Hymn 30 come from the Griggs translation. For a second English translation, Zboyovski, *Saint Symeon the New Theologian* which is a compilation of two works by George Maloney.

and self-conceit and when the light shines, it increases the soul's comprehension of spiritual mysteries and chases away the swarm of passions.[23]

Certainly the most magnificent gift bestowed by the divine fire of the Holy Spirit is the union of the soul with the Creator. "When the fire shines . . . it purifies the house of your soul, then the fire mingles with her [the soul] without mixing, and unites inexpressibly, and unites essentially to the essence of this soul, the whole by all means to the whole, and little by little illuminates the soul; it utterly consumes and enlightens her, and—I do not know how to express it—the two become one, the soul with her Creator, and in the soul the Creator is completely alone with the alone, He who embraces all creation in his palm."[24] In order to heighten the monks' appreciation of this great gift, Symeon asks them to consider the existence of those souls who have lost this gift and now are in hell, a place of "terrible darkness" that is "filled full of unclean and poisonous reptiles."[25] "Thus everyone who sees these terrors will groan, and lament, and will want to fall in with Christ who makes the light shine forth!"[26] Orthodox theologians place much greater weight on the Transfiguration than commonly found in Western theology. In the process of deification, believers participate in the light of Tabor, not only spiritually but physically as well. Symeon stands in this tradition. When next inviting his fellow monks to consider the souls who share in Christ's glory, Symeon remarks, "Strange marvel, my flesh, I mean the essence of my soul, yes, and of my body, participates in divine glory and flashes forth divine radiance (1 Pet 5:1)."[27]

Throughout the remainder of Hymn 30, Symeon puts the image of fire to use in various ways to describe the relationship of the soul with the Creator. First, he depicts the soul's desire to be with God as a fire. Symeon takes the soul on a journey that resembles the journey that Dante will take centuries later. Symeon envisions his soul being led from hell to heaven by God. Symeon describes the scene in terms of the prodigal son who has returned home. "He dressed me in an immaterial and radiant robe, (Luke 15:22) likewise sandals, and a ring, and a crown incorruptible, and eternal, and all foreign to the things here below."[28] The soul's time in heaven, however, is limited for as the journey continues, "the Creator led me into a perceptible and bodily tent (2 Cor 5:4), and He enclosed me in it . . . [and] led me down

---

23. Symeon the New Theologian, Hymn 30, 233–34.
24. Ibid., 234–35.
25. Ibid., 236–37.
26. Ibid., 237.
27. Ibid., 238.
28. Ibid., 239–40.

CHAPTER EIGHT: ELEMENTS OF NATURE IN THE BIBLE 139

into the perceptible and visible world, and he determined that I should live and be with those in darkness."[29] In this visible world, the soul yearns for God. "And sitting in the middle of my tent, as though enclosed in a basket or in a jar, (Exod 2:6) I cried, I wailed very much, not at all looking outside. For I was seeking Him, Him Whom I desired, (Song 3:1) for Whom I had passionate love, by Whose youthful beauty I was wounded. I was enflamed and burning, all of me set on fire."[30]

Second, not only does Symeon speak of the soul's desire for union with God as a fire, but he uses the same language to describe the union itself. "Again I saw Him within my house and within my earthen jar where suddenly He became whole, ineffably united to me, unspeakably joined, and mixed in me without mixing, like a fire in the iron itself and the light in the crystal, and He made me like a fire."[31] Later Symeon speaks in starker terms about this union: "I am a human by nature, and God by grace."[32] Symeon contends that the divine fire resides in the soul in the same way that the element of fire resides in iron. "Take a clear image for me, the image of stone and iron, for certainly there is in them the nature of fire, but it is not seen at all. But yet, when they are struck together they continually send out sparks of fire and they are immediately seen by everyone."[33] When the iron hits the stone, a spark flies and ignites the kindling. In the same way, "a spark of divine nature" can ignite the blaze within the human soul.[34] The resulting flame is a union of both human and divine essences.

The third way Symeon relates fire to the Christian life is in its power to purify, as for example, in the process of refining precious metals. Through fasting, repentance, and patient endurance, the soul is threshed so that it may ignite more quickly when touched by the divine fire. "And before you have been purified, how will your mind receive the divine illuminations? And how, tell me, from whence, from what other means shall the divine fire, (Luke 12:49) by falling into your heart, light up and ignite it, and burn, and unite it, and join, and make the creature inseparable with the creator?"[35] In his *Seventh Ethical Discourse*, Symeon compares the soul that has been cleansed of "the filth of the passions" to a clay pot being baked in the kiln. The smoke at first blackens the pot, but as it continues to bake "it becomes

29. Ibid., 240.
30. Ibid., 241.
31. Ibid., 242–43.
32. Ibid., 243.
33. Ibid., 245.
34. Ibid., 246.
35. Ibid., 247–48.

all translucent and like the fire itself, and the smoke can communicate none of the blackness to it. Just so, indeed, does the soul which has begun to burn with divine longing see first of all the murk of passions within it, billowing out like smoke in the fire of the Holy Spirit." After the impurities of the soul have been destroyed, "the divine and immaterial fire unites itself essentially to the soul" and shares in the fire like the clay pot does in the visible fire.[36]

Gustavo Gutiérrez, *We Drink from Our Own Wells*

In his *We Drink from Our Own Wells*, Gustavo Gutiérrez organizes his spiritual theology around the image of water. The title comes from a saying by Bernard of Clairvaux that in matters of spirituality all people "must drink from their own well," that is, they must draw upon their own most intimate, life-giving experiences of the Lord. Gutiérrez locates his own experiences of the Spirit at work in the lives of the poor. "In our insertion into the process of liberation in which the peoples of Latin America are now engaged, we live out the gift of faith, hope, and charity that makes us disciples of the Lord. This experience is our well. The water that rises out of it continually purifies us and smooths away any wrinkles in our manner of being Christians, at the same time supplying the vital element needed for making new ground fruitful."[37] Gutiérrez expands the image of the well to include Christ himself, the spirituality that emerges from and sustains our lives of discipleship, and the Christian community itself as it journeys throughout history.

The primary spiritual meaning of the image of the well is Christ himself who is the wellspring of eternal life (John 4:14). "The life signified in the image of water comes to us through encounter with the Lord: 'Whoever drinks of the water that I shall give him will never thirst; the water that I shall give him will become in him a spring of water welling up to eternal life' (John 4:14). In these texts [John 4:14 and 7:38] 'living water' refers to the gift of the Spirit that Jesus makes to his disciples. Drinking from one's own well, then is a 'spirit-ual' experience in the fullest sense of the word."[38] Our experience of the Spirit in Christ "is not only a point of departure but a permanent wellspring of life."[39] In his spiritual reading of the call of the first disciples, Andrew and Simon Peter, in John's Gospel, Gutiérrez reflects on the detail recorded in the Gospel account that it was "the tenth hour" or "about four o'clock in the afternoon" (John 1:39). Gutiérrez comments,

---

36. Symeon the New Theologian, *Seventh Ethical Discourse*, 99.
37. Gutiérrez, *We Drink from Our Own Wells*, 5.
38. Ibid., 37.
39. Ibid., 52.

"In its insignificance this mention of the tenth hour conveys a profound message, for we all have these 'tenth hours' in our lives, intense moments of encounter with the Lord in which our spiritual lives are nourished. They are the well from which we drink every so often."[40]

Gutiérrez also relates the image of the well to spirituality "because a spirituality is indeed like living water that springs up in the very depths of the experience of faith."[41] He outlines five themes of the spirituality that he sees emerging from the experience of the poor in Latin America: conversion, gratuitousness, joy, spiritual childhood, and community. All five themes are very traditional, but Gutiérrez gives each of them a unique treatment from a liberation perspective. Conversion is not purely a change in our inner disposition, but includes a movement into solidarity with the oppressed. Sin is both a misuse of our personal freedom and a failure to create a more just and peaceful world. The personal and social dimensions of conversion and sin are not mutually exclusive. "The encounter with the Lord in the inmost recesses of the individual does not exclude but rather calls for a similar encounter in the depths of the wretchedness in which the poor of our countries live."[42] Likewise, the profound awareness that all human action is only possible because of the grace of God does not eliminate the need for the messy work of improving the living conditions of the poor. "Many Latin American Christians are attempting to live the gratuitous love of God by committing themselves to a liberative undertaking."[43] Gutiérrez also situates joy in the midst of the struggle for justice. Despite toiling in "entrenched death-dealing conditions" of injustice caused by "the unjust hand and the greedy heart" of their oppressors, the poor live in a joy "born of the conviction that unjust mistreatment and suffering will be overcome."[44] Spiritual childhood, marked by an absolute openness to God, is the very attitude that makes possible an identification with the poor among us. "The Magnificat, which Luke places on [Mary's] lips, gives profound expression to what the practice of Latin American Christians is bringing to light once again in our day. The canticle of Mary combines a trusting self-surrender to God with a will to commitment and close association with God's favorites: the lowly, the hungry."[45] The presumption that underlies Gutiérrez's entire spiritual theology is community. The journey

---

40. Ibid., 42.
41. Ibid., 37.
42. Ibid., 99.
43. Ibid., 109.
44. Ibid., 114–15.
45. Ibid., 127.

of discipleship is essentially communitarian; there is a "basic ecclesial dimension of walking according to the Spirit."[46]

It is in the life of the community that we find the third sense in which Gutiérrez employs the image of the well in his theology. "Spirituality is a community enterprise. It is the passage of a people through the solitude and dangers of the desert, as it carves out its own way in the following of Jesus Christ. This spiritual experience is the well from which we must drink."[47]

The experience of the individual within the community is not one free of loneliness, weariness, or despair. Neither is the life of the community immune from exploitation, eternal threats, and even killings. Despite the realities of both personal and communal existence, the Christian community walks by a faith in the Risen Lord. The sharing in the Eucharist celebrates the hope that the God of life will have the final word in human history. "The faith and hope in the God of life that provide a shelter in the situation of death and struggle for life in which the poor and oppressed of Latin America are now living—they are the well from which we must drink if we want to be faithful to Jesus."[48]

The Revitalization of the Biblical Imagery of the Elements of Nature

In his fifteenth *Tractate on the Gospel of John*, Augustine reflects on the story of the Samaritan woman at the well (John 4:4–42), an episode that he describes as "full of mysteries and pregnant with symbols."[49] Like the "evangelist John [who] soars to greater heights like an eagle," Augustine hopes to lead his listeners from an earthly, carnal reading of the story to a heavenly, spiritual understanding of this encounter.[50] Underlying this hope is Augustine's theology of the Incarnation. As John Norris writes, "Augustine interprets Scripture in the *Tractatus in Evangelium Ioannis* according to his understanding of God's revelation to humanity through the incarnation of the Word . . . In the Incarnation, the Word accommodates himself to humanity's capacity for knowledge, dwelling beneath the cover of flesh so that humanity can progress from a knowledge of Christ in the flesh to a knowledge of the Word in the beginning . . . God speaks to humanity in signs and figures, and the greatest of these sacra-

46. Ibid., 129.
47. Ibid., 137.
48. Ibid., 32.
49. Augustine, *Tractate 15*, 80.
50. Ibid., 78.

ments is the Incarnation."[51] Through a spiritual reading of the signs and figures revealed in the Gospel of John, the reader can soar to the heights of understanding regarding Christ's offer of living water.

Augustine wastes no time plunging into the mystery of the Incarnation reflected in the story. "'Jesus, therefore, wearied from the journey, was sitting thus at the spring. It was about the sixth hour.' Now the mysteries begin."[52] The first mystery is the weariness of Christ. For Augustine, Christ's weariness signifies the journey of the Word. "So therefore Jesus was weak, wearied from the journey. His journey is his flesh, assumed for us... Therefore, because he deigned to come to us in this manner, that he appeared in the form of a servant by assuming flesh, the very assumption of flesh is his journey."[53] The second mystery is the reference to the sixth hour, which Augustine takes to mean the sixth age of the world. Human history follows into six ages: Adam to Noah, Noah to Abraham, Abraham to David, David to the Babylonian captivity, the Babylonian captivity to John the Baptist and the time of Christ onward. This scheme echoes Paul's contention that "when the fullness of time had come, God sent his Son" (Gal 4:4). Finally, the well represents the earth. As Augustine explains in his commentary on the Samaritan woman at the well found in his *Eighty-Three Different Questions*, "I see in the well a gloomy depth. I am therefore led to understand [by this] the lowest parts of the universe, i.e. the earth."[54]

Having presented the orthodox understanding of Christ's two natures, Augustine next turns his attention to Christ's offer of living water to the woman. According to Augustine, the woman mystically represents the church and the living water of which Christ speaks is the Holy Spirit. Over the course of her conversation with Christ, the woman slowly realizes the magnitude of the gift being offered to her. When Christ offers her living water, the woman misunderstands. "What is clearer, that he promised not visible water, but invisible? What is clearer, that he spoke, not in a physical sense, but in a spiritual one? Yet that woman still understands the physical sense; she was delighted not to thirst and thought that this was promised her by the Lord according to the flesh."[55] For Augustine, the well represents the pleasures of this world and the water jar is a symbol of human desire. The woman's previous five husbands that Jesus mentions spiritually represent the five senses, so Christ's comment to the woman that she should call

---

51. Norris, "Theological Structure of Augustine's Exegesis," 385.
52. Augustine, *Tractate 15*, 81.
53. Ibid., 82.
54. Augustine, "Question 64," 128.
55. Augustine, *Tractate 15*, 86.

her husband is actually taken to mean, "bring forth your understanding."[56] There is to be sure a patriarchal element in Augustine's interpretation on this point, but with the gift of understanding, the soul begins to truly grasp the significance of Christ's offer. "It is still a weak soul which is ruled by these five senses and lives under these five husbands," but if the soul is properly trained in wisdom, later it embraces the one "true and licit husband, both better than they [the five senses], and who may rule better, and who may rule for eternity, cultivate for eternity, instruct for eternity."[57] As her understanding increases, the woman recognizes that Jesus is a prophet and indeed the Messiah, so she leaves her water jug (human desire) behind to proclaim the good news. "Therefore she cast aside the water jar which was no longer useful, but a burden; for she was eagerly longing to be satiated with that water [the Holy Spirit]."[58] The people of the town proclaim Christ as the Savior of the world. On a final note, Christ remaining with them for two more days represents for Augustine the two commands of love.

Just as Augustine's spiritual reading of the story of the Samaritan woman captures many of the concerns of the orthodox school of thought, Robert C. Neville ably defends the indispensable role that symbols such as water and light play in liberal theology in connecting us with the divine. Neville describes theology as "symbolic engagement" with "ultimacy." "The general thesis of the 'symbolic engagement hypothesis' is that reflection on ultimate matters takes place by means of symbols through which ultimacy is engaged and thereby interpreted."[59] The complex process of interpretation involves a number of elements ranging from the interpreter's own temperament to the culture's network of signs, but it is only through the act of interpretation that we "transform brute stimuli into the means for shaping intelligent, discrimination, and imaginative life."[60] Symbols play a pivotal role in this act of interpretation. Religious symbols in particular refer to what Neville labels "finite/infinite contrasts." A finite/infinite contrast" such as heaven and earth demarcates the sacred from the profane, and in doing so, provides the framework in which persons can discern the meaning and purpose of their lives, understand their place in the universe, and determine what is of ultimate value. Christians speak of the infinite or the ultimate in, for example, spatial terms (a "schema"), when they say that the goal of human existence is to go to heaven. Fur-

---

56. Ibid., 88.
57. Ibid., 91.
58. Ibid., 97.
59. Neville, *On the Scope and Truth of Theology*, 1.
60. Neville, "Contextualization," 76.

CHAPTER EIGHT: ELEMENTS OF NATURE IN THE BIBLE 145

thermore images ("schema-images") of heaven may include a garden, a throne room, a mansion, or a banquet table.[61]

We can gain a better understanding of Neville's theoretical points by examining one of his sermons. Delivered during Advent, the sermon "Waiting for the Light" focuses on three texts dealing with the theme of light: Isaiah 2:1-5, Romans 13:11-14, and Matthew 24:36-44. Turning to Paul's admonition to the church at Rome to wake from their sleep, lay aside their works of darkness, and put on the armor of light (Rom 13:11-14), Neville states, "The dream time and space, said Paul, is not some mythic future place but rather our present life as sleepwalkers. Even we who are believers are dreaming now, said Paul. Wake up to the morning light of true time and peace."[62] The juxtaposition of "dream time" and "true time" suggests that there are two ways of perceiving present reality, one illusionary, the other genuine. "As dreaming, we think that the powers of the world must sweep aside our puny efforts and that no effort is worth it; were we awake, we would see that salvation comes from God, not from our efforts, and that the power of our lives is divine light-power."[63] The finite/infinite contrast appears here as the contrast between "the powers of the world" and the "divine light-power." The goal of human existence is "to awaken to the presence of the king of love" and walk in the light of the Lord. "For when we have passed from sleep to waking, we know that our true time, our numbered set of days, is in the eternity of God and that our true place, our field of battle, of duty and love, is only in God's immensity. We are real only within the power of God's creative act, and the illusion that can exist apart from God, where God can be kept at a distance or postponed, is only a dream that enslaves. The divine light of salvation shines through us and makes us incandescent."[64]

Neville identifies Hauerwas's Gifford Lectures, *With the Grain of the Universe*, as "a magisterial presentation of a conception of theology apparently in almost diametrical opposition to my own."[65] Neville criticizes Hauerwas and other postliberals for making Christian theology primarily a matter of describing Christian identity. "Hauerwas and the people in his line can use the argument that a Christian theologian who disagrees with them is not really a Christian because he or she does not conform to their

---

61. Neville, *Religion in Late Modernity*, 48. Natural elements—fire, water, the abyss, and light—appear in variety of religious traditions, see Neville, *Truth of Broken Symbols*, 94–95.

62. Neville, "Watch for the Light," 35.

63. Ibid.

64. Ibid., 36.

65. Neville, *On the Scope and Truth of Theology*, xiii.

canon of orthodox Christian identity... Christian identity, I argue, should follow the truth rather than substitute self-proclamation of some identity for criteria of truth."[66] Neville also faults postliberals for not providing a stronger mechanism for correcting errors within the Christian tradition itself. Despite the clear differences in theological method between Neville and Hauerwas, there is some overlap in the role that interpretation plays in Neville's theology and the role that vision plays in Hauerwas's. Interpretation and vision both involve seeing the world in a specific way. Neville states, "Interpretation is the intentional act of taking reality to be the way the symbols say it is."[67] In a similar vein, Hauerwas writes, "Christianity can be understood as but one set of coherent metaphors and stories that constitute an understanding of the nature of the world and a possible life plan," and concludes, "to be 'moral' involves learning to see the world in a way that our lives have coherence and unity."[68]

Both Neville's liberal emphasis on interpretation and Hauerwas's postliberal emphasis on vision intersect with the interests of theologians who are exploring more fully the relationship of rhetoric and Christian theology. David S. Cunningham argues that "Christian theology is best understood as *persuasive argument*. Theologians are involved not in the exchange of propositions, nor even in edifying 'conversations,' but in debates, disputes, and arguments. Theologians are always seeking to persuade others—to persuade themselves—of a particular understanding of the Christian faith."[69] Certainly Cunningham's emphasis on the rhetorical nature of theology could move in an orthodox, liberal, or postmodern direction, but I will follow one postliberal thread: the relationship between rhetorical theology and the postliberal claim that rationality is narrative-dependent. William Placher admits, "I do not know how to defend Christian faith—or any belief system—in terms that all rational human beings would have to accept. We are within the context of some tradition, and we begin with the rules and assumptions a particular conversation partner happens to share."[70] How, then, should Christian theology proceed? It must, according to Placher, take the form of "a description of the world as seen from a Christian perspective that draws what persuasive power it has from the coherence and richness of the whole."[71]

---

66. Ibid., xv.
67. Neville, *Religion in Late Modernity*, 59.
68. Hauerwas, "Vision, Stories, and Character," 169–70.
69. Cunningham, *Faithful Persuasion*, 5. Emphasis original.
70. Placher, *Unapologetic Theology*, 123.
71. Ibid., 135.

Drawing upon the image of water, Cunningham offers what he hopes is a persuasive Christian reconceptualization of the doctrine of the Trinity. Cunningham notes, "The practice of trinitarian theology is an attempt to make important claims about the nature of God and of God's relationship to the world ... New language cannot be accepted simply because it 'speaks to us today'; it must be tested in both theory and practice. We thus need to develop language that not only addresses the contemporary rhetorical context, but also remains attentive to the central claims of trinitarian doctrine."[72] To that end, he asks us to "imagine a spring of water coming up out of the ground and then flowing out to nourish the surrounding landscape. Here we have movement, procession, a going-out-from-itself-to-itself."[73] Attentive to the traditional elements of Trinitarian doctrine (e.g., mutual coinherence, processions, relations), Cunningham proposes that we speak of God as Source, Wellspring, and Living Water. "The Wellspring is always coming forth from the Source (again: 'eternally begotten of the Father,' in the most common English translation of the creed), and the Living Waters always flowing out to nurture the believing community."[74] Such an image, argues Cunningham, is "intelligible, concrete, and persuasive" and rightly describes the world as "created, redeemed, and sustained by God."[75]

Marcus Borg puts the image of water to use in a postmodern vein when he compares faith to floating.[76] "Faith as *fiducia* is trusting in the buoyancy of God. Soren Kierkegaard (1813–55), one of the most important nineteenth-century thinkers in religion and philosophy, said faith is like floating in seventy thousand fathoms of water ... If we are fearful and struggle as we float in an immeasurably deep body of water, we sink and drown. But if we trust that the water will keep us up, we float."[77] This understanding of faith emphasizes that it is matter of trust and not belief. Borg warns, "You can believe all the right things and still be miserable. You can believe all the right things and still be relatively unchanged. Believing a set of claims to be true has very little transforming power."[78] Faith is trust (*fiducia*), fidelity (*fidelitas*), and a vision

72. Cunningham, *These Three Are One*, 73.
73. Cunningham, "What Do We Mean," 83–84.
74. Ibid., 85.
75. Ibid., 90.
76. Borg's work defies classification. Many of his positions would easily fall into the liberal camp. He draws upon Lindbeck in *Speaking Christian*, 6, and *The Heart of Christianity*, 213–14 (and see 192 on Christian identity). I will focus on his postmodern tendencies in *Reading the Bible*; however, he also makes it clear that "some postmodern movements strike me as dead ends" (17).
77. Borg, *Speaking Christian*, 122.
78. Borg, *Heart of Christianity*, 30–31.

(*visio*) of the totality of life. Citing the example of Luther, Borg writes, "His transformation occurred through an experience of radical grace that transformed how he saw (*visio*), led him to see that faith was about trusting God (*fiducia*), and led him to a life of faithfulness (*fidelitas*) to God."[79] In terms of our own lives, faith as trust rather than belief changes how we view both life and death. "In this life, a radical centering on God leads to a deepening trust that transforms the way we see and live our lives . . . And in our deaths, dying means trusting in the buoyancy of God, that the one who carried us in this life is the one into whom we die."[80]

Borg believes that not only is faith understood as trust more in keeping with the original sense of the term, but it is more responsive to the present cultural mind-set of the West. "*We live on the boundary of postmodernity*," claims Borg.[81] He highlights three characteristics of this emerging postmodern outlook. "First, postmodernity is marked by the realization that modernity itself is a culturally conditioned, relative historical construction." With the passage of time, we can see how worldviews assumed to be true by past generations gave way to new understandings of the universe, and we have no reason to expect that our present worldview might itself eventually be added to the scrap heap of history. "Second, postmodernity is marked by a turn to experience. In a time when traditional religious teachings have become suspect, we tend to trust that which can be known in our experience." This accounts for the weight given to faith understood as trust rather than belief. "Third, postmodernity is marked by a movement beyond fact fundamentalism [the belief that truth consists only of facts, not metaphors] to the realization that stories can be true without being literally and factually true."[82]

The image of floating in postmodern thought can be taken in one of two ways. In one sense it can imply being set adrift. We have no moorings and so we drift intellectually, morally, and spiritually. With no fixed point by which to navigate our course, we simply float from place to place.[83]

---

79. Ibid., 37.
80. Ibid.
81. Borg, *Reading the Bible*, 17. Emphasis original.
82. Ibid.

83. I certainly claim no expertise in the area of American postmodern literature, but I do find it interesting that the idea of floating and meaningless are joined in *The Floating Opera*. "A text that we might readily identify as the first work of American postmodernism, *The Floating Opera* [by John Barth] an overtly metafictional piece that articulates its own *raison d'être*, for the text as well as the main character/narrator, by denying the possibility of ever locating a purpose, a meaning, for the text (or character)" (Toth, *Passing of Postmodernism*, 129).

There is no real progress, only change. In a second, more positive sense, floating suggests resting comfortably on the surface of the great unknown. Commenting on the nature of mystical experience, Borg writes, "The most abstracted generic terms for what is experienced include 'reality itself,' 'ultimate reality,' or 'Reality' with a capital *R*; 'what is' when our words fall away, or 'is-ness without limits'—without the limits created by our language and categories. Buddhists sometimes speak of it as 'suchness'—the way things are before our categorizations. Williams James called it 'a more,' a stupendous wondrous 'more' that is more than what we had imagined even as it also is present everywhere and capable of being experienced anywhere."[84] The "more" to which James referred is powerfully conveyed by images of the vast ocean's waves crashing on the shore, the heat emanating from a crackling fire on a cold winter's night, or the dawn's light that breaks across the horizon at the start of each day.

Discussion Questions

1. In what way is Christ's baptism rightly called "the Day of Lights"?
2. Why is light imagery associated with Christ?
3. How is the soul a lamp?
4. Why is it that fire is associated with both God (as we see in the stories of the burning bush and Pentecost) and Satan (as in the passage regarding hell)?
5. In what poems or stories does water play a prominent role? What does water symbolize in these works?
6. What is your assessment of Augustine's interpretation of the story of the Samaritan woman at the well?
7. Is Cunningham's analogy of water, in discussing the Trinity, compelling?

Suggested Reading

For an introduction to Gregory of Nazianzus, see Brian E. Daley, "Introduction" to *Gregory of Nazianzus* (New York: Routledge, 2006). On specific areas of Gregory's theology, see Christopher Beeley, *Gregory of Nazianzus on the Trinity and the Knowledge of God* (New York: Oxford University

84. Borg, *Convictions*, 42–43.

Press, 2008) and Andrew Hofer, *Christ in the Life and Teaching of Gregory of Nazianzus* (Oxford: Oxford University Press, 2013). For an introduction to Symeon the New Theologian, see David Griggs, "Introduction" to *Divine Eros* (Crestwood, NY: St. Vladimir's Seminary Press, 2010). See also John Anthony McGuckin, "The Luminous Vision in Eleventh-century Byzantium: Interpreting the Biblical and Theological Paradigms of St Symeon the New Theologian" in Margaret Mullett and Anthony Kirby, *Work and Worship at the Theotokos Evergetis 1050-1200* (Belfast: Belfast Byzantine Enterprises, 1997). For a helpful study of Gutiérrez's spiritual theology, see Margaret McDonald, *Christian Life and Liberation: The Basis for a Christian Spirituality in the Thought of Gustavo Gutiérrez* (PhD diss., Catholic University of America, 1996).

Chapter Nine: Persons in the Bible

THE GREAT CHARACTERS IN both fiction and non-fiction entertain us, inspire us, and on occasion, haunt us. In the same way, the characters in the biblical narrative—whether we regard them as fictional (Jonah) or historical (Paul) or somewhere in between—enjoy an exalted status in the minds of Christian readers. Some of them are moral examples to be emulated, others are tragic figures in a cautionary tale or pivotal players in the plan of salvation. Whatever their role, readers see in these characters' stories a larger spiritual truth that transcends the particularities of time and place. In this chapter we will examine three works by thinkers for whom the biblical characters of Jacob, Elijah, and Mary symbolize in some way the deeper dynamics of the Christian journey to God: Richard of St. Victor's *The Twelve Patriarchs*, Edith Stein's "On the History and Spirit of Carmel" (1935), and Elizabeth Johnson's *Truly Our Sister* (2003).

Richard of St. Victor, *Twelve Patriarchs*

Like Achard whom we discussed earlier, Richard was one of the celebrated biblical expositors of the Abbey of St. Victor near Paris where he served as prior from 1162 until his death in 1173. Like his Victorine counterpart, Hugh, who developed itineraries of the spiritual journey focused on the descriptions of Noah's ark and the ark of the covenant, Richard developed a spiritual theology based on the birth order of Jacob's thirteen children with his wives Rachel and Leah and their maidservants, Bilhah and Zilpah. As Grover Zinn notes: "The history of Jacob's children yields in its deeper sense the moral history of the soul as it moves along the path toward the realization of a life of asceticism and contemplation."[1] The name of each of Jacob's children or the events in each child's life provide a clue to the sequence of steps along the soul's journey, culminating with the birth of Benjamin who, based on the Vulgate translation of Ps 67:28, was a "young man in ecstasy of mind."

---

1. Zinn, "Personification Allegory and Visions of Light," 192.

Richard's reading of the Jacob story tests the patience of many modern readers, but the effort typically yields some interesting insights. With that, we begin. Jacob, or Israel ("the one who sees God"), represents the intellectual soul and Rachel and Leah represent the major division of the soul's powers, reason, and affection (including the will, feelings, and desires) respectively.[2] "Just as it belongs to Rachel to meditate, to contemplate, to distinguish and to understand; so certainly it pertains to Leah to weep, to groan, to grieve and to sigh."[3] Rachel symbolizes the pursuit of truth and wisdom; Leah represents the cultivation of virtue and the pursuit of justice. Jacob ardently desires Rachel who is wisdom (Wis 7:29 and 8:1–2), but must labor for seven years for the privilege of marrying her. Leah (who is "laborious") represents perfect justice under whose demands (e.g., forgiving our enemies) we toil. Leah's poor eyesight may suggest that she errs in her judgement, but in fact she will produce the most offspring with Jacob. Despite this, Jacob values his relationship with Rachel above all else. "What can be sweeter or more joyful than to raise up the eye of the mind to contemplation of highest wisdom? When reason is extended for this contemplating it is deservedly honored with the name of Rachel. Rachel is interpreted 'beginning of vision' or 'a sheep.'"[4] Scripture, furthermore, is "Rachel's bedchamber" where "divine wisdom is hidden beneath the veil of attractive allegories . . . Rachel is sought in such a chamber as often as spiritual understanding is sought out in sacred reading. But so long as we are incapable of penetrating sublime things, we do not find the long-desired, diligently sought Rachel."[5]

Richard introduces the next layer of complexity into his narrative when he discusses the role played by the handmaids Bilhah (Bala) and Zilpah (Zelpha). Bilhah (imagination) serves Rachel (reason) while Zilpah (sensation) serves Leah (affection). Bilhah whose name means "inveterate" is true to her name and constantly brings thoughts and images to reason (Rachel). Even in a darkened and silent room, when the activity of the senses subsides, Bilhah (imagination) continues to be "garrulous."[6] Zilpah, whose name means "gaping mouth" represents sensation.[7] "It is sensation who is accustomed to season foods of carnal delights, to serve them to affection, to invite enjoyment of them before the proper time and to provoke beyond

---

2. McGinn, *Growth of Mysticism*, 402.
3. Richard of St. Victor, *Twelve Patriarchs*, 57.
4. Ibid., 55.
5. Ibid., 56.
6. Ibid., 58–59.
7. Ibid., 59.

measure."[8] The handmaids perform indispensable roles in the life of the soul. "For without imagination, reason would know nothing; without sensation, affection would have sense of nothing."[9] Despite the invaluable roles Bilhah and Zilpah play in the life of the soul, they also have the potential to disrupt the soul. Sensation can inflame "the affection of the soul with longing for carnal pleasures" and imagination "makes noise in the ears of the heart with so much importunity" that reason cannot escape their influence.[10]

The figures of Rachel, Leah, Bilhah, and Zilpah represent the basic framework of Richard's psychology. In the order of the children born to these four women, Richard finds a sequence in the spiritual maturation of a person that allows him/her to enter into a contemplative state. Each woman represents a specific type of development according to Zinn: "the children of Leah discipline the will; those of Bilhah thoughts; those of Zelpha deeds; and Rachel's two children govern the entire life of asceticism and signify contemplation."[11] The first four children are born to Leah: Rueben (fear of the Lord), Simeon (grief), Levi (hope of forgiveness), and Judah (love of justice). Rueben represents the fear of the Lord which is the beginning of wisdom (Ps 111:10). His life, of course, is a cautionary tale. Despite being "son of vision . . . he is blind. . . and does not foresee future evils, is not ashamed of his depravity and is not terrified of divine power." (Gen 35:22, 49:4). As the fear of punishment increases so too does the soul's grief over his or her sins in the birth of Simeon. Again we find a cautionary tale in that Jacob will rebuke Simeon and Levi who will be born next, for their act of revenge against Hamor and Shechem (Gen 34:30–31, 49:5–7). Levi representing hope of forgiveness, follows after fear of the Lord and grief over one's sins. Perhaps with Levi's act of revenge in mind, Richard warns, "For whoever compliments himself with impunity after committing crimes without satisfaction is not so much raised by hope as he is thrown down by presumption."[12] Following forgiveness comes love. An intimacy of the soul with God begins to develop as represented by the birth of Judah ("confessing"). Love confesses both the blessings bestowed by God and the sins that we have committed, but above all, it professes the truth.

8. Ibid., 58.

9. Richard of St. Victor, *Twelve Patriarchs*, 57. Richard clouds the issue a bit by having imagination (Bilhah) serve both reason (Rachel) and sensation (Zilpah): "Therefore the imagination (inasmuch as she is a handmaid) runs between mistress and servant, between reason and sense" (58).

10. Ibid., 58–59.

11. Zinn, "Personification Allegory and Visions of Light," 192.

12. Richard of St. Victor, *Twelve Patriarchs*, 62.

Seeing that Leah is so fruitful, Rachel (reason) desires offspring of her own. Judah is the love of the highest good and now Rachel wants to know the highest good. Bilhah (imagination) gives birth to Dan and Napthali, who represent the two functions of the imagination, judgment and understanding. "Dan knows nothing except corporeal things, but nevertheless he examines things that are far removed from bodily sense. Naphtali rises to the understanding of invisible things by means of the form of visible things."[13] Dan reminds the soul of the judgement that is to come. It is Naphtali who allows us to move from the literal to a spiritual understanding of Scripture. When, for example, Scripture speaks of a land flowing with milk and honey or the heavenly Jerusalem having walls of precious stones, Naphtali understands this spiritually and "seeks what is contained there mystically."[14] Zilpah now gives birth to Gad (abstinence) and Asher (patience). "Therefore, rigor of abstinence is rightly called Gad, that is happiness, who everywhere tramples underfoot the allurements of the world that he despises."[15] Asher patiently endures the trials and tribulations of life. The four children born to Bilhah and Zilpah are the guardians of the "city of our conscience."[16] Bilhah's children (Dan and Naphtali) keep watch on the internal life of the soul while Zilpah's children (Gad, Asher) guard against enemies attacking the person from outside.

With the city of conscience properly guarded, the soul can begin to experience joy represented by Leah's next son, Issachar ("reward"). In Genesis Issachar is described as "a strong ass, living between boundaries."[17] The joyful soul lives on the boundary between heaven and earth. Issachar's younger brother, Zebulun, who is a "dwelling place of fortitude" lived near the shore. "Therefore he sets himself against the perils of those whom he perceives to be fatigued by constant storms of persecution."[18] The last of the "ordered affections"[19] represented by the children of Leah is Dinah who stands for shame. As Bernard McGinn makes clear: "Ordered shame is not the external shamefulness we feel before other people for some fault or solecism, but the internal judgment by which conscience accuses us because of our continuing sinfulness."[20] For Richard, Simeon and Levi's

13. Ibid., 70.
14. Ibid.
15. Ibid., 79.
16. Ibid., 84.
17. Ibid., 92.
18. Ibid., 99.
19. Ibid., 60.
20. McGinn, *Growth of Mysticism*, 403–4.

slaughter of the men of Shechem in retaliation for the rape of Dinah illustrates "how evil it is for grief and hope [of forgiveness] to exceed the limit."[21] The virtues, if not properly directed in specific situations, can become vices that produce calamitous results.

The last two children born to Jacob and Rachel are Joseph and Benjamin. Joseph represents discretion. While belonging to reason, discretion develops through trial and error. "But we only deserve such a son late since we are not educated to the perfection of discretion without a great deal of practice nor except by a great deal of experience."[22] It is discretion that is rewarded by the soul as it is Joseph who receives a coat of many colors from his father. "This is that Joseph who alone among the brothers is clothed in a tunic reaching to the ankles because only that action which is moderated by the prudence of discretion is brought to such a limit of consummation and of its necessary end."[23] The birth of Benjamin is the culmination of the soul's journey to contemplation of God. The death of Rachel in childbirth symbolizes the "death" of reason as the soul passes over into contemplation. "And so when Benjamin is born, Rachel dies, because the mind, having been carried away to contemplation, experiences how great the failure of human reason is."[24] Benjamin's descent into Egypt is the soul's return to the world of change, and the embrace of the brothers Joseph and Benjamin is the embrace of understanding and prudence. "In the death of Rachel contemplation ascends above reason; in the entry of Benjamin into Egypt contemplation descends to the imagination; in the affectionate kissing of Benjamin and Joseph human reason gives applause to divine showing."[25]

Edith Stein, "On the History and Spirit of Carmel" (1935)

In *Twelve Patriarchs*, the Augustinian Richard of St. Victor presents a moral, allegorical reading of the story of Jacob's children. In "On the History and Spirit of Carmel" the Carmelite Edith Stein offers an example of what Kierkegaard called "contemporaneity" with a biblical figure. Rather than merely imitating the example of a figure who lived centuries ago, Stein describes Elijah as a living presence within her Carmelite monastery. For Stein, "Mt. Carmel" refers not only to the site in Israel, but to the Carmelite communities spread throughout the world. "We who live in Carmel and

21. Richard of St. Victor, *Twelve Patriarchs*, 123.
22. Ibid., 124.
23. Ibid., 125.
24. Ibid., 131.
25. Ibid., 147.

who daily call on our Holy Father Elijah in prayer know that for us he is not a shadowy figure out of the dim past. His spirit is active among us in a vital tradition and determines how we live."[26] The figure of Elijah would have particular resonance in the life of Stein who was born into a Jewish family in 1891 in Breslau, Germany (present-day Poland). In her teen years, she didn't believe in God, but her study of phenomenology under Edmund Husserl opened her thinking up to the possibility of religious faith. She was one of the first women in Germany to earn a doctoral degree, but the sexism and anti-Semitism of her day stalled her academic career. It was her reading Teresa of Avila's *Life* that proved the catalyst for her decision to be baptized into the Catholic faith in 1922. In 1933 she entered the Carmelite monastery at Cologne. With the rising Nazi repression, Stein transferred to the Carmelite community in Echt in the Netherlands in 1938. In response to a pastoral letter composed by the bishops of the Netherlands condemning the Nazi persecution of the Jews, the Nazis ordered the deportation of all Catholics of Jewish descent from the Netherlands. In August 1942, Stein and her sister, who also had converted, were sent to Auschwitz where they were soon executed in the gas chamber.

Elijah has always figured prominently in the history and theology of the Carmelites. Unlike religious orders such as the Franciscans or the Dominicans, the Carmelites have no original founder. In the late twelfth century, Christian pilgrims to the Holy Land began to live in loosely knit communities on the western slopes of Mount Carmel. Eventually the community approached Albert, the Latin Patriarch of Jerusalem, for a "formula of life," which was the basis for the eventual Rule of the Carmelites. When the political situation around Carmel began to shift, the Carmelites migrated westward to Europe and were forced to redefine their way of life in this new urban environment. In 1281 the Carmelites took stock of their evolving tradition and produced their *Constitutions*, the Introduction to which is known as the *Rubrica Prima*. The Fourth Lateran Council (1215) had prohibited the establishment of new religious orders, and so in the *Rubrica Prima* we find the bold claim that the Carmelites stand in a direct line of succession with Elijah himself.

> Since some young brothers in the Order do not know how to reply truthfully to those who wish to know how and where our Order originated, we want to provide them with a written account of how to respond to such demands. We say that, on the evidence of trustworthy witnesses, that from the time of the prophets Elijah and Elisha, the holy fathers of both the Old and

---

26. Stein, "On the History and Spirit of Carmel," 1.

> the New Testaments have lived devotedly on Mount Carmel, true lovers of the solitude of that mountain for the contemplation of heavenly things. There near the fountain of Saint Elijah, without any doubt, they lived praiseworthy lives, and their successors continuously thereafter.[27]

The claim that the Carmelites stand in a direct line of succession with Elijah would be regarded as dubious to modern historians, but it expresses the deep impression that Elijah and Mt. Carmel made on the psyche of the early Carmelites and the influence that they continue to exert on Carmelite self-understanding to this day.

A century after the *Constitutions* were composed, Felip Ribot, a Carmelite prior from the Catalonian province compiled a history of the Carmelites entitled, *The Ten Books of the Way of Life and Great Deeds of the Carmelites*. The Carmelite Wilfrid McGreal notes, "After the Rule it is possibly the key work in any understanding of Carmelite spirituality and certainly from 1400 onwards dominated the Carmelites' historical thinking of their vision of the Order."[28] In Book One, Ribot presents a conversation between John XLIV, bishop of Jerusalem, and the monk Caprasius. In this account, John identifies Elijah as the first monk. "This prophet of God, Elijah, was the first leader of monks, from whom this holy and ancient way of life took its origin. For he, having reached divine contemplation and filled with the desire for higher things, withdrew far from the cities, and laying aside all earthly and worldly things, was the first to begin to devote himself to following the religious and prophetic eremitical life, which, under the inspiration and command of the Holy Spirit, he initiated and formulated."[29] This is the tradition in which Edith Stein stands—one that views Elijah as the prototype of the monk who takes vows of poverty, chastity, and obedience. In her piece "On the History and Spirit of Carmel," Stein writes,

> Holy Father Elijah succinctly says what is most important in the first words of his that Scriptures give us. He says to King Ahab who worshiped idols (1 Kgs 17:1), "As the Lord the God of Israel lives, before whom I stand, there shall be neither dew nor rain these years, except by my word."
>
> To stand before the face of the living God—that is our vocation. The holy prophet set us an example. He stood before God's face because this was the eternal treasure for whose sake he gave up

---

27. Quoted in Bergstrom-Allen, *Climbing the Mountain*, 116.
28. McGreal, *At the Fountain of Elijah*, 38–39, 216.
29. Ribot, *Ten Books on the Way of Life*, 9.

all earthly goods... So he is for us an example of the gospel poverty that we have vowed, an authentic prototype of the Savior.[30]

Elijah trusts entirely in the Lord for his sustenance. Whether it be from a raven or a widow, Elijah receives his daily bread through divine workings. Elijah's poverty, in short, is the outward expression of his spiritual reliance on the Lord. Stein emphasizes the solitariness of Elijah's existence. "Elijah stands before God's face because all of his love belongs to the Lord. He lives outside all natural human relationships. We hear nothing of his father and mother, nothing of a wife or child."[31] This solitary existence enables Elijah to confront Ahab and Jezebel without fear of reprisal against his family.

Along with Edith Stein, another prominent Carmelite thinker of the twentieth century was Titus Brandsma. In 1935, Brandsma became the chaplain of the Dutch Catholic journalists and gradually became an outspoken critic of the Nazis. When the Nazis invaded the Netherlands in 1940, Brandsma pressed Catholic publishers to refuse advertising or propaganda from the Nazis. In January, 1942, the Nazis arrested him and after being detained in a series of facilities, he was eventually moved to Dachau where in July of that year he was given a lethal injection. In McGreal's estimation, "Titus offered a prophetic voice at a time when the gospel values were under attack. Like Elijah, he was called to face and challenge the establishment. I believe he was conscious that his calling had to include this social-political dimension."[32] Free from the natural bonds of marriage and family, figures like Elijah and Brandsma are uniquely positioned to speak truth to power.

In addition to his poverty and chastity, Stein highlights Elijah's life of obedience to the commands of God. "The prophet, who serves the Lord in complete purity of heart and completely stripped of everything earthly, is also a model of obedience. He stands before God's face like the angels before the eternal throne, awaiting God's sign, always ready to serve. Elijah has no other will than the will of his Lord."[33] This obedience to the will of the Lord can bring with it a heavy price. Not only does Elijah call down fire from heaven, he is also the broken man under the broom tree in the desert asking the Lord to take his life. It was this "dark night" in the spiritual journey that was so poignantly described by the Carmelite, St. John of the Cross. While clear-eyed about the struggles of the spiritual life, Stein doesn't allow those dark nights to define the spirit of Carmel: "The walls of our monasteries

---

30. Stein, "History and Spirit of Carmel," 1–2.
31. Ibid., 2.
32. McGreal, *At the Fountain of Elijah*, 100–101. I am relying on chapter 8 of McGreal for biographical information on Brandsma.
33. Stein, "On the History and Spirit of Carmel," 2.

enclose a narrow space. To erect the structure of holiness in it, one must dig deep and build high, must descend into the depths of the dark night of one's own nothingness in order to be raised up high into the sunlight of divine love and compassion."[34]

Elizabeth Johnson, *Truly Our Sister* (2003)

In the opening pages of her work *Truly Our Sister*, Elizabeth Johnson poses the question: "What would be a theologically sound, ecumenically fruitful, spiritually empowering, ethically challenging, and socially liberating interpretation of Mary for the twenty-first century?"[35] In her engagement with that question, Johnson explores the history of Catholic theology about Mary as well as modern feminist critiques of certain past versions of Marian theology, modern historical findings on life in first-century Galilee, and the exegetical issues involved in each of the stories involving Mary in the New Testament. We will focus on Johnson's commentary on three of the biblical accounts featuring Mary in Luke and Acts.

The Annunciation (Luke 1:26–38) scene, especially Mary's "fiat" ("Let it be"), plays a vital role in the development of Marian theology in both the Catholic and Orthodox traditions. Johnson argues that "no other text has had more influence on the development of mariology, for better or worse. At its worst, the emphasis of some interpreters on the phrasing of Mary's response, 'be it done to me according to your word,' has led to that ideal of woman as obedient handmaid, passively receptive to male commands, which women today find so obnoxious."[36]

Johnson, however, contends that not all is lost; we can "draw this rich scene into a liberating memory replete with 'lessons of encouragement'"[37] if we focus on the passage's literary structure, the working of the Holy Spirit, and the essential role that Mary's consent plays in this pivotal scene.

First, the literary structure of the Annunciation story recalls earlier biblical announcements of extraordinary births as well as classic scriptural stories of divine commissioning to leaders who led the Israelites out of oppression. The typical pattern is that an angel appears, the person reacts with fear, the angel makes a disclosure about the future, the person questions the angel, and a sign is given to reassure the person. These elements are found in the angel's appearance to Elizabeth as well as the wife of Manoah. These

---

34. Ibid., 6.
35. Johnson, *Truly Our Sister*, 3.
36. Ibid., 248.
37. Ibid.

are the elements founding the story of Moses at the burning bush (Exod 3:1–14) and the call of Gideon (Judg 6:11–24). Second, the "overshadowing" of the Holy Spirit recalls the descent of God's presence on the dwelling place during the Israelites' sojourn in the desert (Exod 40:34). Third, Mary's consent signals for Johnson the relationship between human freedom and divine grace. Rather than a zero-sum game in which an increase in one requires a decrease in the other, Mary's free consent does not diminish the gracious nature of God's action.

For Johnson, the problematic element of the Annunciation story centers on Mary's self-description as the "handmaid [*doulē* Gk] of the Lord." Johnson insists that "centuries of patriarchal interpretation have labeled Mary's response as submissive obedience and have held up this stance as the proper ideal for all women in relation to men, a view antithetical to women's hopes for their own human dignity ... Traditional demands for conformity to patriarchal order and for obedience to male religious authority figures, be they God, husband, or priest, make women shudder before this text and reject it as dangerous to physical and psychological health as well as to a liberating spirituality."[38] The text does nevertheless contain a liberating message. "Very carefully we peel off the layers of saccharine humility and forced subordination. This young peasant girl discerns the voice of God in her life commissioning her to a momentous task. Exercising independent thought and action, she asks questions, takes counsel with her own soul."[39] She determines, without the assistance of any male authority figure, that she will play this decisive role in the redemption of humanity. Rather than a submissive, passive figure, Mary embodies courageous self-determination as a woman of Spirit.

In a second story, the visitation of Mary to Elizabeth (Luke 1:39–56), we find in Elizabeth's canticle a praise of Mary, but it is Mary's canticle, the Magnificat, the longest passage on the lips of any woman in the New Testament, that garners the most attention in Johnson's analysis.[40] Following the structure of a psalm of thanksgiving, the Magnificat falls into two sections: the first praises God (vv. 48–50) and the second recounts the marvelous deeds that God has done (vv. 51–55). In the first section, Mary identifies with the lowly. "Mary's self-characterization as lowly is not a metaphor for spiritual humility but is based on her actual social position. Young, female, a member of a people subjected to economic exploitation by powerful ruling groups, afflicted by outbreaks of violence,

38. Ibid., 254–55.
39. Ibid., 256.
40. Ibid., 263.

she belongs to the semantic domain of the poor in Luke's gospel, a group given negative valuation by worldly powers."[41] In the second section, Mary proclaims God's steadfast concern for the poor, the lowly, and the outcasts. "In the psalms and the prophets, the Holy One of Israel protects, defends, saves, and rescues these 'nobodies,' adorning them with victory and life in the face of despair. Proclaiming the Magnificat, Mary continues this deep stream of Jewish faith in the context of the advent of the Messiah, now taking shape within her."[42] Mary expresses her solidarity with the marginalized, the oppressed, the "lowly" who struggle to survive in a world controlled politically and economically by powers who have no interest in raising the poor from their lowly status.

The third scene is Pentecost (Acts 1:14–15; 2:1–21). This is an important element in Johnson's mariology as it serves as a springboard into her discussion of the communion of saints. The one hundred twenty disciples gathered in Jerusalem include "Mary the mother of Jesus, as well as his brothers" (1:14). Johnson herself takes no firm position on the issue of the perpetual virginity of Mary or whether the brothers and sisters are her biological children or the children of Joseph's first marriage or cousins of Jesus. Johnson emphasizes instead that "their repeated presence yoked to the mother of Jesus in the gospels indicates closeness of multiple children in a blended family . . . When these children are taken into account, the romanticized picture of an ideal 'holy family' composed of an old man, a young woman, and one perfect child does not hold up. There is a lot of noise, a lot of mess, a lot of work, a lot of conversation, perhaps a lot of laughter."[43] Whatever the relation between Mary and "the brothers and sisters" of Christ, Luke numbers her as one of the one hundred twenty upon whom the Holy Spirit came to rest at Pentecost. "From her peasant domicile in Nazareth to the house church in Jerusalem, both of which labored to survive under oppressive economic and political circumstances; from youth to marriage to widowhood; from the birth of her firstborn to his horrendous death to hearing him proclaimed Lord, Messiah, and Savior—she walked her life's path keeping faith with her gracious God, the Holy One of Israel."[44]

Johnson weaves the stories dealing with Mary into the larger concept of the communion of saints. At its most fundamental level, the communion of saints is comprised of "all women and men who have been brushed with the fire of divine love and who seek the living God in their

41. Ibid., 265.
42. Ibid., 266.
43. Ibid., 198–99.
44. Ibid., 303–4.

lives."⁴⁵ The saints are first of all the holy ones living among us. In the early church, a second meaning becomes associated with the saints, as the early Christians included the martyrs and others Christian who had died in the "cloud of witnesses" (Heb 12:1) within the larger Christian community. While Johnson laments the traditional understanding of the saints that developed along patronage lines in which the saints were petitioned for certain benefits or protections, she finds the notion of saints as companions on the journey of life as compelling. "To use a spatial metaphor, here the saints in heaven are not situated *between* God and those on earth, with some more or less powerful in intercessory pull. Rather, they are *with* their sisters and brothers in the one Spirit."⁴⁶

Mary, then, for Johnson is one of the paradigmatic figures, i.e., persons "whose lives embody one or more central values of the faith in a strikingly concrete form."⁴⁷ In the three stories highlighted from Luke-Acts, the historical portrait of Mary that emerges is of a young woman who gives birth to a child whom many of his followers would later identify as the long-awaited Lord and Messiah. She lives in the small village of Nazareth at a time in which Israel is under Roman rule, and the Second Temple has not yet been destroyed. From the archaeological and literary evidence that we possess, we can speculate on her economic and religious status within Galilee, as well as reconstruct a picture of her daily existence (typical housing, methods of food preparation, etc.). In terms of the claims made about Mary in the thirteen stories of the New Testament in which she appears, Johnson highlights her religious observance, her consent to the angels who announce that she is to give birth to the Lord and Messiah, and her rightful place in the history of prophets and friends of God. Still, Mary is a woman shrouded in mystery. Commenting on one of Johnson's early works on Mary, the theologian Barbara Hilkert Andolsen writes, "Johnson advocates a reading of Miriam's [Mary's] story that serves to 'highlight her intelligence, initiative, independence, and personal identity.' However, the very limited historical record about Mary gives us a very shaky basis for an image of a woman marked by initiative and independence. Johnson's description of Mary as a woman of initiative and independence seems to me to be another example of theologians' unfortunate tendency to project onto the historically obscure Miriam of Nazareth the character traits that the theologian values."⁴⁸ Andolsen's question recalls the critique of Feuerbach: Is the imaginative

45. Ibid., 306.
46. Ibid., 318. Italics original.
47. Ibid., 313.
48. Andolsen, "Our Companions Enfolded," 90.

engagement with the text, whether it be that of Richard of St. Victor, Edith Stein, or Elizabeth Johnson, disclosing a treasure long hidden from view or creating a crown from fool's gold? How would we even know if our answer to that question is correct? In answering these questions, we might identify in advance whether our theological sympathies lie with the orthodox, the liberals, the postliberals, or the postmoderns.

The Revitalization of the Biblical Imagery of Persons in the Bible

Jonathan Edwards's treatment of the figure of King David as a "type" of Christ provides a helpful illustration of how "America's Theologian" incorporated Old Testament figures into a theology of redemption. Out of Edwards's enormous body of work, we will focus on *A History of the Work of Redemption*, a work based on sermons that Edwards delivered in 1739 but were not published until after his death, and "Types of the Messiah" composed between 1744 and 1749. While the Old Testament abounds with characters who prefigure the Messiah, according to Edwards, David "was the greatest personal type of Christ of all under the Old Testament."[49] Furthermore, "David was not only a king, but a great prophet (2 Sam 23:2), and also was a priest,"[50] so David also foreshadows in his own career the traditional "three offices of Christ."

David foreshadows the priesthood of Christ by offering sacrifice, by serving as a mediator between God and Israel, and by moving the ark to Jerusalem and making alterations to the ceremonial laws. First, "David was anointed king after offering sacrifice (1 Sam 16). So the prophecies represent the Messiah's exaltation to his kingdom, after he had by his offerings offered up a sacrifice to atone for the sins of men."[51] Second, "David was a mediator to stand between God and the people, both to keep off judgments and the punishment of sin, and also to procure God's favor towards them . . . So the Messiah is spoken of, as in like manner, the mediator, being himself peculiarly God's elect and beloved, is given for a covenant of the people (Isa 42:6 and 49:8) and the messenger of the covenant, and a prophet like unto Moses, who was a mediator."[52] Third, he altered the worship of Israel by housing the ark in Jerusalem and by reorganizing the priests and Levites (1 Chron 23—26). "The law was given by Moses but yet all the institutions of the Jewish worship were not given by Moses. Some were added by David, by divine direction. So this greatest

---

49. Edwards, *History of the Work of Redemption*, 204.
50. Edwards, "Types of the Messiah," 269–70.
51. Ibid., 262.
52. Ibid., 273.

of all personal types of Christ did not only perfect Joshua's work in giving Israel the possession of the promised land, but he also finished Moses' work in perfecting the instituted worship of Israel."[53]

David likewise is a prophet. "David was himself endowed with the spirit of prophecy. He is called, 'a prophet,' Acts 2:29–30, 'Let me speak freely to you of the patriarch David, that he is both dead and buried, and his sepulcher is with us to this day. Therefore being a prophet, and knowing that God had sworn with an oath, etc.' So that herein he was a type of Christ that he was both a prophet and a king."[54] The Spirit rushed upon David after being anointed by Samuel. "The oil that was used in anointing David was a type of the Spirit of God."[55] Edwards was a great admirer of the Psalms and he speculates that it is probably the case that David received his gift of prophecy when he was anointed by Samuel. "And the way that this Spirit influenced him was to inspire this soul to show forth Christ and the glorious things of his redemption in divine songs. Sweetly expressing the breathings of a pious soul full of admiration of the glorious things of the Redeemer, inflamed with divine love and lifted up with praise, and therefore he is called 'the sweet psalmist of Israel' 2 Sam 23:1."[56] Not only are the Psalms the most quoted Old Testament text found in the New Testament,[57] they are "a book of divine songs for [the church's] use in that part of their public worship, viz. singing his praises throughout all ages to the end of the world."[58]

The kingship of David mirrors the Lordship of Christ. First, neither had a stately bearing in appearance. "David's outward appearance was not such as would have recommended him to the esteem and choice of men as a person for rule and victory, but on the contrary such as tended to cause men to despise him as a candidate for such things."[59] Second, though humble in appearance, both David and Christ were victorious in their battles. God "preserved [David] from [Goliath], and gave him the victory over him, so that he cut off his head with his own sword and made him therein the deliverer of his people, as Christ slew the spiritual Goliath with his own weapon, the cross, and so delivered his people."[60] Finally, David reigns over the holy city of Jerusalem which is a type of the church. "This city of Jerusalem is

---

53. Edwards, *History of the Work of Redemption*, 218.
54. Ibid., 209.
55. Ibid., 210.
56. Ibid.
57. Ibid.
58. Ibid., 211.
59. Edwards, "Types of the Messiah," 261.
60. Edwards, *History of the Work of Redemption*, 206.

therefore called the 'holy city,' and it was the greatest type of the church in all the Old Testament. It was redeemed by David, the captain of the hosts of Israel, out of the hands of the Jebusites to be God's city, the holy [place], the place of his rest forever, where he would dwell, as Christ the captain of his people's salvation redeems his church out of the hands of devils to be his holy and beloved city."[61]

The womanist theologian Delores Williams focuses her theological attention not on Abraham, Moses, or David, but Hagar. While the majority of thinkers in the Western tradition have focused their attention on Abraham and Sarah, Williams reads Genesis through the eyes of Hagar and relates Hagar's story to the experience of women whose lives were lived in many of the same circumstances. "A very superficial reading of Genesis 16:1–16 and 21:9–21 in the Hebrew testament revealed that Hagar's predicament involved slavery, poverty, ethnicity, sexual and economic exploitation, surrogacy, rape, domestic violence, homelessness, motherhood, single-parenting and radical encounters with God."[62] Add to this Paul's negative comparison of Hagar and Sarah in Galatians (4:21–5:1) and "Hagar and her descendants represent the outsider position par excellence."[63] Yet, argues Williams, Hagar's resistance, shrewdness, and endurance—her very survival in a world of oppression—is resonant with the history and lived experience of African-American women.

The choice to view Genesis through the perspective of Hagar rather than Sarah, argues Williams, highlights the great divide in biblical hermeneutics. Williams identifies "two traditions of African-American biblical appropriation."[64] The first emphasizes the theme of liberation. The exodus serves as the paradigmatic event in which God hears the cries of the oppressed and rescues them, revealing the divine will for all people at all times. The Hagar story, however, does not fall comfortably into his tradition. In Genesis 16 after Hagar has fled from Sarai to escape her abusive treatment, the angel tells Hagar, "Return to your mistress, and submit to her" (16:9). Williams notes, "The angel of Yahweh is, in this passage, no liberator God."[65] Interestingly, "the harshness of the force Sarai exerts upon Hagar is indicated in the passage by the verb ('nh), which is also used in Exodus to indicate the suffering experience of all Hebrews when they were slaves in Egypt."[66]

61. Ibid., 213.
62. Williams, *Sisters*, 4.
63. Ibid.
64. Ibid., 1.
65. Ibid., 20.
66. Ibid., 19.

However, God's command to the slave of Egyptian descent is the exact opposite of the command to the Israelite slaves in Egypt. The concern in the story of Hagar is survival rather than liberation. Williams labels this approach to the Bible "*the survival/quality-of-life tradition of African-American biblical appropriation.*"[67] The angel's command to Hagar to return to Sarah is borne out of the practical assessment of her situation. The chances of a pregnant Hagar, who has no resources of her own, surviving in the wilderness with a newborn baby were slim. Her best hope for survival required that she return to her state of bondage. Hagar's only assurance is that God has promised numerous descendants for her son (Gen 16:10; 21:18). Vision plays a key role in the story. Hagar "sees" God and names God (Phyllis Trible notes that Hagar is the only person who names God in the Bible)[68] El-roi ("Have I really seen God and remained alive after seeing him?" Gen 16:13). The Lord "gave her new vision to see survival resources where she had seen none before."[69] It is survival, then, not liberation that is the primary category in Williams's womanist theology. "In black consciousness, God's response of survival and quality of life to Hagar is God's response of survival and quality of life to African-American women and mothers of slave descent struggling to sustain their families with God's help."[70]

The "wilderness experience" of Hagar provides yet another point of contact between the story of Ishmael's mother and the history of African-American women. "Hagar and African-American women (and their children) meet God there in the midst of trouble and what appears to be impending death and destruction."[71] Williams notes that in American writing, the image of the wilderness functions at times as a symbol of chaos that must be tamed or "civilized" and at other times as a symbol of pristine beauty that should be treasured. Slaves in antebellum American "had a positive concept of wilderness. It was a free and friendly space where one received from Jesus the strength needed to rise above one's ailments (sadness, sin, affliction, backsliding, etc.) . . . Evidently slaves thought an environment supporting solitude and reflection conducive to gaining a true connection with Jesus and to strengthening the kind of God-consciousness needed to support their journeys through life."[72] For slaves the "wilderness experience" was transformative; in finding a personal relationship with Jesus, slaves found

67. Ibid., 5. Emphasis original.
68. Ibid., 22.
69. Ibid., 4.
70. Ibid., 5.
71. Ibid., 96.
72. Ibid., 99–100.

CHAPTER NINE: PERSONS IN THE BIBLE 167

the strength to persevere. It is for this reason that Williams concludes, "No other biblical image could have been more appropriate than Hagar in the wilderness for presenting the African-American past and present."[73]

Typology or figural interpretation also plays an important role in Hans Frei's account of eighteenth- and nineteenth-century hermeneutics. In pre-critical readings of the Bible, "the several biblical stories narrating sequential segments in time must fit together into one narrative. The interpretive means for joining them was to make earlier biblical stories figures or types of later stories and of their events and patterns of meaning."[74] As scholars in the modern age increasingly understood the referent of the biblical narrative to be history (understood as a reality separate from the biblical narrative), the figural method of interpretation was discredited. Frei argues that Barth's way of reading the Bible provides the way forward and cites "Barth's remarkable use of figural interpretation of the Old Testament in *Church Dogmatics* II,2, pp. 340–409" as one example of how the Bible should be read.[75]

In the midst of his treatment of the doctrine of election, Barth offers over fifty pages of small print commentary on a number of biblical passages, including Leviticus 14 with the procedure the priest should follow to cure someone of leprosy, and Leviticus 16 in which we find the rituals relating to the scapegoat on the Day of Atonement. In the case of leprosy, the priest is to gather two clean birds. One bird is slain, and its blood falls into a vessel containing spring water. The living bird is dipped in the blood of the sacrificed bird, and the water is sprinkled seven times on the leprous person. The living bird is set free. On the Day of Atonement, Aaron is instructed to take two male goats to the entrance of the tent of meeting and, by casting lots, determine which goat is to be sacrificed. Aaron is to lay hands on the other goat and confess over it the transgressions of the people. This second goat is then to be cast out in the wilderness for Azazel.

Both stories in Leviticus involved the chosen and the rejected, the condemned and the freed, the elect and the non-elect. Barth adds "Let us gratefully know ourselves to be elect in the picture of the first goat of Lev 16—grateful that we are accepted to sacrifice ourselves, grateful that we may suffer the saving judgment of the wrath of God, which is the wrath of His Love, as only the elect can and may do! But let us with equal gratitude recognize ourselves as the non-elect in the picture of the second bird of Lev 14—grateful because there is ordained for us the life for whose painful birth the other is elected, the resurrection for whose sake the elect must go to his

---

73. Ibid., 104.
74. Frei, *Eclipse of Biblical Narrative*, 2.
75. I discovered this in Higton, *Christ, Providence, and History*, 155–63.

death!"[76] But, asks Barth, how can we see ourselves as both at the same time? "If man may die by the grace of God, how then can he still live, whether in the realm of Azazel or in the realm of freedom? And if by the grace of God he may live, first in the darkness and then in the light, first a wretched life and then a joyful life, why then must he still die?"[77] Christian readers of the text are then confronted with a choice. We must either consider that the Bible has no answer, or at least any answer that we can discern, or "the subject of the Old Testament witness may be accepted as identical with the person of Jesus Christ as it is seen and interpreted and proclaimed by the apostles because He had Himself revealed and represented Himself to them in this way."[78] Barth asked, "How can we believe in Jesus Christ and not of necessity recognize Him in these passages?"[79] To recognize Christ in the stories in Leviticus is obviously a figural or typological reading, and it is precisely this reading that Barth fully endorses. "The elect individual in the Old Testament, so impressively and yet in so many ways distinguished, set apart and differentiated in the Old Testament stories and pictures, is always a witness to Jesus Christ, and is indeed a type of Christ Himself. It is He, Jesus Christ, who is originally and properly the elect individual. All others can be this only as types of Him . . ."[80]

The postmodern biblical scholar Yvonne Sherwood examines the history of interpretation regarding Jonah in her *A Biblical Text and its Afterlives: The Survival of Jonah in Western Culture*. She begins with a review of the early church thinkers' typological readings of Jonah. The variety of interpretations stem from the cryptic teaching of Christ: "For just as Jonah became a sign to the people of Nineveh, so the Son of Man will be to his generation" (Luke 11:30). Christ further comments that "something greater than Jonah is here" (Luke 11:32). Matthew adds a typological parallel between Jonah's three days in the belly and Christ's three days in the tomb (12:40). Jerome believed that Jonah sleeping in the ship is a foreshadowing of Christ asleep in the boat on the stormy lake (Mark 4:38). Ambrose and Cyril see Jonah's slumber as a prefiguration of Christ in the tomb. The interpretations grew in number: the Ninevites are the Gentiles; the ship is the church; the sea creature is the Devil, and so on.[81] Sherwood faults all the early Christian interpreters for missing the vital element of Jonah's

---

76. Barth, *Church Dogmatics*, 361.
77. Ibid., 362.
78. Ibid., 363.
79. Ibid., 364.
80. Ibid.
81. Sherwood, *Biblical Text and Its Afterlives*, 14–18.

resistance to his calling. "What disappears, specifically, is any sense of Jonah's resistance to God. As his 'flight' slides into 'incarnation', a gesture of rebellion is converted to one of submission; as the storm scene is engulfed by the gospel version, we lose any sense of the storm as an act of divine discipline and punishment. The narrative is drained of all residual friction between the prophet and the deity."[82]

Sherwood claims that her own reading of Jonah "places itself on the postmodern side of the postmodernist/modernist divide."[83] We find the postmodern emphasis on the central role that the reader plays in determining the meaning of a text. "The bottom line seems to be that all readers are always involved, in some sense, in textual management: we cannot let meaning ricochet in all directions . . . We feel the compulsion to bring the text into a manageable whole."[84] Despite our efforts to attach a single meaning to the text, "a considerable residue leaks out of that neat, framing metastory."[85] The traditional views regarding the nature of God, for example, are challenged in the Book of Jonah. "My premise is that the as yet vaguely defined 'strangeness' of the book derives from a lack of closure and of enclosure—from a feeling that Jonah and the reader are held neither within a stable and univocal framework, nor within an environment peacefully circumscribed by the predictability of tradition and the guaranteeability of God."[86] Jonah's search for shelter on the ship or under the leafy plant in Nineveh fails, "and the fact that each shelter ultimately fails to protect him, imitates the structure of the plot: the plot that does not shelter him, the plot that expresses the desire that (to plunder more words from Jeremiah) God would become his 'refuge' and not his 'terror' (Jeremiah 17:7). It is not simply that the edifice of the plot crumbles in good (overtly) deconstructive fashion, but that it fails to protect or please Jonah, or indeed the sailors, creates a sense of the fragility and insecurity of life."[87] Sherwood sees Jonah as a tale about the unpredictability of life rather than a moral lesson about the providence of God. Jonah is an "Everyman, or baby man, living a brief life between shade/protection and the assault of smiting/striking things, between being consumed and being regurgitated, between danger and survival, exile and safety, and life and death."[88] In pondering the lives of both the

82. Ibid., 17.
83. Ibid., 214.
84. Ibid., 215.
85. Ibid., 284.
86. Ibid., 233–34.
87. Ibid., 280.
88. Ibid.

major and minor characters in the biblical narrative we confront the deepest questions about the meaning and purpose of human existence.

Discussion Questions

1. Is seeing the near-sacrifice of Isaac as a foreshadowing of the Crucifixion a legitimate way of reading the Bible? Why? Why not?
2. Could the birth order of Jacob's children be a clue to the spiritual life of Christians? Is Richard simply creating ideas that aren't really there in Genesis? Is Richard's reading of Genesis spiritually useful?
3. What are some parallels between Elijah and Christ? Why do Moses and Elijah appear in the Transfiguration story (Mark 9:2-13)?
4. Is David a foreshadowing of Christ as priest, prophet, and king? Does his sin with Bathsheba disqualify him as a figure for Christ?
5. How does reading Genesis through the eyes of Hagar rather than Sarah change your perception of Genesis?
6. Is the scapegoat (Lev 16) a foreshadowing of Christ? Why? Why not?
7. Does the fictional quality of the Jonah story enhance or detract from its typological use?

Suggested Readings

For an overview of Victorine theology and spirituality, see Steven Chase, *Contemplation and Compassion* (Maryknoll, NY: Orbis, 2003) and chapter 9 of Bernard McGinn, *The Growth of Mysticism* (New York: Crossroad, 1994). For an introduction to Edith Stein's work, see Sarah Borden, *Edith Stein* (New York: Continuum, 2003) and Marian Maskulak, *Edith Stein: Selected Writings* (Mahwah, NJ: Paulist, 2016). For a review symposium on *Truly Our Sister*, see *Horizons* 31 (2004) 160-86. On Edwards's typological reading, see Tibor Fabiny, "Edwards and Biblical Typology" in Gerald McDermott, *Understanding Jonathan Edwards* (Oxford: Oxford University Press, 2009). For a discussion of womanist theology and the story of Hagar, see Anna Fisk, "Sisterhood in the Wilderness: Biblical Paradigms and Feminist Identity Politics in Readings of Hagar and Sarah," esp. 115-21, in A. K. M. Adam and Samuel Tongue, eds., *Looking Through a Glass Bible* (Boston: Brill, 2014). For a helpful study of Frei, see chapter 7 of John David Dawson, *Christian Figural Reading and the Fashioning of Identity* (Berkeley: University of California Press, 2002). For a critical engagement with Sherwood and other postmodern thinkers, see Ronald Hendel, "Mind the Gap: Modern and Postmodern in Biblical Studies," in the *Journal of Biblical Literature* 133 (2014) 422–43. For a collection of writings on figural interpretation, see Stanley D. Walters, ed., *Go Figure!* (Eugene, OR: Pickwick, 2008).

Chapter Ten: Parables in the Bible

IN MANY KEY RESPECTS our entire examination of various biblical images that have sparked the imagination of countless theologians has been an exercise in parabolic thinking. At the heart of a parable lies a comparison between an element in human experience (as ordinary as baking bread or extraordinary as finding buried treasure) and the nature and activity of God (the kingdom of God). When reflecting on a biblical image, the theologian proposes a specific relation between the person, event, or object in the biblical narrative and the belief and practices of Christians. Just as the biblical image functions in a variety of ways in theology, so too the parable can be used to serve any number of ends: to shock the hearer into a new view of human relations (parable of the Good Samaritan), to reverse the hearer's priorities (parable of the merchant's pearl), or to indict the hearer (Nathan's parable to David). In this chapter we will examine how the parables functioned to advance the cause of orthodoxy in the commentary of Jerome (347–420), to assert the ethical demands of Christianity in the preaching of John Chrysostom (347–407), and to shed light on Jesus' teaching regarding the kingdom of God in the exegetical work of John Dominic Crossan (1934–).

Jerome, *Commentary on Matthew* (398)

Around the age of eighteen or nineteen, while in Trier, a well-educated and well-connected Jerome experienced a religious conversion that would set him on the path of a scholarly, ascetic existence. He moved first to Aquileia in northern Italy and then to Antioch and the nearby town of Chalcis before moving to Constantinople. In 382 he returned to Rome where he had studied as a teenager. Jerome had long enjoyed the financial support of patrons and patronesses, and in Rome he had the support of Pope Damasus who commissioned him to produce an authoritative Latin translation of the Psalms and the Gospels. Later he translated the entire Old Testament into Latin to produce the Vulgate text for which he is best known today. After the death of Damasus, Jerome was forced to leave Rome because of his satirical

CHAPTER TEN: PARABLES IN THE BIBLE

attacks on some of his fellow clergy and traveled briefly to Egypt before settling in Bethlehem in 386 where he would spend the rest of his life. He was joined in Bethlehem with Roman aristocrats Paula and her daughter Eustochium who provided Jerome with financial support and built a monastery, convent, and hospice for pilgrims. It was in Bethlehem that Jerome produced his *Commentary on Matthew* in 398.[1]

Jerome dictated the *Commentary on Matthew* in two weeks. His friend Eusebius of Cremona was planning on sailing to Italy and asked Jerome for some edifying reading material for the voyage. Of the many angles from which we could approach Jerome's work, we will focus on his analysis of three sets of parables: the treasure buried in the field and the merchant's search for the pearl (Matt 13); the two sons, the vineyard, and the wicked tenants (Matt 21); and the wise and foolish virgins and the talents (Matt 25). Our attention will be focused on both the spiritual interpretation that Jerome offers in his commentary and the polemical points that he makes against those deemed heretical teachers. As Jerome explained in the prologue to his work *Against the Pelagians*, "I have never spared heretics, and I have done my best to make the enemies of the Church my own."[2]

At the heart of both the parable of the treasure and the parable of the pearl lies a comparison between the value of a singular highest good and the value of multiple lesser goods. In terms of the treasure, Jerome mentions two possible interpretations. The treasure "is either the Word of God, who is seen to be hidden in the flesh of Christ, or it is the Holy Scriptures, in which the knowledge of the Savior is stored away. When anyone finds him hidden in them, he should despise all the gains of this world in order to be able to possess the one he has found."[3] Jerome then adds that the parable of the pearl is making the same point, but is simply using different language. This is in keeping with Jerome's earlier identification of the mustard seed and the leaven as knowledge of Scripture, as well as his teaching that in some sense all scriptural stories can be taken to be parables because "[n]ot only does the obvious meaning of the letter ring out, but hidden mysteries are found there."[4]

Jerome, however, does not simply offer his spiritual interpretation of the mysteries hidden within the parables of the treasure and the pearl, but he also refutes the teachings of Marcion and Mani who regarded the Old

---

1. I am relying upon Part One of Rebenich, *Jerome* and Scheck, "Introduction" for biographical information.
2. Quoted in Scheck, "Introduction," 32 n. 114.
3. Jerome, *Commentary on Matthew*, 163.
4. Ibid., 162.

Testament as either utterly dispensable or inferior to the New Testament. Jerome asserts,

> The good pearls that the salesman seeks are the Law and the prophets. Listen, Marcion; listen, Manicheus; the good pearls are the Law, and the prophets and the knowledge of the Old Testament, but the one pearl of very great price is the knowledge of the Savior and the concealed mystery of the Passion and Resurrection . . . It is not the case that the finding of the new pearl means that old pearls are condemned. Rather, it means that in comparison with it, every other gem is rather cheap.[5]

Jerome argues that a number of biblical interpretations can be acceptable, but that no matter how wide the field of possibilities, it is surrounded by a fence beyond which the Christian thinker should not stray into heresy. In Jerome's day, the question of the canon was not settled. Athanasius's Festal Letter listing the current twenty-seven New Testament canonical texts was only penned in 367. Irenaeus's second-century battle with the Gnostics revolved around the Rule of Faith, those core beliefs found in the biblical narrative (codified in creeds) that serve as the standard against which any interpretation should be measured. In addition to the canon and the Rule of Faith, the bishops and councils displayed increasing authority in the resolution of theological debates. Of course, these markers of orthodoxy would be debated again in the Reformation over discussions of the Old Testament canon, theological debates over the perspicuity of Scripture, and controversies over church governance. The issues involved in orthodoxy, how it is defined, how challenges to it from within the church are handled, and how it is enforced, are matters each church handles in its own way. These battles are an unavoidable, though oftentimes divisive, element in the life of the church.

We find Jerome offering more spiritual interpretation of Scripture as well as inveighing against another heresy in his commentary on the parables of the two sons and the wicked tenants. Again, Jerome allows for more than one interpretation regarding the identity of the two sons. They may be understood to refer to Jews and Gentiles, or to sinners and the just. Jerome identifies the father of the two sons as the vineyard owner, thus linking the two parables. In Jerome's reading of the vineyard parable, the vineyard is the house of Israel (Isa 5:7), the hedge could be a wall or the help of angels, and the tower is the temple. However, when Jerome turns his focus to when the vineyard owner decides to send his son, thinking that the wicked tenants will respect him, Jerome takes aim at the Arians.

5. Ibid., 164.

> What is further added: "They will respect my son," does not imply that he was ignorant [of the outcome]. For what would the householder not know, since in this passage he represents God the Father? But God is always *said to be* uncertain, so that free will in man may be preserved. Let us put a question to Arius and Eunomius. Behold, the Father is said to be ignorant. He delays his decision, and as far as it pertains to us, it is proven that he has lied. Whatever answer they give on the father's behalf, let them understand this answer as well on behalf of the Son, who claims to be ignorant of the day of the consummation.[6]

The Arians who argued that the Son was created and sent by the Father, hence not of the same substance as the Father, pointed to Christ's ignorance regarding the end of the world (Mark 13:32) in support of their position. The Arians argued, "He who knows and he who does not know cannot be equal."[7] Jerome counters by noting that by the literal wording of the parable, the vineyard owner (i.e., God the Father) does not realize that the tenants will in fact kill the Son. Any solution that the Arians can provide to explain how the Father would not be omniscient, argues Jerome, should also be applied by them to Christ's apparent lack of omniscience. Furthermore, if God the Father (and by extension, the Son) is *said to be* unsure, then the free will of the parties involved is preserved.

A third illustration of the combination of Jerome's spiritual reading and his polemics can be found in his commentary on the parables of the ten wise and foolish virgins and the talents. For Jerome, "the ten virgins embrace all men who seem to believe in God," but the virgins with oil for their lamps "are those who are adorned with works as well as with faith."[8] In the same way, those in the parable of the talents who double their entrusted sums may refer to those believers who "fulfill in deed whatever they have learned in words."[9] He adds that the number of wise and foolish virgins is five, which corresponds with the five senses. Scripture speaks of the senses in spiritual terms ("O taste and see that the Lord is good" Ps 34:8), and so the lamps "stand for the senses" and the oil is "the oil of knowledge" and the light is the virtue that shines forth before the Judge.[10] Following the admonition to be on watch for we know not the day or hour, Jerome once again turns his attention to his opponents. "I always warn the wise reader not to subscribe to superstitious

---

6. Ibid., 246. Emphasis original.
7. Ibid., 278.
8. Ibid., 282.
9. Ibid., 288.
10. Ibid., 283.

interpretations and those that are spoken 'line by line' by people who fabricate things by their own arbitrary will. Instead, let the reader consider what precedes, what is in the middle, and what follows. And let him connect to one another all the things that are written."[11] The target of Jerome's attack seems to be Origen. In the preface to the *Commentary* Jerome notes, "I confess that very many years ago I read Origen's twenty-five books on Matthew and just as many of his homilies and a kind of verse-by-verse interpretation."[12] Jerome clearly borrows from Origen, but here he seems to be distancing himself from the great Alexandrian exegete. In Jerome's lifetime the teachings of Origen (d. 254), especially his teaching regarding a "universal restoration" (Acts 3:21) of all creation with God at the end of time that may well include Satan's reconciliation with God, became the source of much controversy. Jerome joined in the denunciation of "Origenism." Whether that was an example of weak-kneed political expediency on Jerome's part or the logical consequence of Jerome's careful separation between Origen's exegetical work (which he admired) and his theological positions (some of which he found suspect) is a matter of scholarly debate.[13]

John Chrysostom, *On Wealth and Poverty*

A member of a prominent family within Antioch, John abandoned a future career in civil service and was baptized around age twenty. After a brief time as a hermit, he returned to Antioch where he served the church in various capacities, eventually being ordained in 386. In the eleven years that he served the church at Antioch as presbyter he developed a reputation as a skilled "golden-mouthed" (Chrysostom) preacher. It was in Antioch around 388–89 that John preached a series of sermons on the parable of Lazarus and the rich man (Luke 16:19–31). In 398 John became the patriarch of Constantinople. His entanglements within both church controversies and palace intrigues made him a polarizing figure. His preaching eventually put him in conflict with the empress Eudoxia which resulted in John being sent into exile twice. It was during his second exile that he died in 407.[14]

John's preaching on the parable of Lazarus and the rich man follows the typical Antiochene method of interpretation that generally focuses on the

11. Ibid., 285.

12. Ibid., 56.

13. For contrasting views, see Rebenich, *Jerome*, 43–51, and Brown, *Via Trilinguis*, 159.

14. For biographical information, I am relying on Roth, "Introduction," and Mayer and Allen, "John's Life and Times" in *John Chrysostom*.

plain sense of the passage. In a straightforward manner, the parable depicts two states of existence: life in the present age and life in the age to come. The rich man (also called Dives, Latin for "rich man") enjoys the pleasures of this world while ignoring the beggar Lazarus who sits at his gate. After their deaths, Lazarus rests with Abraham and the rich man is tormented in Hades. The conclusion sounds a warning as the rich man begs for relief, which he does not receive and for a chance to warn his five brothers, which he is not permitted, but instead is simply told "If they do not listen to the Moses and the prophets, neither will they be convinced even if someone rises from the dead" (16:31).

The imagery that John employs in his series of seven sermons on the parable is always in service of advancing the plain meaning of the text. The themes of the obligation to care for the poor, the reward and punishment of the afterlife, and the need for repentance remain dominant, and the imagery helps illustrate the major themes. For instance, in the first sermon John compares the actions of the rich man with those of a ship's captain. "The rich man had his ship full of merchandise, and it sailed before the wind. But do not be surprised: he was hastening to shipwreck, since he refused to unload his cargo with discretion."[15] Lazarus, by contrast, weathered the storm of the rich man's indifference. The rich man "passed him by like a stone shamelessly and mercilessly ... think how he was likely to sink the poor man's soul as if with a series of waves." All the while, Lazarus lay at the gate, "alive only enough to be able to perceive his own ill fortune, enduring shipwreck while in the harbor, tormenting his soul with the bitterest thirst so near the spring."[16] Although "the waves were so great and came so close together," Lazarus endured the tumultuous voyage and reached safe haven.[17]

One of John's favorite images in the sermons is that of the masks worn by actors in the theater.[18] "For just as on the stage actors enter with the masks of kings, generals, doctors, teachers, professors, and soldiers, without themselves being anything of the sort, so in the present life poverty and wealth are only masks."[19] Outward appearances in this life, such as one's social standing, are not to be mistaken as indicators of a person's virtue or vice. "Just as the man who acts the part of a king or general on the stage often turns out to be a household servant or somebody who sells figs or grapes in the market, so also the rich man often turns out to be the poorest

---

15. John Chrysostom, *On Wealth and Poverty*, 23.
16. Ibid., 30–31.
17. Ibid., 32.
18. See Cardman, "Poverty and Wealth as Theater."
19. John Chrysostom, *On Wealth and Poverty*, 46.

of all. If you take off his mask, open up his conscience, and enter into his mind, you will often find there a great poverty of virtue: you will find that he belongs to the lowest class of all."[20] When the performance has ended, the actors return to their occupations. In the same way, the afterlife is the great unmasking of each person's identity. Lazarus and Dives "departed to the other world, and the play ended; the masks have been removed, and the faces appear from now on."[21]

Another contrast between appearance and reality that Chrysostom frequently employs centers on the health or sickness of the rich man and Lazarus. Lazarus's sores were visible, afflicting only the body, but the rich man "was full of sores within. Just as the dogs licked the wounds of the poor man, so demons licked the sins of the rich man; and just as the poor man lived in starvation of nourishment, so the rich man lived in starvation of the every kind of virtue."[22] Following Christ's teaching, "Those who are well have no need of a physician, but those who are sick; I have come to call not the righteous but sinners" (Mark 2:17), many patristic writers drew the parallel between sin and disease. The course of treatment varied from simply preventative medicine to major surgery. To help prevent the disease of sin, "we need the divine medicines to heal the wounds which we have received and to protect us from those which we have not yet received but will receive." There is no greater preventative measure, insists Chrysostom, than "the continual reading of the divine Scriptures. For it is not possible, not possible for anyone to be saved without continually taking advantage of spiritual reading. Actually, we must be content, if even with continual use of this therapy, we are barely able to be saved."[23] On the other end of the spectrum, serious illnesses require intense treatment. "What the [medicines], surgery, and cautery are for the physician, chastisement is for God. Just as fire is often used to cauterize, to prevent the spread of infection, and as the steel removes decayed flesh, bringing pain but providing benefit, so hunger and disease, and other apparent evils, are used on the soul instead of steel and fire to prevent the spread of disease, by analogy with the body, to make it better."[24]

Chrysostom also conveys the need for perseverance through his use of athletic imagery. His writing recalls Paul's exhortation, "Do you not know that in a race the runners all compete, but only one receives the prize? Run

20. Ibid., 47.
21. Ibid., 110.
22. Ibid., 35.
23. Ibid., 59.
24. Ibid., 103.

in such a way that you may win it. Athletes exercise self-control in all things; they do it to receive a perishable wreath, but we an imperishable one" (1 Cor 9:24–25). Commenting on the rich man's request to the Lord to have Lazarus warn his brothers that this horrible fate awaits those who neglect the poor, Chrysostom notes, "He asks for Lazarus to be sent into his father's house, where Lazarus had his arena and the stadium of his virtue. 'Let them see him crowned for victory,' he says, 'who watched him in his struggle; let the witnesses of his poverty, hunger, and innumerable troubles become witnesses of his honor, his transformation, and of all his glory.'"[25] Instead of questioning God's providence, Lazarus pressed on. "His body was lying down, but his mind was running forward, his will had grown wings. He was reaching for the prize, putting off evil things, becoming a witness of good things." While the rich man's death signaled his defeat, "the poor man's death was a journey, a change for the better, a run from the mark to the prize ... from the sweat of the contest to the crown."[26]

John Dominic Crossan, *In Parables* (1973)

The quest to discover the historical Jesus of Nazareth and the message that he taught continues unabated in both scholarly and popular circles. In one of his earliest books, *In Parables*, John Dominic Crossan argued that the parables offered the best avenue for approaching the historical Jesus. "The term 'historical Jesus' really means the language of Jesus and most especially the parables themselves. But the term is necessary to remind us that we have literally no language and no parables of Jesus except and insofar as such can be retrieved and reconstructed from within the language of their earliest interpreters. One might almost consider the term 'Jesus' as a cipher for the reconstructed parabolic complex itself."[27] Crossan emphasized that the parables offer the closest approximation to "the historical Jesus," but that in their canonical form they have been altered by early Christian interpreters. The proper interpretation of the parables, then, according to Crossan involves two elements: the reconstruction of the parable's original form and the correlation between the parables and the kingdom of God as preached by Jesus. The first task necessitated the use of the tools of modern critical study of the Gospels (e.g., redaction criticism). The second drew upon the insights of modern literary criticism (e.g., the function of poetic metaphors). Crossan highlights the role that metaphors play in drawing us into a

25. Ibid., 83.
26. Ibid., 108.
27. Crossan, *In Parables*, xiii.

new vision of the world. "When a metaphor contains a radically new vision of world it gives absolutely no information until after the hearer has entered into it and experienced it from inside itself. In such cases the hearer's first reaction may be to refuse to enter into the metaphor and one will seek to translate it immediately into comfortable normalcy of one's ordinary linguistic world."[28] *In Parables* is Crossan's effort to shake the readers of Jesus' parables out of their "comfortable normalcy" and recover the original power of Christ's parabolic teachings.

Crossan's interpretation of Jesus' parables hinges on his understanding of what is meant by "the kingdom of God." Unlike scholars who dispute whether Jesus expected the kingdom to arrive at some future date (either imminent or distant) or whether he proclaimed God's reign as arriving in his ministry, or some combination of both ("already, but not yet"), Crossan contends that these positions fail to recognize that Jesus is not speaking in terms of linear time. Rather, Crossan advances the thesis "that Jesus is proclaiming what might be termed *permanent eschatology*, the permanent presence of God as the one who challenges the world and shatters its complacency repeatedly."[29] The coming of the kingdom is not observable, but rather takes place in our consciousness. It is cataclysmic, but not in an apocalyptic sense. It is a shattering of our present understanding of God's activity. Crossan speaks of this disruption taking place in three modes: as *advent* of a new world, a *reversal* of past understanding, and as *action* in response to this world-shattering event.

One of the parables that Crossan uses to illustrate the "advent" dimension of Jesus' teaching is that of the mustard seed. He proceeds by first identifying what he takes to be the original form of the parable. The parable appears in Mark 4:30–32, Matt 13:31–32, Luke 13:18–19 as well as the Gospel of Thomas, logion 20. Crossan sees the evangelist's redactional hand at work in the version of the parable that appears in the Gospel of Mark. He notes that there is a redundancy in the wording. "It is like a mustard seed, which, when sown *upon the ground*, is the smallest of all the seeds on earth [literally in Greek *"upon the ground"*]. Crossan further believes that "the entire small*est*/larg*est* contrast in this superlative form is from Mark himself and not the original parable."[30] The final redactional touch appears in the phrase, "so that the birds of the air can make nests in its shade." Both Matthew and Luke (which is probably closer to the Q version) mention that birds came and nested in the branches, not in its shade. Mark's mention of birds nesting

---

28. Ibid., 13.
29. Ibid., 26. Emphasis original.
30. Ibid., 46. Emphasis original.

under the large branches has led commentators to link this parable with the image of the Messiah as a mighty tree in Ezekiel 17:23: "On the mountain height of Israel I will plant it, in order that it may produce boughs and bear fruit, and become a noble cedar. Under it every kind of bird will live; in the shade of its branches will nest winged creatures of every kind" (see also Dan 4:10–12). Crossan maintains that the allusions refer not to the noble cedar of Ezekiel, but simply to God's care for creation as expressed in Ps 104:12: "By the streams the birds of the air have their habitation; they sing among the branches." The "shrub" in Mark's parable is closer, insists Crossan, to the original parable than the "tree" in Luke and Matthew. Crossan adds that the version of the parable in the Gospel of Thomas lacks the smallest/largest comparison and avoids the shrub/tree problem by simply saying that the seed "produces a large branch." Based on this the reconstruction of the original parable, Crossan offers his interpretation. The traditional interpretation focuses on the growth of the small seed into the large shrub or tree. Crossan, however, argues that "miracle" rather than "growth" is at the heart of the original parable. The comparison of the seed to the fully grown shrub "does not wish to emphasize growth but miracle, not organic and biological development but the gift-like nature, the graciousness and the surprise of the ordinary, the advent of bountiful harvest despite the losses of sowing, the large shade despite the small seed. It is like this that the Kingdom is in advent. It is surprise and it is gift."[31]

The parable of the Great Supper is one of the parables of reversal. The parable appears in Matt 22:1–10, Luke 14:16–24, and the Gospel of Thomas, logion 64. In the Matthean version a *king* is inviting guests to his *son's wedding*, two elements lacking in the Lukan account. Crossan maintains that Matthew has made two important additions to the parable: the first involves the killing of the servants and the king's subsequent reprisal in sending troops and burning the city (vv. 6–7), and the second appears at the end when he appends an originally independent parable regarding the guest who is not wearing the appropriate attire (vv. 11–13). Matthew, according to Crossan, has "allegorized the parable into an image of the history of salvation, as he sees it, and by his addition of 22:11–13 he has actualized it in application to the internal tensions within the Matthean community."[32] Luke's modification, by contrast, takes an ethical turn by adhering to Christ's earlier instruction that "when you give a banquet, invite the poor, the crippled, the lame, and the blind" (Luke 14:13; 14:21). The larger problem, however, in both versions is that the guests seem uninformed that the

---

31. Ibid., 50–51.
32. Ibid., 71.

banquet was being served at that time. The version of the parable in the Gospel of Thomas has four invited guests who decline the offer, but the host seems to have suddenly decided to prepare a banquet and they have been caught off guard by the host's spur-of-the-moment decision. The servants are then instructed to bring back whomever they meet so that the food will not be wasted. The force of the original parable rests with the reversal of fortunes. "Can you imagine, asks Jesus, a situation in which all the invited guests are absent from a banquet and all the uninvited ones are present? This is fundamentally amoral and invites the hearers to recognize a situation of total reversal: the invited are absent, the uninvited are present. As parable it provokes their response to the Kingdom's arrival as radical and absolute reversal of their closed human situation."[33]

Where Jerome used the parable of the wicked tenants to respond to the Arians, Crossan categorizes it as "a parable of action." The parable appears in Mark 12:1–12, Matt 21:33–46, Luke 20:9–19, and the Gospel of Thomas, logia 65–66. Crossan argues that this parable was allegorized by Christian preachers before it was committed to writing in the synoptic tradition. In Mark, the first servant sent to collect some the produce of the vineyard was beaten and sent back empty-handed, the second was beat over the head, and the third was killed. The owner then sent his "beloved son" (12:6). Thinking that they could take possession of the inheritance, the tenants kill the beloved son. The owner retaliates by killing the tenants and giving the vineyard to others. Mark concludes with a citation, Ps 118:22–23: "The stone that the builders rejected has become the cornerstone; this was the Lord's doing, and it is amazing in our eyes." The citation of a verse or two of Psalm 118 appears in the other synoptic accounts and the Gospel of Thomas. In this way, the parable reads as an allegory of the Christian account of salvation, not unlike that found in the parable of the Great Supper. The vineyard represents Israel; the servants are the prophets; and the beloved son is Christ (the rejected stone who has become the cornerstone). Crossan, however, offers a more unorthodox interpretation. The Gospel of Thomas has "Let him who has ears hear," before the citation of Psalm 118. Crossan maintains that the original parable did not include the Psalm 118 verse(s) and in fact was not presented as an allegory.

> When, however, it is decided that Gos. Thom. 93:1–15 [Logion 65] is the best version of the original parable which we have extant at the moment, its meaning is quite clear as a parable of action. It is a deliberately shocking story of successful murder. The story is certainly possible and possibly actual in the Galilean

33. Ibid., 73.

turbulence of the period. It tells of some people who recognized their situation, saw their opportunity, and acted resolutely upon it. They glimpsed a way of getting full possession of the vineyard by murdering the only heir and, with murderous speed, they moved to accomplish their purpose.[34]

In offering her assessment of Crossan's interpretation, the biblical scholar Tania Oldenhage notes that "Crossan reads the tenants' behavior not as wicked but as smart action. However, it is not self-evident what precisely the parable is achieving in Crossan's view." Crossan opposes the reduction of the parables to moral lessons, and any attempt to make moral sense of this particular parable (e.g., take decisive action when the opportunity presents itself) seems strained. "Strictly understood within Crossan's framework, the parable of the Wicked Husbandmen is not 'making a point' but is effecting a subversion of moral expectation," concludes Oldenhage.[35] The shock wave that was unleashed in the advent and experienced in the reversal now reverberates through the action.

The Revitalization of the Biblical Imagery of Parables

The theologian Thomas F. Torrance (1913–2007) was one of the most ardent defenders of the Trinitarian theology promulgated at the early church councils, and it is within this context of faith that he offered his views on Jesus' parables in his 1938/39 lectures at Auburn Theological Seminary in New York.[36] Torrance's approach differs from many of the current treatments regarding parables in that he identifies the preacher of the parables as the Second Person of the Trinity rather than a reconstructed "historical Jesus." Second, Torrance equates Christ himself with the kingdom of God. The kingdom to which Jesus referred was not a political entity as some ancients sought or an ethical commonwealth as some moderns thought, but rather Christ was "thinking of the transcendent Kingdom of God which breaks into history in his own Person. It is not too much to say that *Jesus Christ is himself the Kingdom of God.*"[37] Third, because Christ is the kingdom, Torrance advances christological interpretations of the parables. According to Torrance, "Jesus himself was the Shepherd come in search for the Sheep, the

---

34. Ibid., 96.

35. Oldenhage, *Parables for Our Time*, 77.

36. Torrance's lectures on Christology and soteriology have been published under the title, *The Doctrine of Jesus Christ*.

37. Torrance, *Doctrine of Jesus Christ*, 32. Emphasis original.

Father in him was welcoming home the lost prodigals; he himself was the heir and the Son, the Savior and Redeemer of Israel."[38]

Torrance insists that the focus of the evangelists is on the divinity of Jesus Christ, not with the self-consciousness of Jesus (Schleiermacher) and certainly not on "the religion of Jesus" understood as "the Fatherhood of God corresponding to a brotherhood of all men based on the infinite value of the soul of each man" (von Harnack).[39] Rather, for the Gospel writers, it "is his *Person* that is important, for that is nothing else than the Gospel or the Kingdom of God among men. This does not mean that for the Evangelists Jesus came between men and God. On the contrary God was in Christ, and his Person meant the immediate confrontation of people by the actual and immediate presence of the Holy God himself."[40] Torrance later repeats the point even more emphatically: "Jesus Christ was God *incognito* on earth."[41] The proclaimer does not become the proclaimed, but is in fact the proclaimed all along.

While Christ is the Second Person of the Trinity, he does not directly reveal this fact at the start of his ministry. It is in the context of the gradual self-revelation of Christ that we can properly understand the reason why Christ taught in parables. "The parables are nothing else than indirect ways which Jesus used to speak about himself and his saving and healing work in the Kingdom of God. Indirect, I say, for he only unravelled them to those about him who really knew who he was."[42] For those with the eyes of faith, the parables, miracles, and teachings reveal the identity of the one who preached the words and performed the actions. For "Jesus does not explicitly state who he is, at least until the end; he only hints it and enlarges on what the disciples have already seen; but at the same time all his teaching and all his actions are calculated to draw attention towards himself . . . [The] whole teaching of Jesus is seen to centre on himself; the parables all tell of him and his work in the Kingdom of God; and further, his work is equivalent to the very Word of God."[43]

The parables force the hearers to make a decision on Christ. "Examine the parables and you will find that they are pointed towards Christ's own Person; they are calculated to place himself on the stage: and decision must be taken accordingly, decision directly in relation to his own Person and

38. Ibid., 38.
39. Ibid., 26.
40. Ibid., 27.
41. Ibid., 30.
42. Ibid., 37.
43. Ibid., 36.

place in the Work of God."[44] Christ does not merely speak of forgiveness or final judgement, but he grants forgiveness for sin and claims authority to sit in judgment. Torrance asks, "Who else was the Shepherd in search of the lost sheep than the Christ now welcoming publicans and sinners into the Kingdom? Who else was the physician of lost and sick souls than Christ, and who else the Savior and Messiah than he?"[45] These questions that Jesus posed to his first hearers, in Torrance's reading of the Gospels, are the same questions that Christ poses to listeners today.

Martin Luther King Jr. drew repeatedly on the parables of Christ in his sermons.[46] Three parables to which King returned on several occasions were the parable of Lazarus and Dives, the parable of the rich fool, and the Good Samaritan. The parable of Lazarus and the rich man served as bookends on his career. In October 1955 (two months before the bus boycott), the young pastor Martin Luther King Jr. preached the sermon, "The Impassable Gulf" at Dexter Avenue Baptist Church in Montgomery. The rich man was condemned, said King, because of his self-absorption and his incapacity to sympathize with others, but his "greatest sin was that he accepted the inequalities of circumstance as being the proper conditions of life." King continued,

> Dives is the white man who refuses to cross the gulf of segregation and lift his Negro brother to the position of first class citizenship, because he thinks segregation is a part of the fixed structure of the universe. Dives is the India Brahman who refuses to bridge the gulf between himself and his brother, because he feels that the gulf which is set forth by the caste system is a final principle of the universe. Dives is the American capitalist who never seeks to bridge the economic gulf between himself and the laborer, because he feels that it is the natural [state?] for some to live in inordinate luxury while others live in abject poverty.[47]

In his last Sunday sermon, delivered at the National Cathedral on March 31, 1968, King once again referenced Lazarus and Dives. "Dives went to hell because he sought to be a conscientious objector in the war against poverty. And this can happen in America, the richest nation in the world—and there's nothing wrong with that—this is America's opportunity to

---

44. Ibid., 40.
45. Ibid.
46. Gowler, *Parables after Jesus*, 223–28.
47. Carson et al., *Papers of Martin Luther King, Jr.*, 237–38. I am using the text from The Martin Luther King, Jr. Papers Project at Stanford.

help bridge the gulf between the have and the have-nots. The question is whether America will do it."[48]

King returned frequently to the parables of the foolish rich man and the Good Samaritan. King hammered home the similarity between the rich man and America in their concern over where to store their abundant quantities of grain.

> Our nation's productive machinery constantly brings forth such an abundance of food that we must build larger barns and spend more than a million dollars daily to store our surplus. Year after year we ask, "What shall I do, because I have no room where to bestow my fruits?" I have seen an answer in the faces of millions of poverty-stricken men and women in Asia, Africa, and South America. I have seen an answer in the appalling poverty in the Mississippi Delta and the tragic insecurity of the unemployed in large industrial cities of the North. What can we do? The answer is simple: feed the poor, clothe the naked, and heal the sick.[49]

King reflected on the parable of the Good Samaritan throughout his ministry, but no more poignantly than in his iconic "I've Been to the Mountaintop" sermon. King was in Memphis to support the sanitation workers' strike when he delivered his famous address.

> And so the first question that the priest asked, the first question that the Levite asked was, "If I stop to help this man, what will happen to me?" But then the Good Samaritan came by, and he reversed the question: "If I do not stop to help this man, what will happen to him?" That's the question before you tonight. Not, "If I stop to help the sanitation workers, what will happen to my job?" Not, "If I stop to help the sanitation workers, what will happen to all of the hours that I usually spend in my office every day and every week as a pastor?" The question is not, "If I stop to help this man in need, what will happen to me?" The question is, "If I do *not* stop to help the sanitation workers, what will happen to them?" That's the question.[50]

In the years since the sanitation strike, the question that King posed could be applied to a variety of social causes, but the price of asking that question, in many cases, remains the same that King paid the next day in Memphis.

48. King, "Remaining Awake Through a Great Revolution," 216. I discovered this in Branch, "The Last Wish of Martin Luther King."

49. King, *Strength to Love*, 53.

50. King, "I've Been to the Mountaintop." For sources on King's preaching on the Good Samaritan, see chapter 2 of Miller, *Martin Luther King's Biblical Epic*.

Charles Campbell illustrates the difference between liberal and postliberal homiletics by reflecting upon Hans Frei's observation that the parables should be "seen in the light of the story identifying Jesus of Nazareth rather than (reversely) providing the clue for the theme of that story. In the context of the *full* narrative—pericopes together with passion and resurrection—Jesus identifies the Kingdom of God and is only secondarily identified by his relation to it: He is himself the parable of the Kingdom."[51] By situating the parables within the context of the Gospel narrative, Frei departs from liberal commentators in two important ways. First, Frei "refuses to dissect the gospels through form and redaction criticism in order to isolate parabolic gems that may serve as aesthetic models for Christian preaching."[52] This problem goes hand in hand with the second problem, which involves the methodology of the preacher. When preachers isolate the parables from the Gospel narrative, they assume that they should preach in parabolic forms as well. "When Jesus becomes primarily a model preacher, as he does in the contemporary emphasis on parables, the stance of preaching changes. The preacher becomes not only one who points to Jesus Christ, but one who stands in the place of Jesus and 'preaches like Jesus preached.' This understanding of the place of Jesus in preaching is not only inconsistent with the content and function of the gospel narratives, but also with the preaching that we find in the rest of the New Testament."[53]

What homiletic implications follow from describing Jesus as "the parable of the Kingdom"? Campbell insists that good preaching focuses on what Frei calls "the singular identity and unsubstitutable history" of Jesus of Nazareth.[54] Preaching should focus on the identity of Jesus and not treat Jesus as a symbol of some general human experience or self-understanding. "The story of Jesus, not the particulars of human experience, is the fundamental reality and starting point. Indeed, to begin with human experience is almost immediately to run the risk of using the story of Jesus as a myth; Jesus easily becomes simply the predicate of some human experience," warns Campbell.[55] Preachers should draw their listeners into the gospel story, for it is only by knowing the identity of Jesus that we can properly understand what he meant by "the Kingdom of God." Campbell notes approvingly, "Frei even goes so far as to suggest that the parable cannot and should not be understood outside

---

51. Frei, "Theology and the Interpretation," 104. Emphasis original.
52. Campbell, *Preaching Jesus*, 178.
53. Ibid., 180.
54. Frei, *Identity of Jesus Christ*, 137.
55. Campbell, *Preaching Jesus*, 193.

the larger narratives that render Jesus' identity. It is the person of Jesus who gives meaning to the parables and not vice versa."[56]

Reading the Gospel of Mark through the lens of reader-response criticism, Robert Fowler sees the parables illustrating the role that the reader plays in generating the meaning of a text. Fowler declares, "A text does not come to us wearing its meaning, like a campaign button, on its lapel. The reader-response critic argues that whatever meaning is and wherever it is found the reader is ultimately responsible for determining meaning."[57] The reader-response critic does not see meaning as a fixed property residing within the text, but a "dynamic, ever-changing creation of the reader in the act of reading."[58] Fowler locates meaning within "the temporal experience of reading." He argues, "In brief, the reading experience, if we stop and think about it, is full of twists and turns, surprises and developments. Our minds change constantly as we read. As our minds change, meaning changes."[59] As we read, we anticipate certain developments and recall past moments in the story, but we as readers also fill in gaps in the story, and in Mark's Gospel this is precisely the case with Jesus' teaching on parables.

Fowler illustrates how the reader's response to the teaching on parables in Mark 4 alters the meaning of the text. The chapter begins with Jesus offering the parable of the sower, after which the disciples ask Jesus about the meaning of the parable. Jesus replies, "To you has been given the secret of the kingdom of God, but for those outside everything comes in parables; in order that 'they may indeed look, but not perceive, and may indeed listen, but not understand; so that they may not turn again and be forgiven'" (4:11–12). Referring to the claim that the disciples have been given the secret of the kingdom, Fowler notes, "The reader has a major problem here. If we review the first four chapters of the Gospel, we cannot find the place in the story where the 'secret of the kingdom of God' was given to Jesus' followers."[60] There is a gap between what the disciples have presumably been told and what the reader knows, and so the reader fills in the gap. We next have the problem of Jesus' reply. Fowler writes, "To add further insult to the exclusion of the reader from the secret of the kingdom, 4:11 goes on to state that 'for those outside everything is in parables.' Apparently the secret of the kingdom is reserved for insiders

---

56. Ibid., 190.
57. Fowler, "Reader-Response Criticism," 51.
58. Ibid.
59. Ibid., 56.
60. Ibid., 63.

only; to outsiders, such as the reader, it is a mysterious puzzle or riddle."[61] This judgment is tempered as the reader discovers that the disciples seem to lack understanding as well (4:13). The ones that the reader presumes to be insiders in 4:11 now seem to be outsiders in 4:13.

> This double reversal in 4:13 encourages us to look back over the preceding verses to reconsider and reevaluate what we have just read. Once we hear Jesus' sharp rebuke of the disciples in 4:13, we may want to reevaluate his comment to them back in 4:11 that they are the recipients of the secret of the kingdom of God. In retrospect, in 4:11 could Jesus have been speaking with tongue in cheek? Could he have been speaking in verbal irony? His words might not have sounded ironic when we were at 4:11, but viewed in hindsight from 4:13, they may have changed in tone.[62]

Sandwiched between 4:11 and 4:13 is the difficult teaching that Jesus speaks in parable to prevent the outsiders from understanding and hence converting. The reader must decide if Jesus is speaking ironically or literally in 4:12, which in turn alters how the reader understands 4:11 and 4:13.

To navigate the parabolic world into which Jesus summons us requires that we develop our capacity for theological creativity. It is the very skill that we sharpen by studying both the profound commentary of past theological masters and the penetrating analysis of present thinkers, as we sit with them reading from the opening verse of the first creation story to the final "Amen" in Revelation. In doing so, we hope to be like "the master of the household who brings out of his treasure what is new and what is old" (Matt 13:52) so that we can continually revitalize our responses to the most critical theological, moral, and spiritual questions of our time.

Discussion Questions

1. What did Jesus mean by "the kingdom of God"? Choose a parable from Matthew 13 and offer your interpretation.
2. Is Jerome's use of the parables to renounce heretical teachings an appropriate or inappropriate use of parables?
3. How does the parable of the rich man and Lazarus apply to a situation in your local community?
4. Is Crossan's approach to the parables appealing or unappealing?

---

61. Ibid., 72.
62. Ibid.

5. What does it mean to say that Jesus is the parable of the kingdom or the parable of God?
6. Are some interpretations of the parables wrong?
7. Does the meaning of a parable change over the course of reading it? If so, does the meaning it has for the reader at the conclusion have priority over earlier readings?

Suggested Readings

For background on Jerome, see Part One of Stefan Rebenich, *Jerome* (New York: Routledge, 2002). For Jerome's exegesis, see the entry and bibliography by Pierre Jay in Charles Kannengiesser, *Handbook of Patristic Exegesis*, Volume II (Boston: Brill, 2004), 1094–1133. For background on Chrysostom, see Wendy Mayer and Pauline Allen, *John Chrysostom* (New York: Routledge, 1999). There are also helpful chapters in Susan R. Holman, ed., *Wealth and Poverty in Early Church and Society* (Grand Rapids: Baker Academic, 2008). For background on Crossan, see Donald L. Denton Jr., *Historiography and Hermeneutics in Jesus Studies* (New York: T. & T. Clark, 2004) and Robert B. Stewart, *The Quest of the Hermeneutical Jesus* (Lanham, MD: University Press of America, 2008). For current approaches to the parables, see Ruben Zimmermann, *Puzzling the Parables of Jesus* (Minneapolis: Fortress, 2015). For a history of the interpretation of the parables, see David B. Gowler, *The Parables after Jesus* (Grand Rapids: Baker Academic, 2017).

Bibliography

Achard of St. Victor. *Sermon XV.* In *Achard of Saint Victor: Works*, edited by Hugh Feiss, 291-351. Kalamazoo: Cistercian, 2001.
Adam, A. K. M., ed. *Postmodern Interpretations of the Bible.* St. Louis: Chalice, 2001.
Adams, Kimberley VanEsveld. "Family Influences on 'The Minister's Wooing' and 'Oldtown Folks': Henry Ward Beecher and Calvin Stowe." *Religion and Literature* 38 (2006) 27-61.
Allen, Rosamund A. "Introduction." In *Richard Rolle: The English Writings*, 9-64. Mahwah, NJ: Paulist, 1988.
Ambrose. *Hexameron, Paradise, Cain and Abel.* Translated by John J. Savage. Fathers of the Church 42. Washington, DC: Catholic University of America Press, 1961.
———. *On the Death of His Brother Satyrus* and *On Faith in the Resurrection.* In *Funeral Orations by Gregory Nazianzen and Saint Ambrose*, 197-259. Translated by John J. Sullivan and Martin McGuire. Washington, DC: Catholic University of America Press, 1953.
Andolsen, Barbara Hilkert. "Our Companions Enfolded in the Love of Spirit—Sophia: Mariology and the Communion of Saints in the Theology of Elizabeth A. Johnson." In *Things New and Old*, edited by Phyllis Zagano and Terrence W. Tilley, 81-90. New York: Crossroad, 1999. 81-90.
Aquino, Maria Pilar. "Feminist Intercultural Theology: Toward a Shared Future of Justice." In *Feminist Intercultural Theology*, edited by Maria Pilar Aquino and Maria Jose Rosado-Nunes, 9-28. Maryknoll, NY: Orbis, 2007.
———. *Our Cry for Life.* Maryknoll, NY: Orbis, 1993.
———. "Theological Method in U.S. Latino/a Theology." In *From the Heart of Our People*, edited by Orlando O. Espin and Miguel H. Diaz, 6-48. Maryknoll, NY: Orbis, 1999.
Aquino, Maria Pilar, and Maria Jose Rosado-Nunes, eds. *Feminist Intercultural Theology* Maryknoll, NY: Orbis, 2007.
Auden, W. H. "Purely Subjective." In *Prose*, Volume II, edited by Edward Mendelson, 184-98. Princeton: Princeton University Press, 2002.
———. "The Seven Ages." Part Two of "The Age of Anxiety." In *Collected Longer Poems*, 274-96. New York: Random House, 1969.
Augustine. *City of God.* Translated by Gerald G. Walsh, Demetrius B. Zema, Grace Monahan, and Daniel Honan. Garden City, NY: Image, 1958.
———. *Instructing Beginners in Faith.* Translated by Raymond Canning. Hyde Park, NY: New City, 2006.
———. *On Christian Teaching.* Translated by R. P. H. Green. New York: Oxford University Press, 1997.
———. "On the Merits and Forgiveness of Sins." In *A Select Library of Nicene and Post-Nicene Fathers* V, edited by Philip Schaff, 11-78. Grand Rapids: Eerdmans, 1956.

———. "Question 64." In *Eighty-Three Different Questions*, 127–35. Translated by David L. Mosher. Fathers of the Church 70. Washington, DC: Catholic University of America Press, 1982.

———. *Tractate 15*. In *Tractates on the Gospel of John 11–27*, 78–99. Translated by John W. Rettig. Fathers of the Church 79. Washington, DC: Catholic University of America Press, 1988.

Bahlke, George W., ed. *Critical Essays on W. H. Auden*. New York: G. K. Hall, 1991.

Balthasar, Hans von. *Truth is Symphonic*. San Francisco: Ignatius, 1987.

Barth, Karl. *Church Dogmatics* II/2. Edinburgh: T. & T. Clark, 1957.

Basil of Caesarea. *Exegetic Homilies: On the Hexameron*. Translated by Agnes Clare Way. Fathers of the Church 46. Washington, DC: Catholic University of America Press, 1963.

Beeley, Christopher, ed. *Re-Reading Gregory of Nazianzus*. Washington, DC: Catholic University of America Press, 2012.

Behr, John. "The Rational Animal: A Rereading of Gregory of Nyssa's *De hominis opificio*." *Journal of Early Christian Studies* 7 (1999) 219–47.

Bergstrom-Allen, Johan, ed. *Climbing the Mountain: The Carmelite Journey*. Faversham, UK: St. Albert's, 2014.

Berkman, John, and Michael Cartwright, eds. *The Hauerwas Reader*. Durham, NC: Duke University Press, 2001.

Boeve, Lieven, Hans Geysels, and Stijn Van den Bossche, eds. *Encountering Transcendence*. Leuven: Peeters, 2005.

Bonaventure. *The Soul's Journey into God*. Translated by Ewert Cousins. Mahwah, NJ: Paulist, 1978.

Borg, Marcus. *Convictions*. New York: HarperCollins, 2014.

———. *The Heart of Christianity*. New York: HarperCollins, 2003.

———. *Reading the Bible Again for the First Time*. New York: HarperCollins, 2001.

———. *Speaking Christian*. New York: HarperCollins, 2011.

Braaten, Carl. "Eschatology and Mission in the Theology of Robert Jenson." In *Trinity, Time, and Church*, edited by Colin E. Gunton, 298–311. Grand Rapids: Eerdmans, 2000.

Branch, Taylor. "The Last Wish of Martin Luther King." *New York Times*, April 6, 2008.

Brock, Sebastian P. "Clothing Metaphors as a Means of Theological Expression in Syriac Tradition." In *Typus, Symbol, Allegorie*, edited by Margot Schmidt and Carl-Friedrich Geyer, 11–38. Regensburg, DE: Pustet, 1982.

———. "Introduction." In *St. Ephrem the Syrian: Hymns on Paradise*, 7–75. Crestwood, NY: St. Vladimir's Seminary Press, 1990.

———. *The Luminous Eye*. Kalamazoo: Cistercian, 1992.

Brown, Dennis. *Via Trilinguis*. Kampen, NL: Kok Pharos, 1992.

Brueggemann, Walter. *Texts Under Negotiation*. Minneapolis: Fortress, 1993.

Buchan, Thomas. "Paradise as the Landscape of Salvation in Ephrem the Syrian." In *Partakers of the Divine Nature*, edited by Michael J. Christensen and Jeffery A. Witting, 146–59. Madison, NJ: Fairleigh Dickinson University Press, 2007.

Bultmann, Rudolf. *History and Eschatology*. Edinburgh: Edinburgh University Press, 1957.

———. *Jesus Christ and Mythology*. New York: Scribner, 1958.

———. *Kerygma and Myth*. New York: Harper and Row, 1961.

Bunyan, John. *The Doctrine of the Law and Grace Unfolded*. In *The Miscellaneous Works of John Bunyan*, Volume II, edited by Richard L. Greaves, 1–226. Oxford: Claredon, 1976.

———. *Grace Abounding to the Chief of the Sinners*. New York: Penguin, 1987.

Burns, J. Patout. "Creation and Fall according to Ambrose of Milan." In *Augustine: Biblical Exegete*, edited by Frederick Van Fleteren and Joseph C. Schnaubelt, 71–97. New York: Peter Lang, 2001.

Calvin, John. *Genesis*. Edited by Alister McGrath and J.I. Parker. Wheaton, IL: Crossway, 2001.

Campbell, Charles L. *Preaching Jesus*. Grand Rapids: Eerdmans, 1997.

Caputo, John D. *On Religion*. New York: Routledge, 2001.

Cardman, Francine. "Poverty and Wealth as Theater: John Chrysostom's Homilies on Lazarus and the Rich Man." In *Wealth and Poverty in Early Church and Society*, edited by Susan R. Holman, 159–75, Grand Rapids: Baker Academic, 2008.

Carson, Clayborne, et al., eds. *The Papers of Martin Luther King, Jr. Volume VI: Advocate of the Social Gospel, September 1948—March 1963*. Berkeley: University of California Press, 2007.

Carson, Clayborne, and Peter Holloran, eds. *A Knock at Midnight: Inspiration from the Great Sermons of Reverend Martin Luther King, Jr.* New York: Warner, 2000.

Casiday, Augustine. *The Orthodox Christian World*. New York: Routledge, 2012.

Christensen, Michael J., and Jeffery A. Witting, eds. *Partakers of the Divine Nature*. Madison, NJ: Fairleigh Dickinson University Press, 2007.

Chryssavgis, John. *John Climacus*. Burlington, VT: Ashgate, 2004.

Costache, Doru. "Christian Worldview: Understandings from Basil the Great." *Phronema* XXV (2010) 21–56.

Cousins, Ewert. "Introduction." In *The Soul's Journey into God*, 1–48. Mahwah, NJ: Paulist, 1978.

Crawford, Nathan. *Theology as Improvisation*. Boston: Brill, 2013.

Crossan, John Dominic. *In Parables*. New York: Harper and Row, 1973.

Cunningham, David S. *Faithful Persuasion*. Notre Dame: University of Notre Dame Press, 1991.

———. *These Three Are One*. Malden, MA: Blackwell, 1998.

———. "What Do We Mean by 'God'?" In *Essentials of Christian Theology*, edited by William C. Placher, 76–92. Louisville: Westminster/John Knox Press, 2003.

Cunningham, Lawrence S., and Keith J. Egan. *Christian Spirituality*. Mahwah, NJ: Paulist, 1996.

Daley, Brian E. "Introduction." In *Gregory of Nazianzus*, 1–61. New York: Routledge, 2006.

Daley, Brian E., ed. *Gregory of Nazianzus*. New York: Routledge, 2006.

Davies, Michael. "*Grace Abounding to the Chief of Sinners*: John Bunyan and spiritual autobiography." In *The Cambridge Companion to Bunyan*, edited by Anne Durnan-Page, 67–79. Cambridge: Cambridge University Press, 2010.

Davies, Oliver. *Graceful Reading: Theology and Narrative in the Works of John Bunyan*. Oxford: Oxford University Press, 2002.

———. "Ruysbroeck, a Kempis and the *Theologia Deutsch*." In *The Study of Spirituality*, edited by Cheslyn Jones, Geoffrey Wainwright, and Edward Yarnold, 321–24. New York: Oxford University Press, 1986.

Davis, Ellen F., and Richard B. Hays, eds. *The Art of Reading Scripture*. Grand Rapids: Eerdmans, 2003.

Dawson, David. "Sign Theory, Allegorical Reading, and the Motions of the Soul in *De doctrine christiana*." In *De doctrine christiana: A Classic of Western Culture*, edited by Duane W. H. Arnold and Pamela Bright, 123–41. Notre Dame: University of Notre Dame Press, 1995.

De Lubac, Henri. *History and Spirit: The Understanding of Scripture according to Origen*. San Francisco: Ignatius, 2007.

de Vries, Pieter. *John Bunyan on the Order of Salvation*. New York: Peter Lang, 1994.

Dorrien, Gary. *The Word as True Myth*. Louisville: Westminster John Knox, 1997.

Edwards, Jonathan. *A History of the Work of Redemption*, edited by John F. Wilson. New Haven: Yale University Press, 1989.

———. "Types of the Messiah." In *Typological Writings*, edited by Wallace E. Anderson and Mason I. Lowance Jr. with David H. Watters, 187–324. New Haven: Yale University Press, 1993.

Egan, Keith. "Guigo II: The Theology of the Contemplative Life." In *The Spirituality of Western Christendom*, edited by Roxanne Elder, 106–15. Kalamazoo: Cistercian, 1976.

Ephrem the Syrian. *Hymns on Paradise*. Translated by Sebastian Brock. Crestwood, NY: St. Vladimir's Seminary Press, 1990.

———. "Letter to Publius." In *St. Ephrem the Syrian: Selected Prose Works*, 338–55. Edited by Kathleen McVey. Fathers of the Church 91. Washington, DC: Catholic University Press, 1994.

Espin, Orlando O., and Miguel H. Diaz, eds. *From the Heart of Our People*. Maryknoll, NY: Orbis, 1999.

Farley, Edward. *Faith and Beauty*. Burlington, VT: Ashgate, 2001.

Farrer, Austin. *The Glass of Vision*. Westminster: Dacre, 1948.

———. *A Rebirth of Images*. Westminster: Dacre, 1949.

Feiss, Hugh. "Introduction." In *Achard of Saint Victor: Works*, 19–58. Kalamazoo: Cistercian, 2001.

Feiss, Hugh, ed. *On Love*. Hyde Park, NY: New City, 2012.

Ferguson, Everett. "Gregory's Baptismal Theology and the Alexandrian Tradition." In *Re-Reading Gregory of Nazianzus*, edited by Christopher Beeley, 67–83. Washington, DC: Catholic University of America Press, 2012.

Fish, Stanley. *Is There a Text in This Class?* Cambridge, MA: Harvard University Press, 1980.

Foster, Charles H. *The Rungless Ladder*. Durham, NC: Duke University Press, 1954.

Fowler, James W. "Faith Development Theory and the Postmodern Challenges." *The International Journal for the Psychology of Religion* 11 (2001) 159–72.

———. *Stages of Faith*. San Francisco: Harper and Row, 1981.

Fowler, Robert M. "Reader-Response Criticism: Figuring Mark's Reader." In *Mark and Method*, edited by Janice Capel and Stephen D. Moore, 50–83. Minneapolis: Fortress, 1992.

Frei, Hans. *The Eclipse of Biblical Narrative*. New Haven: Yale University Press, 1974.

———. *The Identity of Jesus Christ*. Philadelphia: Fortress, 1975.

———. "Theology and the Interpretation of Narrative: Some Hermeneutical Considerations." In *Theology and Narrative*, edited by George Hunsinger and William C. Placher, 94–116. New York: Oxford University Press, 1993.

Freiss, Horace Leland. *Schleiermacher's Soliloquies.* Chicago: Regent Court, 1957.
Fuller, John. *W.H. Auden: A Commentary.* Princeton: Princeton University Press, 2000.
Gilkey, Langdon. *On Niebuhr.* Chicago: University of Chicago Press, 2001.
Golitzin, Alexander. *On the Mystical Life: The Ethical Discourses*, Vol. 2. Crestwood, NY: St. Vladimir's Seminary Press, 1996.
Gowler, David B. *The Parables after Jesus.* Grand Rapids: Baker Academic, 2017.
Greaves, Richard. *John Bunyan and English Nonconformity.* London: Hambledon, 1992.
Greer, Rowan. "Introduction." In *Origen*, 1–37. New York: Paulist, 1979.
Gregory of Nazianzus. Oration 38 and Oration 39. In *Gregory of Nazianzus*, edited by Brian Daley, 117–38. New York: Routledge, 2006.
———. *Oration 40.* In *Festal Orations*, edited by Nonna Verna Harrison, 99–142. Crestwood, NY: St. Vladimir's Seminary Press, 2008.
Gregory of Nyssa. *The Great Catechism*, edited by H. Wace and P. Schall, 471–509. A Selected Library of Nicene and Post-Nicene Fathers, sec. series, vol. 5. Grand Rapids: Eerdmans, 1954.
———. "On the Making of Man," edited by H. Wace and P. Schall, 387–427. A Selected Library of Nicene and Post-Nicene Fathers, sec. series, vol. 5. Grand Rapids: Eerdmans, 1952.
———. *On the Soul and the Resurrection.* Translated by Catharine P. Roth. Crestwood, NY: St. Vladimir's Seminary Press, 1993.
Griggs, David. *Divine Eros: Hymns of St. Symeon the New Theologian.* Crestwood, NY: St. Vladimir's Seminary Press, 2010.
———. "Introduction." In *Divine Eros*, 9–29. Crestwood, NY: St. Vladimir's Seminary Press, 2010.
Gschwandtner, Christina M. *Reading Jean-Luc Marion.* Bloomington: Indiana University Press, 2007.
Guigo II. *The Ladder of Monks.* Translated by Edmund Colledge and James Walsh. Kalamazoo: Cistercian, 1981.
Gunton, Colin E., ed. *Trinity, Time, and Church.* Grand Rapids: Eerdmans, 2000.
Gustafson, James. *Ethics from a Theocentric Perspective*, vol. 1. Chicago: University of Chicago Press, 1981.
———. *An Examined Faith.* Minneapolis: Fortress, 2004.
Gutierrez, Gustavo. *We Drink from Our Own Wells.* Maryknoll, NY: Orbis, 2003.
Harkins, Frank T., and Frans van Lierre, eds. *Interpretation of Scripture: Theory.* Turnhout, BE: Brepols, 2012.
Harrison, Nonna Verna. *Festal Orations.* Crestwood, NY: St. Vladimir's Seminary Press, 2008.
Hauerwas, Stanley. *Against the Nations.* San Francisco: Harper and Row, 1985.
———. *Christian Existence Today.* Durham, NC: Labyrinth, 1988.
———. *Cross-Shattered Christ.* Grand Rapids: Brazos, 2004.
———. *The Peaceable Kingdom.* Notre Dame: University of Notre Dame Press, 1983.
———. *Vision and Virtue.* Notre Dame: University of Notre Dame Press, 1974.
———. "Vision, Stories, and Character." In *The Hauerwas Reader*, edited by John Berkman and Michael Cartwright, 165–70. Durham, NC: Duke University Press, 2001.
Hauerwas, Stanley, and William H. Willimon. *Resident Aliens.* Nashville: Abingdon, 1989.
Haynes, Carolyn A. *Divine Destiny.* Jackson: University Press of Mississippi, 1998.

Hedley, Douglas, and Brian Hebblethwaite, eds. *The Human Person in God's World*. London: SCM, 2006.

Hefling, Charles, C. *Jacob's Ladder: Theology and Spirituality in the Thought of Austin Farrer*. Cambridge, MA: Crowley, 1979.

Heintz, Michael. "Ambrose of Milan." In *Dictionary of Major Biblical Interpreters*, edited by Donald K. McKim, 118–23. Downers Grove, IL: IVP Academic, 2007.

Henriksen, Jan-Olav. *Desire, Gift, and Recognition*. Grand Rapids: Eerdmans, 2009.

Henry, Patrick. "What was the Iconoclastic Controversy About?" *Church History* 45 (1976) 16–31.

Higton, Mike. *Christ, Providence, and History*. New York: T. & T. Clark, 2004.

Hildebrand, Stephen M. *The Trinitarian Theology of Basil of Caesarea*. Washington, DC: Catholic University of America Press, 2007.

Hofer, Andrew. *Christ in the Life and Teaching of Gregory of Nazianzus*. Oxford: Oxford University Press, 2013.

Holman, Susan R., ed. *Wealth and Poverty in Early Church and Society*. Grand Rapids: Baker Academic 2008.

James, William. *The Varieties of Religious Experience*. New York: Modern Library, 1902.

Jeffrey, David Lyle, ed. *A Dictionary of Biblical Tradition in English Literature*. Grand Rapids: Eerdmans, 1992.

Jenson, Robert. "The End is Music." In *Edwards in Our Time*, edited by Sang Hyun Lee and Allen C. Guelzo, 161–72. Grand Rapids: Eerdmans, 1999.

———. *Systematic Theology*, Volume II. New York: Oxford, 1999.

St. Jerome. *Commentary on Matthew*. Washington, DC: Catholic University of America Press, 2008.

John Chrysostom. *On Wealth and Poverty*. Crestwood, NY: St. Vladimir's Seminary Press, 1984.

John Climacus. *The Ladder of Divine Ascent*. Mahwah, NJ: Paulist, 1982.

John of Damascus. *On the Divine Images*. Translated by David Anderson. Crestwood: St. Vladimir's Seminary Press, 1980.

———. *Three Treatises on the Divine Images*. Translated by Andrew Louth. Crestwood, NY: St. Vladimir's Seminary Press, 2003.

Jones, Arthur. "'No time for glorifying and exalting': Two Perspectives." *National Catholic Reporter* (April 14, 2005). http://www.nationalcatholicreporter.org/update/conclave/pto41405aj.htm.

Jones, Cheslyn, et al., eds. *The Study of Spirituality*. New York: Oxford, 1986.

Johnson, Elizabeth. *Truly Our Sister*. New York: Continuum, 2003.

Keeble, N. H., ed. *John Bunyan: Conventicle and Parnassus*. Oxford: Claredon, 1988.

Kawashima, Robert S. "A Revisionist Reading Revisited: On the Creation of Adam and Then Eve." *Vetus testamentum* 56 (2006) 46–57.

Kearney, Richard. *Anatheism*. New York: Columbia University Press, 2010.

———. "Imagining the Sacred Stranger." In *Politics and the Religious Imagination*, edited by John Dyck, Paul Rowe, and Jens Zimmermann, 15–30. New York: Routledge, 2010.

Keller, Catherine. "Eyeing the Apocalypse." In *Postmodern Interpretations of the Bible*, edited by A. K. M. Adam, 253–77. St. Louis: Chalice, 2001.

King, Martin Luther, Jr. "The Impassable Gulf." https://swap.stanford.edu/20141218225617/http://mlk-kppo1.stanford.edu/primarydocuments/Vol6/2Oct1955TheImpassableGulf-TheParableofDivesandLazarus.pdf.

———. "I've Been to the Mountaintop." http://kingencyclopedia.stanford.edu/encyclopedia/documentsentry/ive_been_to_the_mountaintop/.
———. "Remaining Awake Through a Great Revolution." In *A Knock at Midnight: Inspiration from the Great Sermons of Reverend Martin Luther King, Jr.*, edited by Clayborne Carson and Peter Holloran, 201–24. New York: Warner, 2000.
———. *Strength to Love*. New York: Harper and Row, 1963.
Kitchen, Robert A. "Ephrem the Syrian." In *The Orthodox Christian World*, edited by Augustine Casiday, 201–7. New York: Routledge, 2012.
Koester, Nancy. *Harriet Beecher Stowe: A Spiritual Life*. Grand Rapids: Eerdmans, 2014.
Koosed, Jennifer L. "Coming of Age in Phyllis Trible's World." *Lexington Theological Quarterly* 38 (2003) 15–19.
Kreeft, Peter. *Jacob's Ladder*. San Francisco: Ignatius, 2013.
———. "The Most Important Argument in Christian Apologetics." In *The Intellectuals Speak Out About God*, edited by Roy Abraham Varghese, 243–53. Chicago: Regnery Gateway, 1984.
Ladner, Gerhart B. "The Philosophical Anthropology of Saint Gregory of Nyssa." *Dumbarton Oaks Papers* 12 (1958) 60–94.
Lamm, Julia. "Introduction." In *Schleiermacher*, 1–100. Mahwah, NJ: Paulist, 2014.
Lawrence, C. H. *Medieval Monasticism*. New York: Longman, 2001.
Lee, Sang Hyun, and Allen C. Guelzo, eds. *Edwards in Our Time*. Grand Rapids: Eerdmans, 1999.
Leinhard, Joseph T., et al., eds. *Augustine: Presbyter Factus Sum*. New York: Peter Lang, 1993.
Leiva, Sam. "An Age of Anxiety: W. H. Auden's Existential Theology of the 1940s." http://chum338.blogs.wesleyan.edu/2014/12/31/w-h-auden-existential-theology-of-the-1940s/.
Lim, Richard. "The Politics of Interpretation in Basil of Caesarea's *Hexameron*." *Vigiliae Christianae* 44 (1990) 351–70.
Lindbeck, George. *The Nature of Doctrine*. Philadelphia: Westminster, 1984.
Louth, Andrew. "Introduction." In *Three Treatises on the Divine Images*, by St. John of Damascus, 7–17. Crestwood, NY: St. Vladimir's Seminary Press, 2003.
———. *The Origins of the Christian Mystical Tradition*. Oxford: Oxford University Press, 2007.
———. *St. John Damascene*. Oxford: Oxford University Press, 2002.
Luther, Martin. *Lectures on Genesis*. In *Luther's Works*, vol. 5, edited by Jaroslav Pelikan. St. Louis: Concordia, 1968.
Lyotard, Jean-Francois. *The Postmodern Condition: A Report on Knowledge*. Translated by Geoff Bennington and Brian Massumi. Minneapolis: University of Minnesota Press, 1984.
MacSwain, Robert, ed. *Scripture, Metaphysics, and Poetry*. Burlington, VT: Ashgate, 2013.
Maesen, Rob. "John Ruusbroec as a Major Contemplative Christian Author." *Sino-Christian Studies* 3 (2007) 61–84.
Maier, Carmen E. *Poetry as Exegesis: Ephrem the Syrian's Method of Scriptural Interpretation Especially as Seen in His Hymns on Paradise and Hymns on Unleavened Bread*. PhD diss., Princeton Theological Seminary, 2012.
Marion, Jean-Luc. *God Without Being*. Chicago: University of Chicago Press, 1991.
Maritain, Jacques. *Art and Scholasticism*. New York: Scribner, n.d.

Martens, Peter W. *Origen and Scripture*. Oxford: Oxford University Press, 2012.
Martin, Dale B. *Pedagogy of the Bible*. Louisville: Westminster John Knox, 2008.
Matz, Brian. "Baptism as Theological Intersection in Gregory Nazianzen's Oration 39." *Sacris Erudiri* 51 (2012) 35–58.
Mayer, Wendy, and Pauline Allen. *John Chrysostom*. New York: Routledge, 1999.
McFague, Sallie. *Life Abundant*. Minneapolis: Fortress, 2001.
McGinn, Bernard. *The Growth of Mysticism*. New York: Crossroad, 1994.
McGrath, Alister. "An Evangelical Evaluation of Postliberalism." In *The Nature of Confession*, edited by Timothy R. Phillips and Dennis L. Okholm, 23–44. Downers Grove, IL: InterVarsity, 1996.
McGreal, Wilfrid. *At the Fountain of Elijah*. Maryknoll, NY: Oribis, 1999.
McGuckin, John A. *St. Gregory of Nazianzus: An Intellectual Biography*. Crestwood, NY: St. Vladimir's Seminary Press, 2001.
———. "Symeon the New Theologian's *Hymns of Divine Eros*: A Neglected Masterpiece of the Christian Mystical Tradition." *Spirtus* 5 (2005) 182–202.
McVey, Kathleen, ed. *St. Ephrem the Syrian: Selected Prose Works*. Fathers of the Church 91. Washington, DC: Catholic University Press, 1994.
Merrill, Timothy F. "Achard of Saint Victor and the Medieval Exegetical Tradition: Rom 7:22–25 in a Sermon on the Feast of the Resurrection." *The Westminster Theological Journal* 48 (1986) 47–62.
Miller, Keith D. *Martin Luther King's Biblical Epic*. Jackson: University Press of Mississippi, 2012.
Mommaers, Paul. *Jan van Ruusbroec: Mystical Union with God*. Leuven: Peeters, 2009.
Moran, Gabriel. *The Present Revelation*. New York: Seabury, 1972.
Murray, Robert. "The Theory of Symbolism in St. Ephrem's Theology." *Parole de l'Orient* 6/7 (1975–76) 1–20.
Nelson, Gerald. *Changes of Heart*. In *Critical Essays on W. H. Auden*, edited by George W. Bahlke. New York: G. K. Hall, 1991.
Neville, Robert C. "Contextualization and the Non-obvious Meaning of Religious Symbols: New Dimensions to the Problem of Truth." *Neue Zeitschrift fur systematische Theology und Religionsphilosophie* 44 (2002) 71–88.
———. *On the Scope and Truth of Theology*. New York: T. & T. Clark, 2006.
———. *Religion in Late Modernity*. Albany: SUNY Press, 2002.
———. *The Truth of Broken Symbols*. Albany: SUNY Press, 1996.
———. "Watch for the Light." In *The God Who Beckons*, 31–36. Nashville: Abingdon, 1999.
Newey, Vincent. "'With the eyes of my understanding': Bunyan, Experience, and Acts of Interpretation." In *John Bunyan: Conventicle and Parnassus*, edited by N. H. Keeble, 189–216. Oxford: Claredon, 1988.
Niebuhr, Reinhold. *An Interpretation of Christian Ethics*. New York: Seabury, 1963.
———. "The Truth in Myths." In *Faith and Politics*, edited by Ronald Stone, 15–31. New York: George Braziller, 1968.
Norris, John M. "The Theological Structure of Augustine's Exegesis in the *Tractatus in Evangelium Ioanni*." In *Augustine: Presbyter Factus Sum*, edited by Joseph T. Leinhard, Earl C. Muller, and Roland J. Teske, 385–94. New York: Peter Lang, 1993.
Oldenhage, Tania. *Parables for Our Time*. Oxford: Oxford University Press, 2002.

BIBLIOGRAPHY

Origen. *Homily XXVII on Numbers.* In *Origen,* 245–69. Translated by Rowan A. Greer. New York: Paulist, 1979.

———. *On First Principles.* Translated by G. W. Butterworth. Gloucester, MA: Peter Smith, 1973.

———. "The Prologue to the Commentary on the Song of Songs." In *Origen,* 217–44. Translated by Rowan A. Greer. New York: Paulist, 1979.

Owens, W. R. "Introduction." *Grace Abounding to the Chief of the Sinners,* by John Bunyan, vii—xxiii. New York: Penguin, 1987.

Pascal, Blaise. *Pensees.* Translated by W. F. Trotte. New York: Dutton, 1958.

Pecknold, C. C. *Transforming Postliberal Theology.* New York: T. & T. Clark, 2005.

Pelikan, Jaroslav. *The Christian Tradition,* vol. 1. Chicago: University of Chicago Press, 1971.

Placher, William C., ed. *Essentials of Christian Theology.* Louisville: Westminster/John Knox, 2003.

———. *Unapologetic Theology.* Louisville: Westminster/John Knox Press, 1989.

Rebenich, Stefan. *Jerome.* New York: Routledge, 2002.

Reventlow, Henning Graf. *History of Biblical Interpretation,* vol. 1. Atlanta: Society of Biblical Literature, 2009.

Ribot, Felip. *The Ten Books on the Way of Life and Great Deeds of the Carmelites,* edited by Richard Copsey. Faversham, UK: St. Albert's, 2007.

Richard of St. Victor. *The Twelve Patriarchs.* Translated by Grover Zinn. New York: Paulist, 1979.

Richardson, Ruth Drucilla, ed. *Schleiermacher in Context.* Lewiston, NY: Edwin Mellen, 1991.

Ricoeur, Paul. *The Symbolism of Evil.* New York: Harper and Row, 1967.

Rohr, Richard. *Falling Upward.* San Francisco: Josey Bass, 2011.

Rolle, Richard. *The English Writings.* Mahwah, NJ: Paulist, 1988.

———. *The Fire of Love.* New York: Penguin, 1972.

Rombs, Ronnie J. *Saint Augustine and the Fall of the Soul.* Washington, DC: Catholic University of America Press, 2006.

Rorty, Richard. *Philosophy and the Mirror of Nature.* Princeton: Princeton University Press, 1979.

Roth, Catherine. "Introduction." In *On Wealth and Poverty,* 7–18. Crestwood, NY: St. Vladimir's Seminary Press, 1984.

Rousseau, Philip. *Basil of Caesarea.* Berkeley: University of California Press, 1994.

Ruusbroec, John. *The Spiritual Espousals.* Translated by James A. Wiseman. Mahwah, NJ: Paulist, 1985.

Ruysbroeck, Jan van. *The Seven Steps of the Ladder of Spiritual Love.* Translated by F. Sherwood Taylor. Westminster: Dacre, 1944.

Scheck, Thomas P. "Introduction." In *Commentary on Matthew,* by St. Jerome, 3–47. Washington, DC: Catholic University of America Press, 2008.

Schmidt, Margot, and Carl-Friedrich Geyer, eds. *Typus, Symbol, Allegorie.* Regensburg, DE: Pustet, 1982.

Schuler, Stephen J. *The Augustinian Theology of W. H. Auden.* Columbia: University of South Carolina Press, 2013.

Scuiry, Daniel E. "The Anthropology of St. Gregory of Nyssa." *Diakonia* 18 (1983) 31–42.

Shakespeare, William. *As You Like It.* Cambridge: Cambridge University Press, 2004.

Sherwood, Yvonne. *A Biblical Text and Its Afterlives: The Survival of Jonah in Western Culture*. Cambridge: Cambridge University Press, 2000.
Slocum, Robert Boak. *Light in a Burning Glass: A Systematic Presentation of Austin Farrer's Theology*. Columbia: University of South Carolina Press, 2007.
Stapert, Calvin R. *A New Song for an Old World*. Grand Rapids: Eerdmans, 2007.
Stein, Edith. "On the History and Spirit of Carmel." In *The Hidden Life*, edited by Lucy Gelber and Michael Linssen, 1–6. Washington, DC: ICS, 1992.
Steinmetz, David C. "Luther and the Ascent of Jacob's Ladder." *Church History* 55 (1986) 179–92.
Stowe, Harriet Beecher. *The Minister's Wooing*. New York: Penguin, 1999.
Sullivan, John J., and Martin R. P. McGuire. "Introduction." In St. Ambrose, *On the Death of His Brother Satyrus*, 159–60. In *Funeral Orations by Gregory Nazianzen and Saint Ambrose*. Washington, DC: Catholic University of America Press, 1953.
Symeon the New Theologian. Hymn 30. In *Divine Eros: Hymns of St. Symeon the New Theologian*, 230–48. Translated by David Griggs. Crestwood, NY: St. Vladimir's Seminary Press, 2010.
———. *Seventh Ethical Discourse*. In Alexander Golitzin, *On the Mystical Life: The Ethical Discourses*, Vol. 2, 81–102. Crestwood, NY: St. Vladimir's Seminary Press, 1996.
Swift, Louis. "Basil and Ambrose on the Six Days of Creation." *Augustinianum* 21 (1981) 317–28.
Tauler, Johannes. *Sermons*. Translated by Maria Shrady. Mahwah, NJ: Paulist, 1985.
Tice, Terrence N. "Schleiermacher's 'Highest Intuition' in Landsberg (1794–1796)." In *Schleiermacher in Context*, edited by Ruth Drucilla Richardson, 18–42. Lewiston, NY: Edwin Mellen, 1991.
Tillich, Paul. *The Courage to Be*. New Haven: Yale University Press, 1952.
Torrance, Thomas. *The Doctrine of Christ*. Eugene, OR: Wipf and Stock, 2002.
Toth, Josh. *The Passing of Postmodernism*. Albany: SUNY Press, 2010.
Torjesen, Karen Jo. "'Body,' 'Soul,' and 'Spirit' in Origen's Theory of Exegesis." *Anglican Theological Review* 67 (1985) 17–30.
Trible, Phyllis. "Depatriarchalizing in Biblical Interpretation." *Journal of the American Academy of Religion* 41 (1973) 30–48.
———. "Eve and Adam: Genesis 2–3 Reread." *Andover Newton Quarterly* 13 (1973) 251–58.
Tugwell, Simon. *Ways of Imperfection*. Springfield, IL: Template, 1985.
Van Nieuwenhove, Rik. "Experience and Mystical Theology in the Fourteenth Century: An Examination of Ruusbroec." In *Encountering Transcendence*, edited by Lieven Boeve, Hans Geysels, and Stijn Van den Bossche, 411–47. Leuven: Peeters, 2005.
Van Fleteren, Frederick, and Joseph C. Schnaubelt, eds. *Augustine: Biblical Exegete*. New York: Peter Lang, 2001.
Varghese, Baby. "Saint Ephrem and the Early Syriac Liturgical Traditions." *St Vladimir's Theological Quarterly* 56 (2012) 17–49.
Viladesau, Richard. *Theology and the Arts*. Mahwah, NJ: Paulist, 2000.
Wakefield, Gordon S. "'To be a Pilgrim': Bunyan and the Christian Life." In *John Bunyan: Conventicle and Parnassus*, edited by N. H. Keeble, 111–35. Oxford: Claredon, 1988.
Ward, Graham. "A Postmodern Version of Paradise." *Journal for the Study of the Old Testament* 20 (1995) 3–12.

Wells, Samuel. *Improvisation*. Grand Rapids: Brazos, 2004.
West, Cornel. "Review of *Philosophy and the Mirror of Nature* by Richard Rorty." *Union Seminary Quarterly Review* XXXVII (1981–82) 179–85.
Williams, Delores S. *Sisters in the Wilderness*. Maryknoll, NY: Orbis, 2013.
Winslow, Donald F. *The Dynamics of Salvation: A Study in Gregory of Nazianzus*. Patristic Monograph Series 7. Cambridge, MA: Philadelphia Patristic Foundation, 1979.
Wolter, Clifton. "Introduction." In *The Fire of Love*, by Richard Rolle, 9–37. New York: Penguin, 1972.
Woolverton, John F. "Hans W. Frei in Context: A Theological and Historical Memoir." *Anglican Theological Review* 79 (1997) 369–93.
Wyschogrod, Edith, and John D. Caputo. "Postmodernism and the Desire for God: An E-Mail Exchange." *Cross Currents* 48 (1998) 293–310.
Young, Andrew. "The Soul of a Nation" in the PBS documentary, *God in America*. http://www.pbs.org/godinamerica/transcripts/hour-five.html.
Zagano, Phyllis, and Terrence W. Tilley, eds. *Things New and Old: Essays on the Theology of Elizabeth A. Johnson*. New York: Crossroad, 1999.
Zecher, Jonathan. *The Role of Death in the Ladder of Divine Ascent and the Greek Ascetic Tradition*. Oxford: Oxford University Press, 2015.
Zboyovski, John M. *Saint Symeon the New Theologian: The Mystic of Fire and Light and Hymns of Divine Love*. Bangalore: I. J. A, 2011.
Zinn, Grover A., Jr. "Personification Allegory and Visions of Light in Richard of St. Victor's Teaching on Contemplation." *University of Toronto Quarterly* 46 (1977) 190–214.

Subject Index

Alexandria, 8
Antioch, 8

beauty, 126–28

David, 163–65
distortion, 36–37
drama, 128–29

ecological economic model, 14

fire, 137–40
floating 147–48

Gustafson, James, 4

Hagar, 165–67
"highest intuition," 53–54

icon/idol, 129–30
improvisation, 18

jazz, 18
Jonah, 168–70

liberal theology, 2–3, 17, 34–35, 53–54, 71–73, 91–92, 107–9, 126–28, 144–46, 165–67, 185–86
Lyotard, Jean-Francois, 110

mind as mirror, 111–12
moon, 9

orthodox theology, 2, 33–34, 52–53, 69–71, 89–91, 105–7, 124–26, 142–44, 163–65, 183–85

Pecknold, C. C., 74–75
Pelagians, 34
postliberal theology, 3–4, 17–18, 35–36, 54–55, 74–75, 92–94, 109–110, 128–29, 146–47, 167–68, 187–88
postmodern theology, 4–5, 18, 6–7, 55–56, 75–76, 94–95, 110–12, 129–31, 147–49, 168–70, 188–89

reader-response criticism, 188–89

Solomon, 52–53
Stranger, 55–56

Tracy, David 122–23

water, 140–42

Young, Andrew, 17

Author Index

Achard of St. Victor, 44–47
Ambrose, 6–12, 83–86
Aquino, Maria Pilar, 86–89
Auden, W. H., 107–9
Augustine, 34, 142–44

Balthasar, Hans Urs von, 16
Barth, Karl, 3, 109, 167–68
Basil of Caesarea, 6–12, 15
Bonaventure, 100–103
Borg, Marcus, 147–49
Brueggemann, Walter, 18
Bultmann, Rudolf, 3, 91–92
Bunyan, John 24–29

Campbell, Charles, 187–88
Caputo, John, 4–5, 36–37
Crossan, John Dominic, 179–83
Cunningham, David, 146–47

Edwards, Jonathan, 163–65
Ephrem the Syrian, 79–83

Farley, Edward, 126–28
Farrer, Austin, xi–xiii
Fish, Stanley, 75–76
Fowler, James, 103–5
Fowler, Robert, 188–89
Frei, Hans, 54–55

Gregory of Nazianzus, 132–36
Gregory of Nyssa, 20–24
Guigo II, 63–66
Gutierrez, Gustavo, 140–42

Hauerwas, Stanley, 91–94, 109–10

Jenson, Robert, 89–91
Jerome, 172–76
John Chrysostom, 176–79
John Climacus, 58–62
John of Damascus, 114–17
Johnson, Elizabeth, 159–63

Kearney, Richard, 55–56
Keller, Catherine, 94–95
King, Jr., Martin Luther, 185–86
Kreeft, Peter, 66–69

Lindbeck, George, 3–4, 36
Luther, Martin, 70–71

Marion, Jean-Luc, 129–30
Maritain, Jacques, 124–26
Martin, Dale, 33
McFague, Sallie, 12–16

Neville, Robert, 144–46
Niebuhr, Reinhold, 34–35

Origen, 39–44

Richard of St. Victor, 151–55
Rohr, Richard, 48–51
Rolle, Richard, 117–21
Rorty, Richard, 111–12
Ruysbroeck, Jan van, 97–100

Schleiermacher, Friedrich, 53–54
Sherwood, Yvonne, 168–70
Stein, Edith, 155–59
Stowe, Harriet Beecher, 71–73
Symeon the New Theologian, 136–40

Tauler, Johannes, 105–7
Tillich, Paul, 108–9
Torrance, Thomas F., 183–85
Trible, Phyllis, 29–33

Viladesau, Richard, 121–24

Wells, Samuel, 128–29
Williams, Dolores, 165–67

Scripture Index

Genesis

1:1—2:4a	6–12
2	29–33
2:4b–25	20–24
2:16–17	25
3:1	37
16:1–16	165–67
21:19–21	165–67
28	58–69

Exodus

2:6	139
3:1–14	160
10:20–21	133
13:21–22	133
20:4–5	115
33–34	50
40:34	160

Numbers

2:9	6
10:1–10	84
33	39–44

Leviticus

14	167
16	167
23:24	84

Judges

6:11–14	160

1 Samuel

16	16

2 Samuel

23:2	163

1 Chronicles

23–26	163

2 Chronicles

13:14	85
27:16–21	81

Psalms

19:1	114
34:8	65
67:28	151
111:10	153
118:22–23	182

Song of Songs

3:1	139

Wisdom

7:29	152
8:1–2	152

Isaiah

2:1–5	145
6:3	119
11:2–3	46, 105
11:6–9	93
42:6	163
49:8	163

Jeremiah

17:7	169

Daniel

10:14	28

Matthew

1–28	172–76
4:1	45
5:8	64
5:45	50
7:14	36
12:40	168
12:43–45	46
13:18–19	180–81
21:33–46	182–83
22:1–10	181–82
24:36–44	145
25:1–13	82
25:35	56

Mark

4	188–89
4:30–32	180–81
4:38	168
10:45	47
12:1–12	182–83

Luke

1:26–38	159
1:38	49
1:39–56	160
10:29–37	186
11:30	168
11:2	168
12:16–21	186
12:49	137, 139
13:18–19	180–81
14:16–24	181–82
15:22	138
16:19–31	176–79, 185–86
20:9–19	182–83

John

1:9	140
1:51	59, 70
3:18	92
4:14	140
4:4–42	142–44
13:3	48
14:16	36

Acts

1:14–15	161
2:1–21	161
2:29–30	164
7:55	36

Romans

5:5	49
5:14	33
5:18–19	26, 34
6:11	34
8:29	47
10:4	91
13:11–14	145

1 Corinthians

8:1	48
10:1–5	134
12:10	61
13:12	78, 90
15:22	84
15:35–38	24

2 Corinthians

5:4	138
5:17	29, 91

Galatians

4:4	143
4:21–51	165

Colossians

3:2	60

1 Timothy

1:15	24

Hebrews

8:8–13	25
12:1	162
13:14	60

James

1:17	125

1 Peter

5:1	138

1 John

3:2–3	78

Revelation

2:10	78
4:6–11	94
4:8	119
5:6	46
5:8	119
7:9–10	81
8:2	84
11:15	84
12:3	46
21:15–21	118